The Sociology of Rural Development and Environment Life

ABOUT THE BOOK

Rural life is the principal pivot around which whole Indian social life revolves. India is a land of agriculture. Its history, customs and traditions, complex social organization and unity in diversity etc can be understood by the study of rural life. Rural sociology is the scientific study of rural society. It involves a systematic study of rural society, its institutions, activities, interactions and social change. It not only deals with the social relationships of man in a rural environment but also takes urban surroundings into consideration for a comparative study.

ABOUT THE AUTHOR

Anjali Garg, born in Kanpur, done B.A (Hons), M.A, M.Phil., in political Science is Presently Assistant Professor at University of Sharjah, Department of sociology, UAE. She is teaching the subject for last 18 Years. She has attended a number of conferences, seminars and has several articles and Journals. She is a member of Ministry of Infrastructure Development in UAE.

The Sociology of Rural Development and Environment Life

Anjali Garg

AMIGA PRESS INC.
DELHI (INDIA)

AMIGA PRESS INC.
H.O.: 28-A, Indra Park,
Chander Nagar, Delhi-110051 (India)
Tel.: 011-22504028, +91-98736-57000
E-mail: amigapress@gmail.com
amigaeditorial@gmail.com
amigapub@gmail.com
info@amigapress.co.in
Website : www.amigapress.co.in

This edition is published by Amiga Press Inc.

ISBN: 978-93-87295-34-6

First Published 2020

Printed and bound in India by Replika Press Pvt. Ltd.

Preface

Rural sociology is a scientific discipline focused on all aspects of a rural way of life, including its customs, demographics, and interactions with urban groups. This specific area of sociology explores rural society's role in the rest of the world, particularly in terms of economics and social theory. Many rural areas are rich centers of resources that sometimes face unique challenges due to changes in technology, infrastructure, and agribusiness. Scholars who study rural sociology often attempt to illustrate the differences between rural and urban life as well as the social issues that both types of populations have in common. Rural life is the principal pivot around which whole Indian social life revolves. India is a land of agriculture. Its history, customs and traditions, complex social organization and unity in diversity etc can be understood by the study of rural life. Rural sociology is the scientific study of rural society. It involves a systematic study of rural society, its institutions, activities, interactions and social change. It not only deals with the social relationships of man in a rural environment but also takes urban surroundings into consideration for a comparative study.

Aspects of rural social life are frequently quite different from those of urban areas. Many geographic regions are classified as rural when the average number of residents per square mile or kilometer falls below a certain benchmark. This population base number can vary according to census policies of different areas. Scholars who study rural sociology are often interested in how people who may live a significant distance from their nearest neighbors develop a sense of community. This area of sociology can also involve examining how rural settings sometimes require residents to become innovative in terms of economic viability in the midst of changes on a larger scale.

The book would be of great value for the students, teachers, trainees, agriculturists, social workers, planners, politicians and common readers.

– Author

Contents

❑❑❑

1.

Panchayati Raj Institutions and Rural Development

Panchayati Raj

Panchayats have been the backbone of the Indian villages since the beginning of recorded history. Gandhiji, the father of the nation, in 1946 had aptly remarked that the Indian Independence must begin at the bottom and every village ought to be a Republic or Panchayat having powers. Gandhiji.s dream has been translated into reality with the introduction of the three-tier Panchayati Raj system to ensure people.s participation in rural reconstruction.

73RD AMENDMENT ACT, 1992

The passage of the Constitution Act, 1992 marks a new era in the federal democratic set up of the country and provides constitutional status to the Panchayati Raj Institutions. Consequent upon the enactment of the Act, almost all the States/UTs, except J&K, NCT Delhi and Uttaranchal have enacted their legislation. Moreover all the States/UTs except Arunachal Pradesh, NCT Delhi and Pondicherry, all other States/UTs have held elections.

As a result, 2,32,278 Panchayats at village level; 6,022 Panchayats at intermediate level and 535 Panchayats at district level have been constituted in the country. These Panchayats are being manned by about 29.2 lakh elected representatives of Panchayats at all levels.

This is the broadest representative base that exists in any country of the world. developed or underdeveloped. The main features of the Act are. a 3- tier system of Panchayati Raj for all States having population of over 20 lakh; Panchayat elections regularly every 5 years; reservation of seats for Scheduled Castes, Scheduled Tribes and women; appointment of State Finance Commission to make recommendations as regards the financial powers of the Panchayats and constitution of District Planning Committees to prepare development plans for the district as a whole. As per the Constitution Act, the Panchayati Raj Institutions have been endowed with such powers and authority as may be necessary to function as institutions of selfgovernment and contains provisions of devolution of powers and responsibilities upon Panchayats at the appropriate level with reference to the preparation of plans for economic development and social justice; and the implementation of such schemes for economic development and social justice as may be entrusted to them.

FINANCIAL POWERS OF PANCHAYATI RAJ INSTITUTIONS

Article 243-G of the Constitution of India provides that the States/UTs may, by law, endow the Panchayats with such powers and authority as may be necessary to enable them to function as institutions of self-government and to prepare plans for economic development and social justice and their implementation including those in relation to the matters listed in the Eleventh Schedule. As per Article 243-H of the Constitution, State Legislatures have been empowered to enact laws;

- To authorise a Panchayat to levy, collect and appropriate some taxes, duties, tolls and fees;
- To assign to the Panchayat, some taxes, duties, tolls levied and collected by the State Government;
- To provide for making grants-in-aid to the Panchayats from the Consolidated Fund of the State; and
- To provide for constitution of such funds for Panchayats for crediting all money received by or on behalf of Panchayats and also the withdrawal of such money therefrom.

CONSTITUTION OF STATE FINANCE COMMISSIONS

Article 243-I of the Constitution provides for constitution of a State Finance Commission to review the financial position of Panchayats and to make recommendations to the Governor regarding the principles governing the major issues mentioned in Article 243-H. All the States/UTs barring Arunachal Pradesh constituted State Finance Commissions and all the SFCs except Bihar have submitted their Reports to the respective State Governments.

The States of Assam, Karnataka, Kerala, Madhya Pradesh, Punjab, Rajasthan, Tamil Nadu, Tripura and West Bengal have accepted most of the recommendations of the SFCs.

Andaman and Nicobar Islands, Dadra and Nagar Haveli, Daman and Diu and Lakshadweep Islands have received Reports of the Finance Commission which will be placed on the table of Houses by the Ministry of Home Affairs being the nodal Ministry.

States such as Andhra Pradesh, Himachal Pradesh, Haryana, Karnataka, Kerala, Madhya Pradesh, Maharashtra, Rajasthan, Sikkim, Tamil Nadu, Tripura, Uttar Pradesh, Assam, Punjab, Orissa and West Bengal have constituted second generation of State Finance Commissions. The Finance Commission for the four UTs has also been constituted by the Central Government. Constitution of State Finance Commission is now due in Goa, Manipur and Gujarat.

ELEVENTH FINANCE COMMISSION

The Eleventh Finance Commission recommended '1600 crores per annum for rural local bodies. Out of total grants, an amount of '197.06 crores was earmarked for development of data base on the finance of the Panchayats and an amount of '98.61 crores for maintenance of accounts of Panchayats as the first charge on these grants.

The Commission also recommended that in cases where elected local bodies are not in place, the Central Government should hold the grants for local bodies in trust on a non-lapsable basis during 2000-05 and that the Central Government would withhold a part of the recommended grants in case of such bodies to whom functions and responsibilities have not been devolved. Besides, the Commission recommended that Audit of accounts of the local bodies should be entrusted to the C&AG who may get it done through his own staff or by engaging outside agencies on payment of remuneration fixed by him and an amount of halfa-per cent of the total expenditure incurred by the local bodies should be placed with the C&AG for this purpose, and the report of the C&AG relating to audit of accounts of the Panchayats should be placed before a Committee of the State Legislature constituted on the same lines as the Public Accounts Committee.

The Ministry of Finance releases Grants recommended by the Eleventh Finance Commission to the States. For the year 2000-2001 ad-hoc grants of '57,186 lakhs were released to the States on.on Accounts. basis to the extent of 50 per cent of allocated grants. EFC Grants were not released during 2000-2001 to the States of Andhra Pradesh, Assam, Bihar, Gujarat, Jharkhand and Punjab as elections were due. During the year 2001-02, funds were released to the tune of '2,06,944 lakhs. However, these grants were withheld for the States of Arunachal Pradesh, Jharkhand, Jammu and Kashmir and Punjab due to pending Panchayat elections. During the current year, an amount of '3,56,822 lakhs has been released as on 4.12.2002.

INITIATIVES TAKEN BY THE MINISTRY

A Conference of the Chief Ministers on Panchayati Raj was held on 2nd August, 1997 at Vigyan Bhavan, New Delhi, under the chairmanship of Hon.ble Prime Minister to review the functioning of the Panchayati Raj Institutions where the outstanding issues like devolution of powers/ functions and responsibilities upon PRIs, setting up District Planning Committees; implementation of the reports of the State Finance Commissions, linkage of DRDAs with Zilla Parishads, training to Panchayati Raj elected representatives/functionaries were discussed in great detail. The Conference also called upon the concerned 8 States to enact the required State Legislation on the Provisions of the Panchayat Act, 1996 before 23rd December, 1997.

Based on the detailed discussions, the Conference recommended setting up of two Committees. the Committee of the Panchayat and the Tribal Development Ministers of the 8 States covered under Schedule V of the Constitution under the then Chairmanship of Minister to examine and to give their recommendations to enact the State legislation in consonance with the Central Act, 1996 before the cut off date *i.e.* 23rd December, 1997; and the Committee of the Chief Ministers under the Chairmanship of Prime Minister to examine the issues regarding the devolution of powers, functions and responsibilities upon PRIs and to recommend measures to streamline the Panchayati Raj system.

The reports of the Committee of Panchayat and Tribal Development Ministers of the Schedule V States and the Committee of Chief Ministers under the Chairmanship of the Prime Minister have been circulated to the States for appropriate action.

The important recommendations of the Committee of Chief Ministers were:

- Leave selection of beneficiaries to Gram Sabha.
- Waive requirement of Technical sanction for works upto '10,000.
- Innovate to provide adequate manpower support to the Gram Panchayats.
- Delegate total control over such manpower to Gram Panchayats.
- Zilla Parishad Chairpersons be made the Chairpersons of DRDAs.
- Panchayati Raj Institutions and Rural Development.
- Provide reasonable opportunity of hearing to the PRIs before suspension/ dismissal.
- Gram Panchayat President to be accountable solely to Gram Sabha.
- Expeditious constitution of District Planning Committees.

In order to ensure that Panchayati Raj Institutions function as instruments of local government, it is important that their functional and financial autonomy is guaranteed and transparency in their functioning is ensured.

This has to be accomplished in most of the States. The role of the Gram Sabha is, perhaps, the most important in ensuring the success of Panchayati Raj Institutions at the village level.

The role of local people in conducting social audit and fixing responsibility on panchayat functionaries will be effectively ensured with Gram Sabha becoming active. It is essential that the village community perceives meetings of the Gram Sabha as useful. The most important factor for that is the empowerment of the Gram Sabha. Another important factor for the success of the Panchayati Raj system is the need for transparency in the functioning of these bodies. Panchayats being closer to the people, their right to information and accessibility to the panchayats must be ensured.

This issue was discussed in the Chief Ministers Conference held on 2nd August, 1997 and the Committee of Chief Ministers as well. The Ministry had written to the States. The Hon.ble Prime Minister too, in his letter to the Chief Ministers, had urged that all relevant information on development schemes taken up by the Panchayat along with the budget for them should be displayed prominently in the Panchayat Office. Relevant records should be made available for inspection by members of the public. Photocopies of documents such as muster rolls, vouchers, estimates etc. can be made available to the public on payment of a nominal fee.

Technical manuals may be prepared for execution of various works at the Panchayat level so that transparency can be ensured. The Ministry convened a Conference of State Ministers of Rural Development and Panchayati Raj on May 13, 1998. This meeting was inaugurated by the Hon.ble Prime Minister. The resolutions adopted in the Conference held on 13.5.98 are. a Task Force for studying the structure and functioning of the Panchayats should be set up; provisions of 73rd Amendment Act and Central Act 40 will be complied with; Gram Sabhas should be convened on a single pre- determined day every quarter and care should be taken to respect the autonomy and independence of each tier of PRIs and to build up capability of the village level Panchayats. In pursuance of the resolution, a Task Force was constituted under the Chairmanship of the then Minister of State, Ministry of Rural Areas and Employment to study the structure and functioning of PRIs. The State Governments have been requested to ensure that the Gram Sabha Meetings are convened once in each quarter preferably on. 26th January- Republic Day; Ist May-Labour Day; 15th August-Independence Day and 2nd October-Gandhi Jayanti.

The Government of India decided to observe the year 1999-2000 as the.Year of Gram Sabha.. This is in recognition that the Gram Sabha is potentially the most significant institution for participatory and decentralised democracy. On 17th March, 1999, all Chief Ministers/Administrators have been requested to initiate measures to energise Gram Sabha in tune with the Seven Point minimal package during the Year of Gram Sabha.: A conference of Ministers of States in. charge of Panchayats Raj was held on 11th July, 2001 in New Delhi to discuss measures for strengthening Panchayati Raj Institutions towards implementation of the Constitution Act, 1992.

The major recommendations adopted in the Conference included:

- Panchayat elections should be regularly held every 5 years.
- The States would issue detailed executive instructions devolving specific and substantial executive powers in respect of the 29 Subjects listed in the 11th Schedule, upon each tier of Panchayats by 31st March,2002.
- A task Force comprising senior officers from the Ministry of Rural Development and the State Governments would be set up suggesting how to operationalise administrative decentralization of powers and submit its report by 31st August, 2001.
- District Planning Committees would be set up by the remaining States/UTs by December, 2001.

- The State Acts would be amended to bring them in conformity with the provisions of Panchayats Act, 1996.
- The scope of State Government.s intervention and control over the PRIs should be minimized and if there is any specific complaint against any Panchayat, it should be referred to a body similar to the. Ombudsman in Kerala.
- The parallel bodies, if any, set by the States, should work under the supervision of Panchayats and the Gram Sabha.
- *It was resolved that the following Four-point strategy for strengthening of Gram Sabhas will be implemented by the States*:

1. Awareness through print and electronic media, street plays and training to the elected Panchayat representatives.
2. Participation of the community in the preparation of need-based action plans, their execution and monitoring.
3. Transparency by displaying all relevant information on a bill board regarding estimates, availability of funds and expenditure on the works taken up by the Panchayats, making available relevant records for inspection by the public, and providing photocopies of documents, on demand, on payment of nominal charges.
4. Social Audit should have binding legal outcome so as to curb corruption and misutilisation of funds.

The Chief Ministers of the States and Administrators of Union Territories were advised to implement the resolutions of the Conference within the time frames agreed upon during the discussion. In pursuance of the resolution of the Conference of State Ministers incharge of Panchayat Raj held in July, 2001 in Delhi, a Task Force on Devolution of Powers and Functions upon PRIs was constituted on 11th July, 2001 under the Chairmanship of Additional Secretary and Financial Advisor in the Ministry of Rural Development consisting of State Secretaries in-charge of Panchayati Raj in Assam, Chhattisgarh, Kerala, Karnataka, Uttar Pradesh and West Bengal and concerned Joint Secretary in the Ministry.

The Task Force submitted its report on 31st August, 2001 within the time frame. The recommendations of the Task Force included: interse distribution of the 29 Subjects into activities/ tasks to be performed by different tiers of Panchayats, enhancement of the financial resources of Panchayats, provision by the State Government of.Untied. grants to enable Panchayats to utilise the same in conformity with local needs and priorities, mandatory Social Audit by Gram Sabhas and availability of qualified/trained personnel, at various level, to assist Panchayati Raj Institutions in day-to-day working.

The Chief Ministers of States and Administrators of UTs were requested to initiate appropriate steps, keeping in view of recommendations of the Task Force, towards the completion of devolution of powers upon Panchayats by the end of March, 2002.

An All India Panchayat Adhyakshas Sammelan was held on 5th and 6th April 2002 in New Delhi with a view to getting a feed back from the Adhyakshas and revitalizing and strengthening the Panchayati Raj Institutions in the country in a timebound manner.

The discussions in the Sammelan focussed on the topics namely:

- Devolution of Powers and Functions to Panchayats,
- Functioning of the Gram Sabha,
- Planning for Development at the Grass-root Level,
- Social Audit,
- Resource Mobilisation by the Panchayats and
- Awareness Generation for the Rural Development Programmes and Capacity Building. Besides the Panchayat Adhyakshas, Union Ministers, State Ministers incharge of Panchayats, Central and State Officials and representatives of NGOs and International Organisation attended this Sammelan, which was inaugurated by the Prime Minister and also addressed by the Leader of Opposition. The National Declaration adopted by the Sammelan indicate, inter-alia that the States and Union Territories would initiate, by the end of December, 2002, the necessary measures:
  - To hold regular and timely Panchayat elections, to devolve funds, functions and functionaries to Panchayats,
  - To constitute District Planning Committees and make them functional,
  - To set up Ombudsman to look into the complaints against the Panchayats,
  - To ensure Parallel Bodies function under the guidance of the Panchayats,
  - To amend the State Legislations to provide Panchayats adequate control over natural resources like, land, water, minor forest produce and minerals,
  - To make legal provisions for accountability and transparency in the functioning of Panchayats in accordance with the 4-Point strategy. Awareness, Participation,
  - To strengthen the Gram Sabhas and Gram Panchayats.
  - To devise an appropriate mechanism to provide significant non-budgetary resources in the form of loans with adequate maturities to pris, specifically to be used for such developmental projects as are planned and executed by pris themselves.
  - To put in place an appropriate structure of incentives to recognise and encourage the Panchayats for outstanding performance, especially in respect of improvements effected in accepted Social Development Indicators.
  - To discuss the need for an appropriate new Amendment to the Constitution to bring about speedy and effective devolution of financial and administrative powers to pris and to quickly initiate the process of

bringing in the much needed new Constitution Amendment. The Sammelan also urges all the Political Parties and Members of Parliament to pass the Amendment and thus usher in the era of Second Generation of Panchayati Raj Reforms.

The Ministry of Rural Development is currently considering ways of securing mandatory devolution of atleast some of the administrative and financial powers to Panchayati Raj Institutions by the State Governments. The Ministry had introduced the Constitution Bill,1999 in the Parliament on 17.12.1999 to amend Article 243-C and of the Constitution to enable the State Legislatures to decide the methodology for election of members and chairpersons of Panchayats at the intermediate level and the district level.

It was decided to have wider consultations with all the political parties and the State Governments on the Bill. Accordingly, the comments of all the State Chief Ministers were sought in this behalf. A meeting of Leaders of all Political Parties in the Parliament was held under the Chairmanship of the Hon.ble Prime Minister on 19th May, 2001 to seek the approval of all Political Leaders in respect of the Constitution Bill, 1999. Since no consensus was arrived at in the Meeting, it was decided to defer the Bill and to study further in wider context of Panchayati Raj in the country.

THE PROVISIONS OF THE PANCHAYATS ACT, 1996

This Act which came into force on 24th December, 1996, extends Panchayats to the Schedule-V areas of States such as Andhra Pradesh, Chhattisgarh, Jharkhand, Gujarat, Himachal Pradesh, Maharashtra, Madhya Pradesh, Orissa and Rajasthan. It intends to enable tribal society to assume control over their own destiny to preserve and conserve their traditional rights over natural resources. The State Governments were required to enact their legislation in accordance with the Provisions of Act before the expiry of one year *i.e.* 23rd December, 1997. All the States barring have enacted State Legislation to give effect to the provisions contained in The Provisions of the Panchayats Act, 1996.

ISSUES ARISING OUT OF IMPLEMENTATION OF PART-IX OF THE CONSTITUTION AND PESA, 1996

While the State Panchayati Raj Acts have been enacted, State Election Commission and State Finance Commissions have been set up and regular Panchayat elections have been held providing reservation for SCs/STs/ Women in Panchayats, the results of actual implementation of the Constitution Act, 1992 have fallen far short of expectations on the ground level.

- Though the political decentralisation has been largely successful, with elections held regularly and with ample participation of people, there is only minimum administrative and fiscal decentralisation, which remain de facto under the control of the State Governments.

- Panchayats have not given adequate responsibilities to levy and collect taxes, fees, duties or tolls. Panchayats should have been granted appropriate powers to generate their own resources.
- Recommendations of State Finance Commissions have been either accepted partially or implemented half-heartedly.
- Powers given to the State Election Commissions vary from State to State. These Commissions should have been given powers to deal all matter relating to Panchayat elections namely, delimitation of constituencies, rotation of reserved seats in Panchayats, finalislation of electoral rolls, etc.
- Gram Sabhas have not been empowered and strengthened to ensure people.s participation and transparency in functioning of Panchayats as envisaged. There are certain problems, both with certain Central laws and State legislations as have been passed in pursuance of Act 40 of 1996.

  Certain crucial issues arise:
- Definition of Minor Forest Produce. the Indian Forest Act, 1927 defines timber as including within its definition, bamboo as well as cane. The Ministry of Environment and Forests define Minor Forest Produce to exclude bamboo and cane. While doing so, they have decided to adopt the definition of timber as given in the Indian Forest Act, 1927.. In most States, tribals have been traditionally depending on bamboo and cane for their livelihood. However, for the last many years, Forest Corporations and Forest Departments have prevented tribals from having access to bamboo and cane while at the same time giving these to private industry at highly concessional rates. In many cases, tribals have been driven to desperation on account of this policy of State Forest Departments. It is felt that the definition of timber in the Central Act, 1927 is neither scientific nor equitable, and goes against the spirit of the provisions of Act 40 of 1996.
- Ownership of Minor Forest Produce:-There are also issues arising from the interpretation by the Ministry of Environment and Forests of the intention of Parliament regarding vesting of ownership of Minor Forest Produce in Gram Sabhas. The proposals made by the Ministry of Environment and Forests interpret the intention of Parliament as giving not ownership *per se*, but making available to the Gram Sabhas, residual profits of State Forest Corporations/ Federations. This necessarily means that according to the Ministry of Environment and Forests, State Forest Corporations/Federations will continue to trade in Minor Forest Produce and if there is any surplus, that surplus will be given to the Gram Sabhas. This Ministry has already taken up these issues with the Ministry of Environment and Forests.

Research and Development Work

A Research Advisory Committee headed by the Secretary approves proposals from voluntary organizations/institutions on Action Research studies related to

Panchayati Raj. The Ministry has commissioned several such studies on issues such as Performance of Panchayats, women empowerment, Awareness Campaign, implementation of PESA, 1996, etc.

TRAINING OF PANCHAYATI RAJ INSTITUTIONS

Under the Scheme Panchayat Development and Training central assistance is provided to the States, NGOs and other institutions for their efforts to impart training to the elected and official functionaries of the Panchayati Raj Institutions.

The funding pattern under the scheme is as follows:

- 20 per cent funding is provided for lodging and boarding and 50 per cent for reproduction of training material and other items to State Governments;
- 100 per cent Central assistance is provided to NGOs and other institutions.

The elements of support by Ministry of Rural Development under this scheme include the following:

- Expenditure on participation for training of elected representatives of Panchayati Raj Institutions including awareness generation programmes.
- Cost of expenditure on accommodation/ hiring of rooms.
- Audio/ Video training equipment expenditure.
- Workshops/Seminars, awareness generation campaigns on Panchayati Raj.
- Support for Mobile training facilities for training in Panchayati Raj.

Proposals received under the scheme are considered by the Training Research and Advisory Committee headed by the Secretary. With the reallocation of work relating to capacity building of PRIs, to Training Division the proposals relating to capacity building of PRIs are being processed by Training Division for consideration by TRAC. The Plan Outlay for this scheme for the year 2002-03 is '5.00 crore. The Central Outlay for training of Panchayati Raj Institutions during the Ninth Plan was '17.00 crores. During 2002-2003 an amount of '3.85 crores was allocated but it has been kept at '1.98 crores only for the current year at RE stage for the Action Research Study/Workshop component.

Rural Development in Panchayat Raj

Perarignar Anna's vision is being translated into reality in Tamil Nadu under the dynamic leadership of our Honourable Chief Minister, Kalaignar M. Karunanidhi. Never before in the history of the State has so much been done for the rural poor in so many different ways as in the past four years. By virtue of the Anaithu Grama Anna Marumalarchi Thittam, every Village Panchayat of Tamil Nadu will have its own library, playground, village pond, and burial ground-cum- cremation shed together with drinking water systems, streetlights and cement concrete streets in every hamlet, by 2011. Under the Mahatma Gandhi National Rural Employment Guarantee Scheme, a sum of '3,352.58 crores has been disbursed as wages till 31.3.2010 to the rural poor, among whom 56 per cent are Scheduled Castes and 76 per cent are women.

Tamil Nadu has won accolades as one of the best-performing States in this Scheme from no less an institution than the Honourable Supreme Court of India. As regards rural roads, the total length of black-topped roads has gone up from about 29,280 kilometres in 2006 to about 54,620 kilometres in 2010. The women's Self-Help Groups movement has been given a fillip as may be seen from the fact that the total Bank Credit disbursed to SHGs during the past 4 years was '6,364 crores as against a sum of only '1,765 crores disbursed to SHGs during the 17 years from 1989 to 2006. The Kalaignar Veettu Vasathi Thittam launched by the Honourable Chief Minister on 3.3.2010 is by far the biggest Statefunded Scheme and aims at replacing all the huts in rural Tamil Nadu with permanent concrete houses over a six year period from 2010-11 to 2015-16, with 3 lakh huts being taken up for replacement during 2010-11 at a cost of '1,800 crores.

In short, there has been a major transformation of the rural landscape in Tamil Nadu during the past four years.

Raj Department is responsible for the implementation of various Centrally sponsored, State-funded, and Externally-aided schemes for poverty alleviation, employment generation, sanitation, capacity building, women's social and economic empowerment, Tsunami rehabilitation, apart from provision of basic amenities and services. The Department is also entrusted with the responsibility of enabling the various Panchayat Raj Institutions (PRIs) to function as effective units of Local Self- Government.

There are 12,620 Village Panchayats, 385 Panchayat Unions (coterminus with Blocks) and 29 District Panchayats under the purview of the Department. The Directorate of Rural Development and Panchayat Raj including the Training wing, the Tamil Nadu Corporation for Development of Women, the Vazhndhu Kaattuvom Project Society and the Tsunami Project Implementation Unit come under this Department. This Department also provides administrative support to the State Election Commission.

History of Panchayat Raj Institutions

Tamil Nadu has a long history of local selfgovernance as is evident from the Uthiramerur stone inscriptions in Kancheepuram district. Tamil Nadu, in those days, was a land of village republics, with community groups undertaking many activities for their area development. This tradition reached its peak during the 10th and 11th centuries under the reign of Cholas when Village Councils used to levy taxes, improve community life and administer justice in their limited area.

These Village Councils had effective links with the Chola rulers."Kuda Olai Murai" was the name of the secret ballot method exercised to elect members to the Village Councils. With the downfall of Cholas, the State experienced a decline of the Village autonomy and rise of the centralized feudal administrative system. This continued till British rulers introduced local selfgovernance primarily as an administrative convenience for the imperial Government. In the post independence era, the first enactment in democratic decentralization in the State was the Madras Village Panchayats Act, 1950. Pursuant to the White Paper on the"Reform of Local Administration" in 1957, the Madras Panchayats Act, 1958 and Madras District Development Council Act, 1958 were enacted with the following salient features:

- A two-tier system of Village Panchayats and Panchayat Unions.
- Creation of Panchayat Unions co-terminus with the Community Development Blocks.
- Village Panchayat Presidents to become exofficio members of the Panchayat Union Councils with the Chairperson of the Panchayat Union Council directly/indirectly elected.
- Entrusting the Panchayat Unions and Village Panchayats with a large umber of developmental and welfare functions.
- Abolition of District Boards.
- Creation of District Development Council as an advisory body.

This two-tier system operated very well till 1975 and elections were held regularly. Subsequently, the tenures of the Panchayat Unions and Village Panchayats were extended up to 1.2.1977 and 12.9.1979 respectively. Thereafter, Special Officers (Block Development Officer for all the Village Panchayats in a Block and Divisional Development Officer for all the Panchayat Unions in a Division) managed the rural Local Bodies till the next elections in 1986. The elected rural Local Bodies continued in office till March 1991. Again, no elections were held till October 1996 and the Special Officers managed the rural Local Bodies.

CONSTITUTION (73RD AMENDMENT) ACT, 1992

Though the Panchayat Raj Institutions were in existence in various forms in various States, these institutions did not acquire the status and dignity of viable and responsive people's bodies due to a number of reasons including absence of regular elections, prolonged supersession, insufficient representation of weaker parts like Scheduled Castes, Scheduled Tribes and Women, inadequate devolution of powers and lack of financial resources.

In the light of the experience gained and the short-comings that had been observed, the 73rd amendment of the Constitution was enacted in 1992, to enshrine in the Constitution certain basic and essential features of Panchayat Raj Institutions to impart certainty, continuity and strength to them. A number of fundamental changes were brought about in the Panchayat Raj System by virtue of this Act. Pursuant to this, the Tamil Nadu Panchayats Act 1994 was enacted and it came into force with effect from 22.04.1994.

Some of the important changes brought about by the 73rd Amendment to the Constitution and the Tamil Nadu Panchayats Act 1994 are:

- Introduction of a three tier system-at the Village, Intermediate (Block) and District levels. [There are 12,620 Village Panchayats, 385 Panchayat Unions (coterminous with Blocks) and 29 District Panchayats in Tamil Nadu].

- Mandatory conduct of Local Body elections every five years and conduct of elections before the expiry of the duration of the Local Body or before the expiry of a period of 6 months from the date of its dissolution.
- Introduction of reservation of seats (*i.e.* ward members) and offices (*i.e.* Chairpersons/Presidents) for Scheduled Castes/Scheduled Tribes in proportion to their population in every Local Body with provision for rotation of the reserved seats and offices.
- Introduction of reservation of one-third of total number of seats and offices for women with provision for rotation.
- Constitution of a State Election Commission as an independent body to conduct elections to both rural and urban Local Bodies regularly.
- Establishment of a quinquennial State Finance Commission to recommend devolution of resources from the State Government to the rural and urban Local Bodies.
- Constitution of a District Planning Committee to consolidate the plans prepared by the rural and urban Local Bodies in the district with a view to prepare a comprehensive development plan for the district.
- Introduction of the concept of' Grama Sabha' comprising all registered voters in a Village Panchayat.

Tamil Nadu's Stand on the 73rd Constitutional Amendment

The Government of Tamil Nadu has had reservations regarding certain aspects of the 73rd Constitutional amendment and our experience of working under the new system for the past 12 years has only confirmed the same. The system prevailing under the old Tamil Nadu Panchayats Act of 1958 wherein the Presidents of Village Panchayats were ex-officio members of the Panchayat Union Council at the Block level ensured organic linkage between the two tiers. Hence, the name'Panchayat Union' and it genuinely functioned as a'union' of Village Panchayats.

Since the Village Panchayat Presidents themselves' doubled up' as ex- officio members of the Panchayat Union Council, there were no separate ward members for the Council. Having separate ward members for Panchayat Unions (6,570 for the State as a whole) and District Panchayats (656) has vastly increased the number of'members' and has paved the way for inter-tier friction and disharmony. Although Article 243 C (3) of the Constitution states that a State may, by law, provide for the representation of Village Panchayat Presidents on the Panchayat Union Council and Panchayat Union Chairpersons on the District Panchayat, this arrangement is not satisfactory because it can render the Panchayat Union Councils and District Panchayats too unwieldy with too many members and can create disharmony between the two distinct power blocs within each Council.

Hence, Tamil Nadu has not invoked Article 243 C (3). The lack of organic linkages between the three tiers results in a scenario where each tier is unaware of what the other two tiers are doing. It often leads to duplication in the selection of works and avoidable paperwork and loss of time in reworking the choices. Tamil Nadu has been pressing for the reversion to the 1958 model where the Presidents of Village Panchayats were ex-officio members of the Panchayat Union Council at the Block level. Under the 1958 Act, the Chairpersons of the Panchayat Union Council could be either directly or indirectly elected. Most of the time, Tamil Nadu had direct elections for the posts of Chairpersons of Panchayat Unions and this arrangement was found to be working well as the Chairperson commanded respect and there was no scope for vexatious noconfidence motions.

But after the 73rd amendment, the Constitution itself stipulates that Chairpersons of Panchayat Unions and District Panchayats should be elected indirectly. Only in the case of elections of Village Panchayat Presidents, the States have the freedom to opt for either direct election or indirect election. The State Government has been pressing that the States should have similar freedom in respect of elections of Chairpersons of Panchayat Unions and District Panchayats.

The Government of Tamil Nadu have, for long held the view that there should have been a single consolidated Amendment to the Constitution covering both rural and urban Local Bodies instead of two Amendments-one covering rural Local Bodies (73rd) and the other urban Local Bodies (74th). This'compartmentalization' has resulted in a scenario whereby the District Panchayat-instead of being a nodal body responsible for coordinating and monitoring all the rural and urban Local Bodies in the district-finds that its jurisdiction is confined only to the rural areas. In a State like Tamil Nadu with about 42 per cent urban population, and with several highly urbanised districts such as Coimbatore (69.1 per cent), Kanniyakumari (66 per cent), The Nilgiris (58 per cent), Theni (54 per cent) and Madurai (52 per cent), the argument that the District Panchayat should become a nodal body responsible for coordinating and monitoring the development activities in the entire district becomes weak.

A system whereby all the Chairpersons of Panchayat Unions, Municipalities and Town Panchayats are ex-officio members of the District Panchayats, with the Chairman of the District Panchayat being either directly or indirectly elected would have been more meaningful and credible. This weakness has been sought to be overcome through the District Planning Committee which has members drawn from both rural and urban Local Bodies, but its composition is flawed because there is no representation for Panchayat Union and Village Panchayat members on it. A mention was made in His Excellency the Governor's Address in the Tamil Nadu Legislative Assembly in 2006 that the Tamil Nadu would press for the amendment of the Constitution seeking a two tier system of Panchayats and the abolition of District Panchayats. Tamil Nadu did have powerful elected District Boards till they were abolished in 1961.

In their place, the District Development Council, an advisory-cum- planning body, comprising all the MPs, MLAs, Chairpersons of Panchayat Unions, Town

Panchayats, Municipalities and Corporations in the district with the District Collector as Chairman were set up. The Government of Tamil Nadu believes that Village Panchayats and Panchayat Unions are the two tiers closest to the people, qualifying for the appellation'local' and represent the'cutting edge' of Local Self- Government. These two tiers need to be strong and vibrant and strengthened further.

This Government is of the opinion that the reasons which led to the abolition of the old District Boards are still valid and applicable to the third tier of District Panchayat, which at present has only an advisory-cum planning role. At the same time, this Government is aware that other States may have different views on this topic based on their own past legacy. For example, some States want Village and District Panchayats but do not want the intermediate tier (Block or Taluk Panchayat).

But there is a general consensus that there is one tier too many under the present system. It may be noted that with regard to the States, the Legislative Assembly is mandatory while the Legislative Council is optional as per the Constitution. Similarly, in order to accommodate divergent needs, the Constitution may be so amended so as to make the Village Panchayats mandatory for all the States and leaving it to the discretion of the concerned State Legislatures whether to have the intermediate Panchayats only or District Panchayats only or both. The State Government would press for such an amendment to the Constitution.

Panchayat Elections

Conduct of 2006 Local Body Elections

Though the Tamil Nadu Panchayats Act was enacted in April 1994, only after the change of Government in May 1996, the first ordinary elections were held to all the rural and urban Local Bodies in October 1996. The second ordinary elections to the Local Bodies were conducted during October 2001. The third ordinary elections to the Local Bodies were conducted in October 2006.

Reservation of Seats and Offices and Rotation

Article 243 D of the Constitution relates to reservation and rotation of seats for Scheduled Castes, Scheduled Tribes and Women in rural Local Bodies. The relevant provisions of Tamil Nadu Panchayats Act, 1994 are Sections 11, 20, 32 & 57. These are supplemented by the Tamil Nadu Panchayats (Reservation of Seats and Rotation of Reserved Seats) Rules, 1995. The Rules provide for the reservation of seats by adopting a list of wards or Panchayats arranged in the descending order of the percentage of SCs, STs and Women and applying a'cut off' at the point where the number of reserved seats and offices is equal to the prescribed ratio. The periodicity of rotation is also fixed under the Rules. The Government amended Rule 7 of the Tamil Nadu Panchayats (Reservation of Seats and Rotation of Reserved Seats) Rules, 1995 Panchayati Raj Institutions and Rural Development 115 vide G.O.Ms. No. 105, RD & PR (C4) Department, dated 1.9.2006 by virtue of which the posts of Presidents of Village Panchayats and Chairpersons of Panchayat Unions and District Panchayats reserved for SCs, STs and Women were rotated-after 10 years-for the October 2006 elections.

While the posts of ward members of all the 3 tiers reserved for Women were rotated-after 10 years-those reserved for SCs and STs were not rotated; in other words, they would continue to be reserved as such until the Government direct otherwise. However, the Government took a conscious decision not to rotate the posts of Presidents of Pappapatti, Keeripatti and Nattarmangalam Village Panchayats in Madurai district and Kottakachiyendal Village Panchayat in Virudhunagar district reserved for SCs where elections could not take place for a prolonged period due to local opposition to reservation.

This Government solved, what appeared to be an intractable problem, by successfully conducting elections to the posts of Presidents and ward members in all the four Panchayats during the ordinary elections held in October 2006. It is gratifying to note that the various communities of these Panchayats have overcome their past differences and have wholeheartedly accepted the newly elected Scheduled Caste Presidents.

Conversion of Multi-Member Wards to Single Member Wards

The system of Multi-Member Wards is in existence only in Village Panchayats and not in any other rural or urban Local Body. It has posed difficulties at the time of voting and also during the counting process. There has also been lack of clear demarcation of responsibility amongst the multiple members. The Third High Level Committee headed by the Hon'ble Deputy Chief Minister has recommended for the conversion of Multi-Member Village Panchayat Wards into Single Member Wards.

On the basis of this recommendation, Section 12 of Tamil Nadu Panchayats Act, 1994, has been amended by abolishing the Multi Member Ward System in Village Panchayats and replacing it with Single Member Wards-vide Tamil Nadu Act No. 20 of 2009. The system of single member wards in Village Panchayats will be brought into effect in 2011 Local Body elections.

DEVOLUTION OF POWERS

Local Government is a State subject figuring as item 5 in List II of the Seventh Schedule to the Constitution of India. Article 243 G of the Indian Constitution enshrines the basic principle for devolution of power to the rural Local Bodies. Subject to the provisions of this Constitution, the Legislature of a State may, by law, endow the Panchayats with such powers and authority as may be necessary to enable them to function as institutions of self-Government and such law may contain provisions for the devolution of powers and responsibilities upon Panchayats at the appropriate level, subject to such conditions as may be specified therein, with respect to the preparation of plans for economic development and social justice; the implementation of schemes for economic development and social justice as may be entrusted to them including those in relation to the 29 matters listed in the Eleventh Schedule.

The Government of Tamil Nadu is committed to ensuring that the Panchayat Raj Institutions function as effective institutions of Local Self- Government. At the same time, since State autonomy is a firm and abiding principle of the Government of Tamil Nadu, it has opposed certain proposals of the Ministry of Panchayati Raj at the Centre which appeared to transgress into the Constitutional space earmarked for States, as for example, by trying to constitute an'Advisory Committee' for each State for monitoring the devolution of powers and functions from State Governments to Local Governments; by seeking a'MOU' between the State Chief Minister and the Union Minister for Panchayati Raj; by trying to get a resolution passed for the transfer of the subject of'Local Government' from the State List to the Concurrent List at a National Convention of Chairpersons of District Panchayats and Block Panchayats in April 2008; and so on. It is a matter of pride that all the three High Level Committees for recommending the devolution of greater powers and functions to rural and urban Local Bodies were constituted only during Kalaignar's tenure as Hon'ble Chief Minister of Tamil Nadu.

In 1996, soon after the conclusion of the first ordinary elections to the three tiers of Panchayats, the Government of Tamil Nadu constituted the First High Level Committee under the Chairmanship of Thiru L.C. Jain, the then full-time Member of the State Planning Commission to give recommendations on the entrustment of powers and functions to the three tiers of Panchayats.

The Committee submitted its report to the Government in April, 1997. Many of the recommendations of the L.C. Jain Committee have been crystallized into action towards empowering the Panchayats. Apart from the Rural Development Department, other departments such as Agriculture, Animal Husbandry, Forests, Social Welfare, Revenue, Khadi and Village Industries, Education, Health and Family Welfare, Adi-Dravidar Welfare, Co- operation, Food and Consumer Protection, have issued Government Orders for devolution of powers and functions in their respective spheres to the three tiers of Panchayats.

Again, the Government in G.O. Ms. No. 320, Rural Development (C1) Department, dated 11.11.1997 constituted the Second High Level Committee under the Chairmanship of Thiru.Ko.Si.Mani, the then Hon'ble Rural Development and Local Administration Minister with experienced persons including sitting MLAs of various political parties as members of the Committee to recommend more devolution of powers and functions to the Panchayats. This High Level Committee submitted its report on 11.1.1999 with 1209 recommendations to the Government. The Government accepted 718 recommendations and issued orders for their implementation. This Government, in continuance of its commitment to devolve greater powers and responsibilities to rural and urban Local Bodies, constituted the Third High Level Committee under the Chairmanship of the Hon'ble Deputy Chief

Minister, Thiru. M.K. Stalin vide G.O. Ms. No.6 RD & PR (C1) Department, dated 22.1.2007 and with select District Panchayat Chairpersons, Panchayat Union Chairpersons and Village Panchayat Presidents besides certain subject experts as members. The Committee was required to study the duties, functions and powers already entrusted to the rural and urban Local Bodies and make recommendations for further devolution of the same in order to make them more effective.

High Level Committee Under the Chairmanship of Thiru M.K.Stalin

The Third High Level Committee was formed under the Chairmanship of Hon'ble Deputy Chief Minister to devolve more powers and functions to the Local bodies. The first meeting of the Committee was held on 7.3.2007. In continuation of this, a conference of Local Body representatives was held in the presence of Hon'ble Chief Minister on 18.3.2007, following which Regional Conferences of local body representatives were held in Erode (24.7.2007), Trichy (25.7.2007), Tiruvannamalai (03.8.2007), and Virudhunagar (23.8.2007) under the Chairmanship of Hon'ble Deputy Chief Minister.

The second meeting of High Level Committee was conducted on 19.9.2007. Further, Hon'ble Deputy Chief Minister conducted discussions on 11.10.2007 and 12.10.2007 with the Secretaries of other departments in order to devolve more powers to the rural Local Bodies. The Committee presented its report to the Hon'ble Chief Minister of Tamil Nadu on 10.12.2007 and submitted a total of 99 recommendations categorized under 39 subjects.

Recommendations of the M.K. Stalin Committee

The important recommendations of the third High Level Committee are highlighted:

- Grama Sabha to act as a forum of Social Audit for all the schemes implemented by various Departments.
- Approval of the list of all individual beneficiary schemes to be done by Grama Sabha.
- Conversion of multi-member wards into single member wards in all the Village Panchayats as is there in the case of the Panchayat Unions and District Panchayats.
- Stability of tenure of rural and urban Local Body representatives by making the moving and passing of No Confidence Motions more stringent.
- Designating November 1st of every year as the'Local Bodies Day'.
- Empowering weaker Village Panchayats by enhancing their State Finance Commission grants and allocating the entire Central Finance Commission grants to Village Panchayats so as to enable them to meet the expenditure relating to water supply, electricity charges and sanitation.

- Pooling of assigned revenues of Local Cess, Local Cess Surcharge, and Surcharge on Stamp Duty and Entertainment tax at State Level and apportioning it to the districts thereafter.
- Giving Panchayat Raj Institutions greater operational independence by enhancing administrative sanction powers of Village Panchayats, Panchayat Unions and District Panchayats for works taken out of their General Funds.
- Rationalisation of Village Panchayat Accounts.
- Issue of Identity Cards to the Heads of three tiers of Panchayat and for the Members of Panchayat Unions and District Panchayats.
- Making BDOs (Village Panchayats) as separate Pay Drawing Officers.
- Provision of Telephone facility to all Village Panchayats.
- Provision of Wireless to Panchayat Unions.
- Vehicles for Panchayat Raj Institutions and key functionaries of Rural Development Department.
- Revival of Namakku Naame Thittam.
- Formulation of Panchayat Union School Renovation Programme.
- Setting up of Libraries and Sports Centres in all Panchayats under AGAMT.
- Designating Village Panchayats as'Village Level Committee' for selecting the beneficiaries and implementing the schemes of various other departments at Village level.

It is important to note that most of the recommendations have already been accepted by the Government and necessary orders issued. It may be noted that as per the rankings of various States in India done by the Ministry of Panchayat Raj, Government of India based on the devolution of powers, functions and funds to the Panchayat Raj Institutions, Tamil Nadu stood fourth in 2006-07; first in 2007-08; third in 2008-09 and second in 2009-10.

DELIMITATION OF LOCAL BODIES

A large number of requests for upgradation, downgradation, bifurcation and amalgamation of rural and urban Local Bodies have been received by Government. Government have issued orders vide G.O.Ms No. 131, RD & PR (C1) Department, dated 16.3.2007 prescribing the procedure for the conduct of public hearings by Collectors/Heads of Departments before making their final recommendations to Government in response to such requests. It has been clarified to all the rural and urban Local Bodies that the terms of office of the present office bearers will not, in anyway, be affected.

The District Collectors have already conducted public hearings pertaining to the requests from various rural and urban Local Bodies and the proposals are under the consideration of the Government. So far, decision has been taken by the Government only in respect of Village Panchayats lying in the vicinity of a few Municipal Corporations. In 2011, it has been proposed to merge 25 Village

Panchayats of Kancheepuram and Tiruvallur Districts with Chennai Corporation, 61 Village Panchayats of Vellore District with Vellore Corporation, 7 Village Panchayats of Erode District with Erode Corporation, 10 Village Panchayats of Thoothukudi District with Thoothukudi Corporation and 8 Village Panchayats of Tiruppur District with Tiruppur Corporation.

Before the recent delimitation of Assembly Constituencies, 278 Panchayat Unions were coming fully within the boundary of an Assembly Constituency; after delimitation, this number has come down to 213. At present, 172 Panchayat Unions are coming under 2 or more Assembly Constituencies. Hence, the Government have taken up steps to study the reorganization of Panchayat Union boundaries in order to ensure that an Assembly Constituency comprises only full Panchayat Unions. However, the alteration of Panchayat Union boundaries will not, in anyway, affect the present term of office of the elected representatives.

This work has been temporarily kept in abeyance due to the ban on changing jurisdictions of administrative units with effect from 1.1.2010 in view of the forthcoming Census operations.

DISQUALIFICATION OF MEMBERS OF PANCHAYATS

In order to bring the procedure for disqualification of elected members of Panchayat Raj Institutions in line with that relating to disqualification of MPs and MLAs under the Representation of the People Act, 1951 certain amendments to Sections 34, 35, 37, 38, 39 and 41 of the Tamil Nadu Panchayats Act, 1994 have been introduced.

As per the amended provisions, the Government will decide the question of disqualification of members of Panchayats in consultation with the Tamil Nadu State Election Commission. New sections 41-A, 41-B, 41-C and 41-D, have been added to the Act enabling the Tamil Nadu State Election Commission to conduct enquiries relating to disqualification of members of the Panchayats.

GRAMA SABHA

The Grama Sabha is the grass root level democratic institution in each Village Panchayat. A vibrant Grama Sabha is essential for the effective functioning of Village Panchayats by promoting transparency and accountability in administration, enhancing public participation in the planning and implementation of schemes and in the choice of beneficiaries, and paving the way for social audit. The Government have ordered the conduct of Grama Sabha meetings a minimum of four times a year *i.e.* on 26th January, 1st May, 15th August and 2nd October.

In order to streamline the procedure for the conduct of Grama Sabha, this Government brought out suitable amendments to the Tamil Nadu Grama Sabha (Quorum and Procedure for convening and conducting of meetings) Rules, 1998 vide G.O.Ms No. 130 RD & PR (C4) Department dated 25.9.2006 and specified that the Grama Sabha shall meet in each of the Village Panchayat wards by rotation.

Since a quorum of 10 per cent of the voters was unattainable and unwieldy for the bigger Village Panchayats, a reduced quorum based on the population of Village Panchayats has been prescribed. It has also been specified that out of the quorum, at least 1/3rd shall be women and the number of SC/ST participants shall bear the same proportion to the quorum as the population of SCs/STs bears to the total population of the Village Panchayat. Recording of Grama Sabha attendance and proceedings through proper registers and keeping photographic record have been made mandatory for the conduct of Grama Sabhas.

The Third High Level Committee constituted under the Chairmanship of Hon'ble Deputy Chief Minister had recommended that the expenditure limit for conducting Grama Sabha may be increased from '500 to '1,000. The Government have accepted the above recommendation and ordered that the Village Panchayat Presidents can incur the expenditure for conducting Grama Sabha to a maximum limit of '1,000 with the approval of the Village Panchayat, vide G.O.Ms.No.160 RD & PR department dated 30.09.2008.

VILLAGE PANCHAYATS

There are 12,620 Village Panchayats in the State spread across the 31 districts, including two new Village Panchayats, *viz.*, Perumathur and Indira Nagar in Kurinjipadi Panchayat Union of Cuddalore District that were notified on 16.8.2008.

There are 385 Blocks. The average number of Village Panchayats per district is 421 and per Block is 32. The Nilgiris (35), Kanniyakumari (99), Theni (130) and Karur (158) are some of the districts with fewer Village Panchayats while Villupuram (1104), Tiruvannamalai (860), Vellore (753), Cuddalore (683) and Kancheepuram (648) are some of the districts with a large number of Village Panchayats. The population of Village Panchayats in Tamil Nadu is widely varying with some Village Panchayats having populations even below 500 while others have populations exceeding 25,000.

Among the three tiers, Village Panchayats assume a pre-eminent role in view of the wide variety of civic duties and other functions entrusted to them under Sections 110 and 111 of the Tamil Nadu Panchayats Act, 1994. This Government have always taken efforts to empower the Village Panchayats further in order to enable them to perform their functions in an effective manner. Various efforts have been taken by this Government to improve the finances of the Village Panchayats. Since the Village Panchayats in Tamil Nadu vary widely in population from below 500 to above 25,000 and as the devolution of State Finance Commission grant is mostly linked to population, the smaller Village Panchayats got less grant and the bigger Village Panchayats got more.

While the needs of the bigger Village Panchayats are also greater, it is a fact that there are certain fixed costs associated with the running of a Village Panchayat irrespective of the size and the SFC grant to a Village Panchayat should be sufficient to cover at least the fixed costs, if not the variable costs. There were cases where some Village Panchayats found it difficult to pay their electricity bills on time; a few couldn't pay the salaries and wages of their employees on time. The State Finance Commission recommended the earmarking of certain percentage of the SFC grant as'Equalisation Fund' to assist such weaker Village Panchayats. But past experience showed that the allocation of the Equalisation Fund by Collectors was by discretion which introduced a certain element of arbitrariness. The Government have thus passed G.O.Ms.No.199 Finance (Finance Commission-IV) Department dated 25.5.2007 wherein a floor amount of '3 lakhs has been earmarked for each Village Panchayat irrespective of the population and only after the apportionment of this amount, the remaining amount is distributed among the Village Panchayats in proportion to population.

By virtue of this decision of the Government, the huge disparity in the income of the Village Panchayats has been reduced and at the same time weaker Village Panchayats have been empowered further towards self- sustainable. The Government have also vide G.O.Ms.No.119 R.D. & P.R.(C2) Dept. dated 26.02.2007 decided to allocate the entire Twelfth Finance Commission grant to the Village Panchayats Alone. It is, hence, seen that the average income levels have not only increased for majority of the Village Panchayats, but also the inequity of the income levels amongst various Village Panchayats has decreased due to the steps taken by the Government.

Functions

Sections 110 & 111 of the Tamil Nadu Panchayats Act, 1994 prescribe the duties and functions of Village Panchayats.

Some of the important functions of a Village Panchayat are:

- Construction, repair and maintenance of all village roads.
- Extension of village sites and the regulation of buildings.
- Lighting of public roads and public places in built-up areas.
- Construction of drains.
- Cleaning of streets and improvement of the sanitary condition of the village.
- Construction and maintenance of public latrines.
- Sinking and repairing of wells, the excavation, repair and maintenance of ponds or tanks and the construction and maintenance of water-works for the supply of water.
- Maintenance of burial and burning grounds.
- Maintenance of parks and reading rooms.
- Implementation of schemes such as Indira Awaas Yojana (IAY) and National Rural Employment Guarantee Scheme (NREGS).
- Such other duties as the Government may, by notification, impose.

Resources

The important sources of revenue for the Village Panchayat are:

- *Tax revenue*: Among the three tiers, the Village Panchayat alone has the power to levy taxes. House tax, Profession tax and Advertisement tax are the commonly levied taxes.
- *Non- Tax revenue*: Licensing fees for building plan and layout approval, fees and charges on Dangerous and Offensive trades, water charges, fees on cartstands, fishery rentals, 2C patta fees, income from markets and fairs, ferries, fines and penalties and so on.
- *Assigned and shared revenues*: These revenues include the items pooled at the State level (Surcharge on Stamp duty and Entertainment Tax) which are released by the Director of Rural Development and Panchayat Raj to all the three tiers of the Panchayats including the Village Panchayats. Other items of Assigned and shared revenues for the Village Panchayats include the seigniorage fees (100 per cent) and lease amount (50 per cent share) on minor minerals and social forestry auctions amount.
- *Grants* : Central Finance Commission Grant, State Finance Commission Grant, development grants under Centrally-sponsored and State schemes.

ADMINISTRATIVE POWERS

The Village Panchayat President himself has been designated as the Executive Authority. Cheques for payment have to be signed jointly by the President and Vice-President. Where the relationship between the two is not cordial, the Collector, in his capacity as Inspector of Panchayats, can designate any other member of the Village Panchayat as joint cheque signing authority along with the President. The Government have brought out Tamil Nadu Panchayats (Preparation of Plan and Estimates for works and Mode and Conditions of works) Rules, 2007 vide G.O.Ms.No.203 R.D. & P.R. (PR.1) Department, dated 20.12.2007, wherein the Village Panchayats have been empowered to give administrative sanction and execute individual works up to '2 lakhs from their General Funds.

Previously the Village Panchayats were empowered to give administrative sanction for works up to '1 lakh only. For all works costing more than '2 lakhs but not more than '50 lakhs, the District Collector is the competent authority to give the administrative sanction and for work costing more than '50 lakhs, the Director of Rural Development and Panchayat Raj will be competent to accord administrative sanction. However, the Collector's prior administrative sanction is necessary in respect of all Centrally sponsored and State funded schemes. Village Panchayats have also been given freedom to execute urgent works up to ' 2,000 at a time and up to ' 5,000 for a year without any technical approval. The President can draw self cheque up to '500 to meet contingent expenditures. The Village Panchayats have been given necessary delegation of powers to enable them to attend to repairs and maintenance of hand pumps, power pumps and street lights promptly. They can spend '600 per hand pump per year and up to '7,500 per power pump per year without reference to engineers for preparation of estimates or passing of bills. They can buy street light materials meeting the prescribed quality norms on their own.

Uthamar Gandhi Village Panchayat Award

Uthamar Gandhi Village Panchayat Award was instituted vide G.O.Ms No. 111, RD & PR (C2) Department dated 5.9.2006. This award is being given each year from 2006-07 onwards for those Village Panchayats which have undertaken outstanding works, special initiatives and innovative efforts during the preceding 5 years. The chosen Panchayats are given a certificate, shield and a cash prize of '5 lakhs each while their Presidents are given a certificate and a medal. Awards can also be given posthumously.

For 2006-07 and 2007-08, 15 Village Panchayats each were conferred with Uthamar Gandhi Village Panchayat Awards by the Hon'ble Chief Minister of Tamil Nadu on 10.10.2007 and 19.12.2008 respectively. For 2008-09, orders have been issued selecting 15 Village Panchayats for Uthamar Gandhi Village Panchayat Award for the year 2008-09.

Corporate Social Responsibility Award

Government instituted an Award to honour the Industrial, Service and Business Organisations that are actively involved in various social and economic upliftment activities as part of their Corporate Social Responsibility, from the year 2007-08 onwards vide G.O. Ms. No.117, Rural Development (SS.2) Department, dated 2.7.2007. The Award consists of ' 5 lakhs cash each and a Certificate. This Award will be given to 5 such commercial and industrial establishments every year.

The Government have issued orders selecting 5 organisations for the Corporate Social Responsibility Award for the year 2007-08 and 4 organisations for the year 2008-09. The Awards were given by the Hon'ble Deputy Chief Minister on 19.10.2009. Five organisations have been selected for the year 2009-10.

Rationalisation of Village Panchayat Accounts

The Government had vide G.O.Ms.No.92 Rural Development Department dated 26.3.1997 issued orders for rationalization of Village Panchayat Accounts and the procedure for operation of the Accounts. This was a great step forward in empowering Village Panchayats since it gave freedom to the President and Vice President to operate the various Accounts of a Village Panchayat free from pre-scrutiny by Block officials as was the earlier practice in which the Village Panchayat Consolidated Fund was maintained and operated in the Block office.

However, certain weaknesses were noticed in this new system of maintenance of Village Panchayat Accounts. Several instances of the State Finance Commission Grant and Central Finance Commission Grant released to the Village Panchayats'

Earmarked Grants Accounts being used for less important purposes and not for payment of dues relating to electricity and water charges came to the notice of the Government.

Due to this practice, in order to avoid diversion of funds meant for current consumption charges and water supply maintenance, the District Collectors were directed to deduct the charges payable to TNEB and TWAD Board at the district level before releasing money to the Village Panchayats.

However this resulted in the following two anomalies:

1. TNEB issued wrong/duplicate bills in some instances which did not get deducted since payment was made at district level without proper check by the Village Panchayat Presidents concerned.
2. The Panchayat Presidents did not evince interest in ways and means of reducing power consumption as they never paid the electricity/ water bills of their own.

Several instances also came to notice, wherein Village Panchayat Presidents and Vice- Presidents issued cheques for Scheme funds works/ National Rural Employment Guarantee Scheme works without the works same being measured and check-measured and bills being passed by the Block Development Officer (Village Panchayats) concerned.

The number of instances of unauthorized drawals was greater on the eve of Local Body elections.

Therefore, the Government issued G.O. Ms.No.146 Rural Development and Panchayat Raj Department dt.17.8.2007 for further rationalizing the Village Panchayat Accounts and streamlining the procedures for operation of the Accounts so as to:

- Empower the Village Panchayat Presidents to pay the TNEB and TWAD Board dues from the funds at their disposal and at the same time prevent them from diverting these funds for less important purposes.
- Prevent unauthorized drawals of money from scheme fund/NREGS fund Accounts without authorization of Block Development Officer(VP) concerned.

The Government have further streamlined the above accounting procedure through issuance of G.O. Ms.No.178, RD & PR Department dated: 25.11.2008 and G.O. Ms.No.180 RD & PR Department dated: 01.12.2008. The Government of Tamil Nadu have also taken a stand opposing the imposition of a uniform Accounting System for Village Panchayats across all the States as proposed by the Ministry of Panchayat Raj, Government of India.

The Accounting structure suggested by Ministry of Panchayat Raj was found to be extremely complicated and difficult to comprehend except by officials with accounting background. It was felt that the accounting system proposed did take into account the field realities *viz.* the level of education and competence of the staff in Panchyat Raj Institutons, especially at Village Panchayat level. In Tamil

Nadu, there are 12,618 Village Panchayat Presidents, who are the Executive Authoriy of the Village Panchayats concerned and each President is assisted by a Panchayat Assistant and a Makkal Nala Paniyalar, both of whom have generally only SSLC qualification.

The suggested Accounting system is too complicated for them and there are no commensurate benefits of adopting the Ministry of Panchayat Raj proposed system. Government of Tamil Nadu has firmly stated that its own Accounting System is much simpler and easier to maintain and has been working well and is suited to the State which has a large number of State funded schemes. Hence, while welcoming any'Models and Best Examples', Government of Tamil Nadu has opposed the imposition of a uniform Accounting System.

Abolition of Jamabandhi

The Annual Settlement of Panchayat Accounts was introduced in 1992 at a time when there were no elected Local Bodies and the Panchayat Administration was managed by the Special Officers. However, consequent to the Constitution (73rd Amendment) Act, 1992 and the enactment of Tamil Nadu Panchayats Act, 1994, elected representatives assumed office in the rural Local Bodies in the year 1996 and the elected Local Bodies have an inbuilt system of checks and balances on the expenditure of the Local body funds. Further, the system of Audit of Village Panchayat Accounts has also been introduced and Deputy Block Development Officers have been designated as the Audit Officers. The post of Assistant Director (Audit) has been created for monitoring the progress of audit and the settlement of audit objections.

Grama Sabha has also been strongly propagated as a forum of Social Audit of Village Panchayat accounts. It was viewed that the Annual Settlement of Panchayat Accounts by the Jamabandhi Officers did not contribute any value addition for the betterment of Panchayat Administration and that Jamabandhi had merely degenerated into a ritual. Thus, the Government issued orders vide G.O.Ms.No.175 RD & PR (PR2) Department, dated 14.11.2008 dispensing the Annual Settlement of Panchayat Accounts.

Telephones for Village Panchayats

Given the need for Block officials as well as Presidents to communicate with each other frequently, lack of land-line telephone in most of the Village Panchayats was a major hurdle in the implementation of schemes and in the administration of Panchayats. Hence, the Government vide G.O.Ms.No.118

RD & PR Department, dated 02.07.2007 issued orders permitting each Village Panchayat to have a telephone connection and prescribing a monthly ceiling of '750/- towards telephones charges. So far, a total of 12,572 Village Panchayats out of 12,620 Village Panchayats of Tamil Nadu have been provided with Telephone connections and the remaining 48 Village Panchayats could not be provided with the telephones due to terrain related problems. Once a telephone connection is made available, the Village Panchayat can also have access to the Internet through a dial-up connection.

Tneb Issues

Maintenance of street lights and water supply are the two major functions of the Village Panchayats. Approximately, 70 per cent of the income of the Village Panchayats used to be spent on payment of electricity charges. It was brought to the notice of the Government that in many cases, TNEB raised the bills on Village Panchayats on commercial rates without proper meter reading and levied 12 per cent interest on the dues pending for more than 45 days. Undue delays were also noticed in obtaining estimation for installation of new street lights from TNEB authorities.

The Government implemented a series of measures to settle some of these long term problems persisting between TNEB and the Village Panchayats. The Government have, vide G.O.Ms.No.95 Energy (D2) Department, dated 12.10.2007 reduced the tariff of the EB service connection utilized for public lighting and water supply connection by Village Panchayats from '3.40 per unit to '3 per unit. The Government have also vide G.O.Ms.No.111 RD & PR Dept. dt.26.6.2007 announced a uniform rate per pole of '9,500/- for installation of new street lights by Village Panchayats. The period of payment for EB charges has been raised from 20 days to 60 days for the Village Panchayats, and the interest rate payable by the Village Panchayats for payments beyond 60 days has been reduced from 12 per cent to 6 per cent.

The surcharge of '18.46 crores prior to 13.3.2007 has been written off. Based on the Government's direction, TNEB has taken steps to provide electricity meters to all those service connections of Village Panchayats which didn't have meters, besides replacing defective meters. Meter cards have been provided to all service connections in rural areas and TNEB has been asked to raise bills based only on the initial and final readings of the meters. Steps have also been taken to pay up all the arrears due from Village Panchayats to TNEB. Where the arrears have been cleared, an entry that"No arrears are due pertaining to this service connection as on....." has been directed to be made on the meter cards in order to enable the Village Panchayats to start with a clean slate in future.

Duty of the President to Mandatorily Implement Schemes Entrusted to the Village Panchayat

Village Panchayats implement various Centrally Sponsored schemes and State funded schemes besides undertaking works out of general funds. However, there was no specific provision in the Tamil Nadu Panchayats Act, 1994, to require the President of the Village Panchayat to mandatorily execute or implement the schemes entrusted to the Village Panchayats. Hence, necessary amendment to Section 46 of the Act has been issued making it mandatory for the Presidents of Village Panchayats to execute or implement the schemes entrusted to the Village Panchayats.

Enhancement of Penalties

Tamil Nadu Panchayats Act, 1994, contemplates imposition of penalties on persons who contravene any of the provisions of the Act specified in Schedule- II or who fail to comply with any directions lawfully given to them or requisition lawfully made upon them. Schedule-III of the Act prescribes penalties for the continuing breaches. Since the penalty amounts provided in the Schedules were prescribed 50 years back and had lost their deterrent effect, amendments were issued to Schedule II and Schedule III enhancing the penalty amounts leviable under the Act. This amendment will aid the rural Local Bodies in the strict enforcement of provisions of the Tamil Nadu Panchayats Act 1994.

Restriction of Exemptions Granted to Educational Institutions from House Tax

The Third State Finance Commission had recommended that all fee collecting institutions like nursery, Matriculation schools, tutorial colleges, self financed engineering, medical/dental colleges, para medical institutions, teacher training institutions, coaching centres etc should be subjected to House tax. The Government accepted the recommendation of the Third State Finance Commission and suitably amended rule 15 (c) of the Tamil Nadu Panchayats (Assessments and Collection of Taxes) Rules, 1999 vide G.O. Ms. No.38 RD & PR (PR.1) Department, dated 5.3.2008 and the amended provision now enables the Village Panchayats to levy and collect House Tax on the buildings used by Self financing educational institutions and also from the Government-aided institutions which are conducting self-financing unaided courses.

PANCHAYAT UNION COUNCIL

At the intermediate level, there are 385 Panchayat Unions (Blocks) in the State. The average number of Panchayat Unions per district is 13. The Nilgiris (4) has the lowest number of Panchayat Unions while Villupuram (22) has the highest.

Functions and Powers

Section 112 of the Tamil Nadu Panchayats Act, 1994 prescribes various powers and functions of Panchayat Union Councils.

Some of the important functions of a Panchayat Union Council are:

- Construction, repair and maintenance of all Panchayat union roads.
- Construction of water works for the supply of water for drinking, washing and bathing purposes.
- Construction and maintenance of elementary and middle schools.
- Control of fairs and festivals under the control of the Panchayat Union.

- Opening and maintenance of Panchayat Union public markets.
- Implementing various Centrally sponsored and State schemes.
- Preventive and remedial measures connected with any epidemic or with malaria.

Resources

Panchayat Unions cannot levy any tax.

The revenues of a Panchayat Union consist of the following:

- *Non- tax revenues*: License fees, market fees, receipt from rentals and properties, fines and penalties.
- *Assigned and shared revenues*: The Pooled Assigned Revenue component of Surcharge, Surcharge on Stamp Duty and Entertainment Tax is proportionately distributed to the Panchayat Unions based on the State Finance Commission Grants formula. Lease amount of mines and minerals (50 per cent share) comes individually to the Panchayat Unions concerned and is adjusted at the district level itself.
- *Grants*: State Finance Commission Grants, development grants under Centrally sponsored schemes and State schemes, grants for maternity centres, rural dispensaries.

By virtue of enactment of the Tamil Nadu Panchayats (Preparation of Plan and Estimates for works and Mode and Conditions of works) Rules, 2007 vide G.O.Ms.No.203 R.D. & P.R. Dept. dt. 20.12.2007, the Panchayat Union Councils have been empowered to give administrative sanction and execute individual works up to '10 lakhs from their General Funds without any external approval.

Earlier the Panchayat Unions were empowered to sanction funds up to '5 lakhs only. For all works costing more than '10 lakhs but not more than '50 lakhs, the District Collector is the competent authority to give the administrative sanction and for works costing more than '50 lakhs, the Director of Rural Development and Panchayat Raj will be competent to accord administrative sanction. However for Centrally sponsored and State funded schemes, prior administrative sanction of the District Collector is necessary.

Wireless to Panchayat Unions

The Government have, vide G.O. Ms.No. 134 R.D. & P.R. (SGS.4) Department, dated 02.08.2007, issued orders for provision of wireless communication equipment to vehicles and Block offices in 24 districts of Tamil Nadu during 2007-08 and earmarked an amount of '3.76 crores for this purpose. The wireless communication facility has been extended to the remaining 6 districts at the cost of '116.55 lakhs during 2008-09 vide G.O.Ms.No.177 RD & PR (SGS.4) Department, dated 21.11.2008.

Vehicles to Panchayat Union Chairpersons

The Third High Level Committee constituted under the Chairmanship of Hon'ble Deputy Chief Minister recommended that the Panchayat Union Chairpersons should be given an independent vehicle like District Panchayat Chairpersons to facilitate better supervision of schemes.

It was, thus, announced on the floor of the Tamil Nadu Legislative Assembly on 16.4.2008 that new vehicles will be provided for 385 Panchayat Union Chairpersons during 2008-09 and 385 Driver posts would be newly created for this purpose. Accordingly, 385 vehicles were purchased and handed over to 385 Panchayat Union Chairpersons on 28.07.2008 by the Hon'ble Chief Minister. The Government also ordered for the creation of 385 drivers for Panchayat Union Chairpersons' vehicles vide G.O.Ms.No.67 RD & PR (E5) Department dated 12.05.2008.

Reconstitution of Appointment Committee of Panchayat Unions

The earlier system of conduct of annual elections to elect a member of Appointment Committee was not conducive to the smooth functioning of the Panchayat Union administration. Hence in order to provide continuity to the Committee and avoid changing the composition every year with one new member, the Government have issued amendment to Section 96(1)(a) of Tamil Nadu Panchayats Act, 1994 by making the Vice-Chairman of the Panchayat Union as one of the members of the Appointment Committee.

Consequent to the amendment, the three members Appointment Committee will consist of the Chairman of the Panchayat Union Council, the Vice- Chairman of the Panchayat Union Council and the Commissioner of Panchayat Union.

DISTRICT PANCHAYATS

There are 29 District Panchayats in the State.

Functions

The functions of the District Panchayats are mainly advisory in nature such as:

- Preparation of development plan for the district.
- Compilation of administration reports of Village Panchayats and Panchayat Union Councils of the district and preparation of Annual Report for the District.
- Planning and review of Agriculture, Land Development, Animal Husbandry, Dairy, Poultry, Fisheries and Rural Industries etc.
- Planning and review of rural housing programmes particularly housing for SC/STs.
- Identification of major water supply schemes.

Resources

The District Panchayat has no taxation powers. Its only source of revenue is from statutory grants like State Finance Commission Grant and development grants under Centrally sponsored schemes. By virtue of enactment of the Tamil Nadu Panchayats (Preparation of Plan and Estimates for works and Mode and Conditions of works) Rules, 2007 vide G.O.Ms.No.203 RD & PR Dept. dated 20.12.2007, the District Panchayats have been empowered to give administrative sanction and execute individual works up to '20 lakhs from their General Funds without any external approval. Earlier the District Panchayats were empowered to sanction funds up to '10 lakhs only.

For all works costing more than '20 lakhs but not more than '50 lakhs, the District Collector is the competent authority to give the administrative sanction and for works costing more than '50 lakhs, the Director of Rural

Development and Panchayat Raj will be competent to accord administrative sanction. However for Centrally sponsored and State funded schemes, prior administrative sanction of the District Collector is necessary.

POOLING OF ASSIGNED REVENUES

The major sources of assigned/shared revenues to the rural Local Bodies are Surcharge on Stamp duty, Entertainment tax, seigniorage fee and lease amount of mines and minerals, and sale proceeds of Social Forestry plantations. The total receipts to rural Local Bodies under these heads in a year is about '250-350 crores.

The surcharge on stamp duty is pooled at the Block level and apportioned among the Village Panchayats in the Block in proportion to their land revenue collection. The entertainment tax is shared between the Village Panchayats and Panchayat Union in the ratio 70:30, after deducting 10 per cent towards collection expenses. The seigniorage fee on minor minerals is credited to the Village Panchayats concerned while in the case of the lease amount, 50 per cent is credited to the Panchayat Union and 50 per cent to the Village Panchayats concerned. In the case of social forestry auction amounts, 60 per cent of the gross proceeds will go to the Village Panchayats concerned and 40 per cent will be retained by Forest department. It was observed that there is considerable delay in adjusting the various assigned/ shared revenues to the Village Panchayats and Panchayat Unions and the paper work involved is disproportionate to the amounts involved.

There was considerable inequity in the distribution of what are essentially Government revenues. In order to overcome the delays in adjusting the various assigned/shared revenues to the Village Panchayats and Panchayat Unions and reduce the disproportionate paper work involved and inequities in the distribution, the Government have vide G.O.Ms.No.168 RD & PR Dept. dt.4.10.2007 ordered for the pooling of the Assigned Revenues due to the rural Local Bodies from the proceedings of the Local Cess, Local Cess Surcharge, Surcharge on Stamp Duty, and Entertainment Tax at the State level and apportionment of the above revenues to the rural Local Bodies thereafter. The above Pooling of Assigned Revenue has facilitated quick and easy disbursement of these revenues and is also equitable.

STATE FINANCE COMMISSION GRANT

To augment the resources of the Local Bodies, financial devolution to the Local Bodies is made on the basis of recommendations of the State Finance Commission (SFC). Based on the recommendations of the State Finance Commission, a higher share of State's own tax revenues for the rural and urban Local Bodies beginning with 9 per cent (it being 8 per cent till 2006-07) has been allocated for the year 2007-08 and 2008-09. For 2009-10, the Government have increased the allocation to 9.5 per cent of the State's own tax revenues to the rural and urban Local Bodies.

The percentage of devolution will be progressively increased to 10 per cent within the award period of the Third State Finance Commission (2007-08 to 2011-12). The ratio of the shares of rural and urban Local Bodies will be 58:42 as before. Since Village Panchayats are entrusted with most of the basic functions such as maintenance of village roads and streets, drinking water supply, street lights, sanitation and solid waste management and they are also the largest in number (12,620), the allocation for the rural Local Bodies is shared in the ratio 60:32:8 among Village Panchayats, Panchayat Union Councils and the District Panchayats from the year 2007-08 onwards. These policy changes are expected to greatly improve the delivery of services at the grass roots level. The quantum of increase in SFC Grants to rural Local Bodies from2006-07 to 2009-10.

Streamlining the Modalities of Release of State Finance Commission Grant

The State Finance Commission Grant is released from the Directorate of Rural Development and Panchayat Raj to the District Collectors electronically through the Core Banking System (CBS). The District Collectors, in turn, had earlier been sending the funds to the Village Panchayats by adopting various methods like Core Banking System, Real Time Gross Settlement (RTGS), Demand draft system etc.

There was lack of uniformity in the procedure and a lot of delays in the adjustment of funds in this process. In order to overcome the above drawbacks, a uniform procedure of transferring the funds through 4 Nodal Banks in each of the Districts to the bank accounts of the Village Panchayats has been prescribed with effect from December 2008. This procedure has significantly speeded up the adjustments of Grants to the accounts of rural Local Bodies.

CENTRAL FINANCE COMMISSION GRANT

On the basis of the recommendations of the Twelfth Finance Commission (TFC), the Government of India have allotted a sum of '870 crores for the 5- year period from2005-06 to 2009-10. For 2007-08, this Government decided that the entire Twelfth Finance Commission Grant should be allocated only to Village Panchayats on the basis of population.

The grants should be _tilized by the Village Panchayats entirely for the operation and maintenance cost of water supply, street lighting and sanitation. This system of allocating entire State Finance Commission grant to Village Panchayats continued in the year 2008-09 also. A sum of '174 crores will be provided for the year 2009-10 under the Twenfth Finance Commission Grant.

INCREASE IN THE ALLOWANCES OF RURAL LOCAL BODY REPRESENTATIVES

Fixed Travelling Allowance (FTA) was initially sanctioned by the Government to the Presidents of Village Panchayats and Chairpersons and Members of the Panchayat Unions and District Panchayats vide G.O.Ms.No.262 Rural Development Department dated 20.12.1997. This amount was enhanced by 10 per cent in the year 1999 and was not revised thereafter. The Government have, vide G.O. (D) No.569 RD & PR(C1) Department, dated 28.09.2007, enhanced the FTA of the rural Local Body representatives and the indicates the FTA rates prevalent previously and enhanced now.

ISSUE OF IDENTITY CARDS TO HEADS OF PANCHAYAT RAJ INSTITUTIONS

Based on the representations given by the Village Panchayat Presidents during the Regional Conferences of Village Panchayat Presidents at Erode and Tiruchirapalli, the Hon'ble Deputy Chief Minister announced to give Identity Cards to all the 12,618 Village Panchayat Presidents which were immediately issued thereafter. Identity Cards were also given to the Chairpersons and members of the Panchayat Unions and District Panchayats.

LOCAL BODIES' DAY

The rural and urban Local Bodies are perhaps the agencies with the maximum public interface. There is need to further strengthen this interface and bring about greater transparency and openness in the functioning of Local Bodies. At the same time, it is also necessary to highlight their achievements and carry out the various information, education and communication campaigns relating to civic administration or implementation of schemes. One method of doing this is to designate a particular day in a calendar year as"Local Bodies' Day" The Government have issued G.O.No.632,RD & PR(C1) Department, dated 26.10.2007 earmarking November 1 as"Local Bodies' Day" to be celebrated by all rural and urban Local Bodies in Tamil Nadu every year. Tamil Nadu is the first State in the country to do this.

ELECTRIFICATION OF BUILDINGS USED BY OTHER DEPARTMENTS

The Rural Development and Panchayat Raj (RD & PR) Department constructs various categories of buildings not only for the usage of rural Local Bodies but also for the usage of a number of other departments. Based on the'user pays' principle, it is for the occupying departments to pay the electricity consumption charges. Since the buildings were owned by RD&PR Department, the user departments were unable to apply for electricity connections in their name. In order to overcome this problem, the Government have, vide G.O.Ms.No.206, RD & PR (SGS.1) Department, dated 31.12.2007 given a blanket'No Objection Certificate' to the other user departments for which the RD & PR Department has built buildings through its schemes, to enable them to apply to TNEB for electricity connections and pay the recurring current consumption charges to TNEB, without any financial commitment to the rural Local Bodies.

STABILITY IN TENURE OF LOCAL BODY REPRESENTATIVES

The Government felt that frequent moving of no-confidence motions on trivial and unjustifiable grounds affected the continuity in planning and implementation of works in rural Local Bodies and are detrimental to public interest. In order to make the provisions for moving and passing the noconfidence motion more stringent, the Government have amended relevant provisions of the Tamil Nadu Panchayats Act, 1994, wherein the minimum strength required for issuance of motion of no confidence against the Vice- President of the Village Panchayat or the Chairperson or the Vice- Chairperson of the Panchayat Union or the District Panchayat concerned has been increased from the existing half of the sanctioned strength to threefifth and the minimum strength required for carrying the motion has been increased from the existing two-third to four-fifth of the strength of the local body concerned.

Also it has been stipulated that no motion of any confidence can be brought within one year of the assumption of the office or during the last year of the term of office of the Vice-President of the Village Panchayat or the Chairperson, Vice-Chairperson of the Panchayat Union or the District Panchayat concerned.

ANNUAL REPORT ON THE FUNCTIONING OF PANCHAYATS

As per the original Section 165 of Tamil Nadu Panchayats Act, 1994, each District Panchayat had to prepare an Annual Report giving a full account of its activities during the previous year and forward it to the Government. The Government used to lay all such reports on the table of the Legislative Assembly. However, as the reports of the District Panchayats did not give a comprehensive view of the functioning of Panchayat Raj Institutions, Section 165(2) was deleted and a new Section 166A was introduced replacing the old system with a single Annual Report for the State as a whole.'Annual Reports on the Functioning of Panchayats in Tamil Nadu' for 2006-07, 2007-08, and 2008-09 have already been placed before the Legislative Assembly, and that for the year 2009-10 will be placed in April 2010.

GUIDELINES FOR DISMANTLING OF OLD BUILDINGS UNDER THE CONTROL OF VILLAGE PANCHAYATS AND PANCHAYAT UNIONS

Village Panchayats and Panchayat Unions are maintaining various kinds of buildings such as School Buildings, Kitchen sheds, Library Buildings, Sanitary Complexes, Panchayat Union Offices, Village Panchayat Offices, Over Head Tanks etc. With the passage of time and due to various circumstances, certain buildings become dilapidated and need to be dismantled for safety considerations. In such cases, there were no specific guidelines and clear delegation of powers, for issuing orders for dismantling the dilapidated buildings of Rural Development and Panchayat Raj Department. Hence, the Government vide G.O. Ms. No.56, RD & PR (SGS-IV) Department, dated 3.4.2008 have issued detailed guidelines to be followed for dismantling of old buildings under the control of Village Panchayats and Panchayat Unions.

CONSTITUTION OF FOURTH STATE FINANCE COMMISSION

The Government have, vide G.O.Ms.No.549, Finance (Finance Commission-IV) Department, dated 01.12.2009, constituted Fourth State Finance Commission to review the financial position of the rural and urban local bodies namely Village Panchayats, Panchayat Union Councils, District Panchayats, Town Panchayats, Municipalities and Municipal Corporations.

The Commission has the mandate to make recommendations as to:

- The principles which should govern:
  - The distribution between the state and the said local bodies of the net proceeds of the taxes, duties, tolls and fees leviable by the government which may be divided between them and the allocation between the said local bodies of their respective shares of such proceeds;
  - The determination of taxes, duties, tolls and fees which may be assigned to or appropriated by the said local bodies;
  - The grants-in-aid to the said local bodies from the consolidated fund of the state.
- The measures needed to improve the financial position of the local bodies and to suggest possible new avenues for tapping resources in rural and urban local bodies keeping in mind the local body tax structure in other States.

In reviewing the financial position of the local bodies, the Commission has been asked to assess the financial position of the local bodies as on 31st March, 2010. The Commission has been asked to make its report available by 31st May, 2011 covering the period of five years commencing on 1st April 2012.

PARTICIPATION BY VILLAGERS IN PANCHAYAT ACTIVITIES

Do all people participate equally in activities associated with constituting and operating gram panchayats, or do some types of people more actively influence the results of elections to panchayati raj institutions and the decisions made by these elected bodies? Are those from higher castes relatively more influential in panchayats than those who belong to scheduled castes and tribes?

Which types of people are included or excluded from determining who exercises authority within panchayats? There are a wide range of political activities that are associated with electing representatives and exercising influence within PRIs.

In addition to voting, other indicators of political participation include campaigning, attending rallies and meetings, and making contact with public representatives. In order to ascertain the levels of participation in a variety of political activities, 2,013 villagers were interviewed about their political behaviours.

Among the villagers interviewed for this intensive exercise, 95 per cent of eligible citizens reported that they had voted in most or all of the panchayat elections. Levels of participation in voting did not differ significantly between men and women, land owners and the landless, or among the different caste groups.

While women turned out marginally less often to vote than men, all groups had voting rates in excess of 93 per cent, and self-exclusion was not reported by any group in significant numbers. By any standards these voting figures are high, but high voting figures are not necessarily indicative of broad po litical participation. The survey results indicate that one reason behind such large voter turnout relates to requests and pressure from contesting candidates. Of the villagers interviewed in the eight case study panchayats, 37 per cent said they had voted at least once for reasons of social solidarity—the candidate formed part of their social network. Nineteen per cent said they had voted one or more times because they wished to avoid later tension or conflict with the candidates.

Eighteen per cent maintained that they voted due to a fear that failure to vote might result in deletion of their names from the list of future beneficiaries for anti-poverty programmes or their ration cards might be cancelled and they would no longer be able to purchase staple grains at subsidized rates. High voter turnout in gram panchayat elections is not fully indicative of high levels of broad political participation or interest. Participation in political activity in fact falls off quite sharply when we consider the other activities that are associated with electing representatives and exercising influence within PRIs.

Slightly more than 29 per cent of those interviewed stated that they had worked on behalf of a candidate or political party, and slightly less than 35 per cent of those interviewed stated that they made contact with any panchayat representative during the past year. Contact with janpad or zilla panchayat members was significantly lower. However, what is perhaps most disturbing from the standpoint of accountability and transparency is the very low levels of attendance reported at gram sabha meetings where budgets, finances, and development plans are discussed.

In all 53 villages in the extensive study, the vast majority of villagers did not attend a single gram sabha meeting during the previous year and barely seven per cent of villagers attended meetings regularly. The 10 per cent quorum requirement stipulated by law in both states for gram sabha meetings is very often hard to meet in many villages, and sarpanchas resort to diverse stratagems in order to record a quorum on object.

ARE PANCHAYATS VALUED?

Even though nearly all villagers participate in voting, far fewer—between 20 and 40 per cent—are involved with the other activities that are associated with influencing decision making in PRIs. Why do so many people feel that it is not worth participating in the panchayat system? Is this because there is little to be gained materially or, as Box 1 indicates, is it because they have no control over decisions made? A ranking exercise was carried out in three panchayats in order to understand the value people attribute to the panchayat as a local political and development body as compared to other development activities in the villages.

A cross-section of 20 villagers in each panchayat were asked individually to rank the existing development activities in their village based on which one they think is "better". The outcome of the exercise indicates that the activities which are valued most highly are those which provide all villagers with the opportunity to benefit, such as education or the award of labour associated with resource development. Activities which were valued somewhat less highly were those that benefited certain groups in the village, such as women's savings groups and farmer's cooperatives.

However, the least valued activity was the gram panchayat, as many villagers felt they had no influence, that there was a lack of transparency, a high level of corruption and that very few individuals had the opportunity to benefit.

ACCOUNTABILITY

The value of benefit and accountability are two key factors influencing people's use of PRI system. How accountable are the PRIs? What mechanisms exist to hold representatives accountable, and are these mechanisms being utilized effectively by the population? The State acts and the rules of the gram panchayat provide for certain mechanisms through which elected representatives can be held accountable for their actions.

In Madhya Pradesh and Rajasthan there are three common mechanisms by which villagers can hold their gram panchayat representatives accountable: the gram sabha; the right of recall; and recourse to higher authority. In Rajasthan there is also the additional mechanism of the vigilance committee at the level of the gram panchayat. The gram sabha is intended to be the main platform for widespread transparency and accountability. Its central function is to take stock of past developments, review expenditures, and to decide which new activities are possible within the sanctioned budget. The purpose of the gram sabha is to provide villagers with the opportunity to obtain clarification from their representatives on all aspects and activities of the gram panchayat. However, data from the extensive survey indicate that the gram sabha, with only an average of seven per cent of members attending, is not yet an effective mechanism of governance.

Through passage of a bill in April 1999, Madhya Pradesh became the first state in the country to empower the people of a gram panchayat to recall an elected representative. The right of recall can only be exercised once a panchayat member has completed half of his or her term and requires that 50 per cent of the total electorate support the vote for the representative's removal. In Rajasthan the right of recall is not vested with the electorate, but with the elected representatives. In order to be valid, a no-confidence motion needs only to be supported by one third of the representatives.

In addition to the gram sabha and the right of recall at the gram panchayat level there is also scope for recourse to higher authority. In both states, the District Magistrate has the authority to remove or suspend an elected representative assessed to bedisqualifiedforthepost. In Rajasthan, the vigilance committee is an additional mechanism of accountability.

The purpose of the committee is to monitor and oversee the work of the gram panchayat, and its membership is comprised of non-elected representatives. Although the committee is not endowed with any formal powers, through its monitoring function it has the potential to enhance accountability by reporting its findings to the gram sabha. Although the extensive survey has demonstrated that the gram sabha is not a sufficient mechanism of accountability, what impact do the other mechanisms have on ensuring responsible governance? When villagers experience exclusion or poor performance do they take advantage of these other provisions for holding panchayat officials accountable? The following case studies, which are derived from the extensive survey and individual discussions, document the experience of villagers and place the problems associated with taking action against PRI representatives in context.

The case studies clearly demonstrate that mounting dissatisfaction with the panchayat does not necessarily result in local action to hold PRI representatives accountable. The limited benefits distributed by the panchayat, preoccupation with daily subsistence, local dependency relationships, corruption, and fear of social exclusion from the community hamper the use of the existing accountability mechanisms. Villagers who have taken recourse to higher authority against their elected representatives have met with limited success as the officials have not shown adequate responsiveness to their complaints or, in some cases, have been allied with the sarpanch. The absence of effective accountability mechanisms is linked to the wider socio-political context prevailing in a gram panchayat, as well as to the need for a more neutral government system that can respond effectively to local allegations of mismanagement.

WHO PARTICIPATES?

Even if the villagers view the gram panchayat with a degree of skepticism, the data demonstrate that between 11 and 40 per cent of villagers participated in political activities such as campaigning, contacting representatives, and attending meetings.

Given the hypothesis that social and economic attributes determine inclusion in panchayat activities, the next question is whether or not it is the same group in each case? Factor analysis was used first to check whether the same group of persons was consistently more active with respect to participation in political activities. Regression analysis was then employed to discern the characteristics of those individuals who participated more actively.

Villagers were asked to respond to six different survey questions relating to the participation variables of campaigning, attending rallies, supporting a candidate, influencing voters, contacting public representatives, and attending gram sabhas. The factor analysis shows that indi viduals who score highly on any one of these variables tend to have high scores on each of the other five variables.

Low scores are similarly correlated. Those who are "high participators" campaign vigourously for political candidates, influence other villagers' choices at election time, attend gram sabhas regularly, and are in frequent contact with panchayat representatives. In contrast, those who are "low participators" are not active in election campaigns, do not usually attend political rallies or meetings of the gram sabha, and have less frequent contact with panchayat representatives than other villagers.

ATTRIBUTES ARE MOST SIGNIFICANT TO PARTICIPATION

Which of the factors identified above—gender, education, wealth, and social group—was most significant to participation? Regression analysis was used to determine the level of significance of various attributes using the broad Index of Political Activity as the dependent variable.

As with our original factor analysis these findings were checked by also regressing against a narrower index constructed from the survey items related to frequency of contact with public representatives and participation in gram sabha meetings.

- *Gender*: Women participate to a much smaller degree than men. Controlling for other factors, women score, on average, 24 points lower than men on our 100-point scale of political participation.
- Social Group Rankings are not significantly associated with participation level. Among the different caste groups, only scheduled tribes have a significantly different participation levels. On average, members of scheduled tribes score about six percentage points lower considerable as that which exists between men and women. This difference disappears, however, when we consider the interaction between gender and tribe.

- Access to Information has a significant association with participation levels—a fact that is extremely relevant for policy purposes. The addition of one more source of information to a person's repertoire tends to increase participation by more than five percentage points.
- *State*: The analysis also indicates that villagers living in the three Rajasthan districts participate, on average, to a level that is five percentage points higher than those who live in the three Madhya Pradesh districts. Whether or not this difference holds true between the two states as a whole cannot be determined using this limited six-district analysis. Age and religion are consistently not significant given any alternative specification of the regression model.

An interactive variable was included to assess the interaction between gender and caste. In particular, we examined whether belonging to a scheduled tribe and being female is likely to reduce participation even further than would be suggested by adding together the individual coefficients of these two variables. The resulting interactive variable was significant and the size of its coefficient was also large. The variable ST loses significance when the interactive variable is brought within the analysis, but the overall gender variable continues to remain significant and high.

What this implies is that participation in political activity is low not so much among all scheduled tribes but mostly among the women of this social group. While all women participate less than men, participation levels among scheduled tribe women are on average 6.45 per cent lower. When the original factor analysis was regressed against the narrower index, a very significant gender difference was found. In quantitative terms, this difference amounted to 25 points on the broad index of participation with a higher magnitude of difference observed on the narrow index where women scored about 60 points lower than men on average.

However, this degree of difference is not surprising to those who have observed meetings of gram sabhas in Rajasthan or Madhya Pradesh and know that these meetings are attended mostly by men. The other variables which were found significant in association with the narrow index include education and access to information. The magnitude of influence attached to education and information is greater in the case of the narrow index.

Each additional year of education is associated with a difference of about two points, implying that a person with 10 years of formal education scores 20 per cent higher on the narrow index, all other things being equal, than a person who has no education at all. Similarly, the influence of information is also quantitatively higher in the case of the narrower index. While each additional information source accounts for a difference of about 5 percentage points on the broad index, this difference is in the range of 10 to 12 percentage points on the narrow index. Gender, education, and information are the three factors that, across the entire population and using both the broad and narrow index of participation, are most closely related to participation in PRIs.

The data also suggest that tribal origin, landlessness and religious group may, in pockets of the study population, play and important role in determining who is party to various activities associated with the gram panchayat. The data do not allow full testing of this hypothesis but they do allow us to state that an excluded person, is likely to be an illiterate scheduled tribe woman, who is relatively poorly informed and not well acquainted with the public representatives of her village.

Education and information, the other significant influences on participation rates, were not found to be closely related to landholding or higher social rank, as education is not the exclusive privilege of those with large landholdings and information is reasonably symmetrically distributed among high-and low-caste villagers. Findings of other studies, however, have indicated a strong association between wealth and education. Far from replicating differences in wealth and caste status our data suggest that education and information tend to mitigate and equalize differences in political participation among villagers in Rajasthan and Madhya Pradesh.

The discrepancy between the findings of this study and of others on the relationship between education and wealth may reflect rapid changes occurring in rural areas, but due to methodological differences between studies these findings may warrant further study.

DECENTRALIZED DEVELOPMENT EFFORTS IN INDIA

Recognizing the importance of democratic institutions at the grass-roots level, the Indian Constitution laid down in Article 40 of Part IV of the Directive Principles of State Policy that the state would take steps to organize village panchayats and endow them with such powers and authority as might be necessary to enable them to function as units of self-government.

The Panchayati Raj institutions became a state subject under the Constitution. The Balwant Rai Mehta Committee was appointed in 1957 to study the Community Development and National Extension Service programmes, especially from the point of view of assessing the extent of popular participation, and to recommend the creation of institutions through which such participation could be achieved. The Committee recommended the constitution of statutory elected local bodies with the necessary resources, power and authority devolved to them and a decentralized administrative system working under their control. It also recommended that the basic unit of democratic decentralization should be located at the block/samiti level.

The Committee envisaged directly elected panchayats for a village or group of villages, an executive body called Panchayat Samiti for a block with directly elected and co-opted members, and an advisory body called Zila Parishad at the district level constituted mainly through ex-officio members from the lower tier and others with the district chief as Chairman. The National Development Council affirmed the objective of democratic decentralization. This was the genesis of the Panchayati Raj system and when ushering it in, Nehru described it as "the most revolutionary and historical step in the context of New India". In 1972, the Planning Commission advised the state governments to set up state planning boards as apex planning bodies with the Chief Minister as the Chairman and the Finance Minister, Planning Minister, and technical experts representing various departments and disciplines as members.

The plans envisaged the decentralization of the planning process to districts and ultimately to the block level. District planning bodies were constituted in all the states except Tripura and Arunachal Pradesh. However, the district planning machinery has not really started functioning in some states. According to the information available, planning at block level has been entrusted to the Panchayati Raj bodies in West Bengal. Block level plans are being formulated in the state by block planning committees which are chaired by Sabhapatis of Panchayati Samitis.

Thus, district plans and block plans and the schemes formulated for execution with the help of district plan funds are mainly implemented by the Panchayati Raj institutions, such as Zila Parishads, Panchayat Samitis, Gram Panchayats, and other local bodies. In Karnataka, Zila Parishads and Mandal Panchayats have been entrusted with the responsibility of formulating and implementing district development plans after these bodies were set up under the Zila Parishads and Mandal Panchayats Act of 1983. The district planning committees function under the Zila Parishad. In some other states, such as Gujarat and Maharashtra, the district and block level agencies have been involved in plan formulation for a longer time.

FERMENT IN THE 1980S

A number of committees and study groups reviewed the situation and made recommendations to strengthen the systems of integrated decentralized planning. The Ashok Mehta Committee reviewed the situation in 1978, recommending an institutional design for the Panchayati Raj in the light of the developmental thrust and technical expertise required for the planning and implementation of rural development programmes. Working groups were appointed by the Planning Commission. The Working Group on Block Level Planning headed by Professor M.L. Dantwala in November 1977, and the Working Group on District Planning headed by Dr C.H. Hanumantha Rao, Member of the Planning Commission in September 1982, studied various aspects of decentralized planning at the district and block levels. Both Working Groups recommended that the basic decentralized planning function had to be at the district level.

The Working Group on District Planning recommended that:

- For decentralized planning to make headway, institutional mechanisms had to be more broad-based with the active involvement of local representatives and endowed with a greater degree of autonomy in local decision-making;
- Panchayati Raj institutions and other local government institutions should play a crucial role in the district planning process.

The Committee to Review the Existing Administrative Arrangements for Rural Development and Poverty Alleviation headed by Dr G.V.K. Rao, Member of the Planning Commission, also went into the question of decentralized planning and recommended that:

- Rural development should be the major component of district planning, though the District Plan should encompass the total activity of the district;
- The district should be the basic unit for policy planning and programme implementation. The Zila Parishad should, therefore, become the principal body for the management of all development programmes that could be handled at that level;
- Panchayati Raj institutions at the district level and below should be assigned an important role in respect of planning, implementation and monitoring of rural development programmes;
- Some of the planning functions at the state level might have to be transferred to the district level for effective decentralized district planning;
- In order to give some leeway and manoeuvrability in planning and decision-making, it was necessary to make some funds available to the District Planning Body, funds which were not tied to any departmental schemes and which might be used towards small schemes meant for the local priorities, needs and aspirations of the local community.

The mid-1980s saw the emergence of an influential movement to revitalize local self-government structures in India and link them with the agricultural and rural development process. There were two basic reasons for this. The first was the belief with the then Prime Minister Rajiv Gandhi that India was too 'large' a country to be ruled from a central place. The responsibility of the centre for many functions had to be at the local level. This would lead to accountability in the long run, although in the short run resources would have to be allocated at the local level (if accountability was to be enforced) and these resources could be misused. Rajiv Gandhi, however, believed that in the long run democratic policies would take care of such abuse and so insisted on the political and economic enfranchisement of poorer groups (Scheduled Castes, Scheduled Tribes and women). The second reason was the fact that India's initial agricultural planning systems were somewhat linear in nature, emphasizing, for example, canal and tube-well irrigation and high-yielding varieties and led to the favoured region, favoured crop strategy. The mid-1980s saw this strategy being questioned and the whole issue of widespread agricultural growth raised in terms of an agro-climatic plan.

This in turn raised the question of local participation and voluntary organizations and the associated question of resource allocation and functioning of decentralized markets. The question raised was the manner in which special programmes for employment and rural development could be integrated with the agricultural development.

The mid-term appraisal of the Seventh Five-year Plan had anticipated these problems, as the following abstract shows:

- "However, it is noticed that wherever the Panchayati Raj institutions have been actively involved, the implementation of rural development programmes has been better and the selection of beneficiaries and designing of schemes have been more satisfactory. The Planning Commission has been impressing upon the states that various rural development programmes will be realistic and meaningful only if people's representatives are actively involved and associated in local level planning, design formulation and implementation of those programmes and the selection of beneficiaries in the anti-poverty and employment programmes such as IRDP, NREP, RLEGP etc. and that there is no better instrument to meet this need other than the Panchayati Raj institutions".

  The original Panchayati Raj Bill (1989) was an initiative not only to decentralize power, but to politically enfranchise the poorer parts of society, such as Scheduled Castes, Scheduled Tribes and women, who form a large part of the landless labourer and artisan populations.

  The Jawahar Rozgar Yojana (JRY), a nationwide employment scheme, attempted to put economic power behind this change.

  The manual of JRY clearly brought out these intentions as follows:

- The construction or renovation of irrigation tanks is one of the important community works which can be taken up under JRY. Similarly, items, such as land shaping, drainage, and field channels on private lands which are part of a project to improve the productivity of an area can be undertaken. However, only those blocks of land would be taken up under the programme if more than 50 per cent of the landholders were small and marginal farmers and they owned not less than 25 per cent of the land in the block. The total number of farmers covered by any such works should not be less than 10. No recovery of the cost of land development will be made from the small and marginal farmers. In the case of large farmers, the recovery pattern will be prescribed by the state government. The rate of recovery will be the same as in a similar scheme being implemented by the state government.

  The original Panchayati Raj Bill tied it all up as follows:

- Seats shall be reserved for the Scheduled Castes and the Scheduled Tribes in every Panchayat and the number of seats so reserved shall bear, as nearly as may be, the same proportion to the total number of seats to be filled by direct election in that Panchayat as the population of the scheduled castes in that panchayat area or of the scheduled tribes in that panchayat area bears to the total population of that area.

  If the population of the scheduled castes or, as the case may be, the scheduled tribes, in a panchayat area is not sufficient for the reservation of any seat, one seat for the scheduled castes or, as the case may be, one seat for the scheduled tribes, will be reserved in that panchayat.

- As nearly as may be, thirty per cent of the total number of seats reserved under Clause (a) shall be reserved for women belonging to the scheduled castes or, as the case may be, the scheduled tribes.

  Subject to the provision of the Constitution, the legislature of a state may, by law, endow the panchayats with such powers and authority as may be necessary to enable them to function as institutions of self-government and such law may contain provisions for the devolution of powers and responsibilities upon panchayats at the appropriate level, subject to such conditions as may be specified therein, with respect to:
- The preparation of plans for economic development and social justice;
- The implementation of schemes for economic development and social justice as may be entrusted to them including those in relation to the matter listed in the Eleventh Schedule.

The organizational structure was to be in position to address the basic problems of underdevelopment in the Eighth Plan. However, the process was delayed and many of the original provisions of the Bill were watered down since discretionary powers were given to the states. However, the central features remained, namely, compulsory election; reservation for Scheduled Castes, Scheduled Tribes and women; devolution of resources and powers as outlined above; and rural development programmes, such as JRY which would directly allocate resources at the village level, depending on the indicators of unemployment. A village can now receive around 60,000 rupees under JRY, or 2,000 person days of employment.

Thus, twenty families can have up to 100 days of employment. This kind of input can desilt a village tank by about 3 feet or meet around 30 per cent of the labour requirements of contour bunding and gully plugging in a medium- sized watershed. Thus, integration possibilities existed with the agro-climatic plan. The agro-climatic plan was to be operationalized at the district level to fulfill the objectives of minimum needs and employment.

A recent ILO review of this programme states the following:

- A number of employment generation schemes had been initiated in India, specially since the mid-1960s, in order to help the poor raise their income levels through additional employment. Most of the initial schemes were tentative and limited in scope. At the end of the 1970s, an attempt was made to rationalize these schemes into two comprehensive nationwide schemes– the National Rural Employment Programme (NREP) and the Rural Landless Employment Guarantee Programme (RLEGP). The operation of these schemes left much to be desired; assets created were usually not economically productive, felt needs of the people were not reflected, funds did not go where they were most needed, the system of project approval was inefficient and time-consuming, and the states tended to use the funds allocated for the programmes for other purposes. All this led to the replacement of NREP and RLEGP with a single scheme–the Jawahar Rozgar Yojana (JRY) towards the end of the 1980s.

JRY, a nationwide programme, is funded jointly by the central (80 per cent) and state (20 per cent) governments. Allocation of funds is based on a formula designed to ensure that the distribution of funds corresponds to the distribution of the poor across the regions. Part of the funds (less than 25 per cent) allocated to a state are earmarked for two sub-schemes of JRY: Indira Awaas Yojana–a scheme for building houses free of cost for the weaker parts (Scheduled Castes, Scheduled Tribes and liberated bonded labour), and the Million Wells Scheme for constructing dug-wells free of cost for small and marginal farmers.

Of the remaining funds, 80 per cent goes to village Panchayats and the balance to the district authorities. The village Panchayats are free to decide on the use of funds, except that 22.5 per cent must be devoted to works that directly benefit the weaker parts of society. Funds allocated to the district, however, must be spent in accordance with a given schedule, including an individual beneficiary scheme for the Scheduled Castes and the Scheduled Tribes. Significantly, 10 per cent of the funds are to be allocated for the maintenance of assets already created.

The choice of community assets to be built is not restricted. Assets that may be owned by a group of individuals can be included in the works if they result in a flow of income for the group. Land development in small and marginal farms is also permissible if the owners are in the poor category, as are works for identified poor individuals among the weaker parts. The responsibility for identifying and executing works rests at the district level with the District Rural Development Agency or the Zila Parishad (district Panchayat) and at the village level with the village Panchayat. The latter is empowered to take up any project that has been technically appraised and approved by the Panchayat Samiti (block Panchayat). To avoid deviation and malpractice, the village Panchayat is required to prepare muster rolls in detail for the labour employed and display them at a public place.

For all works under JRY, the wage paid is the minimum wage as prescribed under the Minimum Wages Act. Two kilograms of foodgrains at subsidized rates are also made available to the workers. All works undertaken are included in the Annual Action Plan. Priority is required to be given to incomplete works from the previous Plan. At the village level, the Plan has to be discussed in the village Panchayat and care has to be taken to ensure that top priority is given to works benefiting the weaker parts of the community.

The village Panchayat must also report on the progress of work to the Gram Sabha (village assembly) at least twice a year. Since its inception in April 1989, an average of 8 to 9 million mandays of employment have been annually created under JRY. An average amount of 32.7 billion rupees was available to JRY in the first two years. In the following two years, the implementation of macroeconomic stabilization measures led to a substantial decline in the resources available to JRY. In 1993/94, however, there was a substantial increase. It is evident that the Panchayats are, in principle, substantially involved in implementing JRY.

However, the Panchayats have so far been ineffective and, consequently, government bureaucracies have played a dominant role in the implementation process. There were several reasons for this, most importantly the inherent weaknesses in the Panchayat system as provided for in the Constitution.

Recently, the government has been able to mobilize political support for bringing the Panchayat system to centre stage and passed the Constitution (Seventy-second Amendment) Bill, 1991 thus removing the system's inherent shortcomings. The new Panchayat system should now provide the much- needed non-bureaucratic institutional support to the poverty alleviation programmes and with a more aware rural population, the prospects for its success are perhaps brighter. The Act enjoins the states to endow the Panchayats with such powers as to enable them to prepare and implement plans for economic development and social justice. Clearly, devolution of power has to be both administrative and financial. It envisages the constitution of a state finance commission once in every five years to review the financial position of thc Panchayats. Thc 11th schedulc in the constitution lists 29 functional areas to be brought within the purview of the decentralized planning level, including agriculture and allied activities, irrigation, social forestry, village and small-scale industries, water supply, housing, roads, education and poverty alleviation programmes. Resources and funds flowing from various departments of the state governments and from centrally-sponsored schemes to the district and sub-district levels can be dovetailed within a local area plan.

This would ensure better utilization of resources under one umbrella with priorities assigned to activities on the basis of the felt needs of the people. State governments have enacted appropriate conformity legislation. Similarly, all the states have set up state finance commissions to review the financial positions of the Panchayats and recommend principles which should govern the distribution of the net proceeds of duties and taxes etc. between the states and Panchayats and between Panchayats at different levels. They also suggest ways of raising their own resources by the Panchayats.

Meanwhile, the government has accepted the recommendations of the Tenth Central Finance Commission to give *ad hoc* grants-in-aid of 43.81 billion rupees to the states in four installments commencing from the financial year 1996/97. Panchayats have been empowered by the Seventy-third Amendment. Access to and effective control over resources is a critical component of this empowerment. The real issues of such access are knowledge and awareness of the needs of the people, legal rights, availability and accessibility of social and economic resources. These changes in procedures and organizations have as yet not fully taken place as envisaged in the legislation. It also requires restructuring relationships including looking at gender issues both at the micro and macro level.

PARTICIPATION IN PANCHAYATI RAJ INSTITUTIONS (PRIS) AND GRAM SABHAS

NREGA is designed to be largely implemented through PRIs – at least 50 per cent of all sanctioned works are to be implemented by the Gram Panchayats. The Gram Sabha too plays a crucial role in the selection of works and the conduct of social audits.

Participation of people at large and women in particular in these institutions and assemblies is, then, critical to realising the participatory potential of the Act. During the survey it was found that women workers did not generally take part in Gram Sabhas. This is partly due to lack of awareness about the significant role to be played by the Gram Sabhas in making a shelf of projects and conducting social audits of NREGA works. Women's participation in Panchayati Raj Institution (PRIs) was also very low - not even 1 per cent of the respondents in all the districts said they were involved in PRI's activities. This is despite the reservation of one third of all seats in local elected bodies for women (under the 73rd and 74th Constitutional Amendment Acts). Most elected women tend to be "rubber stamp" leaders, the vast majority of them are illiterate and politically untrained.

While women are increasingly visible as part of the NREGA workforce, there is still much scope to increase their involvement in PRIs to tackle issues like water, sanitation, health, education and of course the implementation of NREGA.

❐

2.

Empowerment, Entrepreneurship and Education in Rural India

Rural Education

The organization president asked the student to go to area schools to assess community residents' perspectives of"what's lacking" in village education systems. In addition to assessing the"missing links," the student's assignment was to"design a model for the future institution of education in rural India" and"provide a module of a new idea" for teachers to change routine. One teacher defined"quality education" as accessible to low income families with"good" teachers who are dedicated to their work." Another asked for improved facilities,"The physical environment confines creativity." A woman from one self-help group said:

- We are illiterate, but we want our daughters and sons to have equal education. We want our daughters to have good character, intelligence, so we can send her any place, like you. You came here because you have education.

The social work student also visited primary schools in two rural districts within the northern Himalayas region of India. She observed curriculum content delivery, school procedures, and overall primary school learning environments.

She talked to teachers, administrators, and parents about rural education in India. Many of these key informants were women parents. She asked these key informants about youth access to education, quality of education, and what they would like for the future of their educational systems. She asked key informants about access to education for girls and young women. The methodology for data collection was similar to that used for the women's self- help groups. Initial questions were also drawn from the practice literature, Empowerment, Entrepreneurship and Education in Rural India programme orientation sessions, and the social work student's observations. They included open-ended questions with flexible probes.

Questioning followed the process and content of information offered by the key informants. Early interview data helped generate discussion questions for subsequent interviewees. Field notes were regularly recorded. They included many direct quotations of key informants and observational data.

ANALYSES

The social work student analysed field notes for topics offered most frequently by the key informants. The student engaged in iterative combing of the data with identification of themes offered by key informants that ranged from broad to specific. Thus data were sorted and assembled using an open, axial, and categorical method consistent with grounded theory analysis. Field note data were triangulated with student observations and literature. Main themes, with supportive data to illustrate each theme, were described within a summary course paper and three presentations to community organizers in India, university study abroad faculty, and American social work students, social work professors, and participants of the 2007 annual conference of the National Rural Social Work Caucus. The outcome themes and supporting data were reviewed by, and discussed at length with, a university social work professor. The data and findings of this study were literally built from the ground up.

OUTCOMES

Three main themes emerged from analysis of the key informant discussions and observational data. Two themes were drawn from the self- help group women. First, the women reported that self-help groups were a beginning step in the empowerment of women within a largely patriarchal society. Second, the women said that self-help group's micro-finance activities increased opportunities for women's entrepr-eneurship that generated income for the women and their families. A third theme was drawn from data about the rural education system reported by the women in the self-help groups, combined with data drawn from the student's school observations, and as reported by educational key informants, *i.e.*, teachers, school administrators, and parents of school age children. Most parents were mothers of the children. Key informants said there was a strong need for increased access to quality education within rural Indian communities, particularly for girls and young women.

Empowerment of Women

The development of mutual aid within self-help groups of rural women appeared to be part of a strengthening social action movement among women in rural India. Although the groups were originally encouraged by the grassroots non-governmental organization, the data suggested that the women made largely autonomous local decisions about what events and enterprises they would support and to what extent. It appeared that the self-help groups were having a significant impact on the empowerment of women in rural areas per the following field note:

- Women repeatedly speak positively about their self-organization, support, and community. During marriage ceremonies, women joined in to help ease the workload. In village K., women expressed that they feel they can talk easily now, have something fun to do, and come out of their houses…Women also said they felt more"in control" after formation of the self-help group. They said they felt"very good" and"important."

Self-help groups provided opportunities for women to serve as models of leadership for the children that were often present in the background during group meetings. Girls and young women watched their mothers, aunts, and grandmothers serve as decision makers and persons that were listened to by others. Several poignant field notes recorded the enthusiasm of the women self-help group participants: Many of the women appeared eager to attend the groups even if they have to walk for hours to get there." [Within the groups], the women"were willing to try new things." The student recorded,"Every woman I talked to had positive feelings towards [the self-help group]" and,"They seem to have a sense of pride and ownership in their group organization."

It appeared that the self-help groups might take on some of the functions of supportive extended family kinship networks. For example, they provided a mechanism for group cohesion expressed through ritual:

- *Song and dance played an integral role in self-help groups*: They [taught] some songs, which appeared to be an effective method to communicate social messages and build cohesion within the group. At first, I was embarrassed and annoyed that the women insisted on me dancing for them. After weeks of Indian dancing in the center of the self-help group meetings, I started to enjoy the event. It made me feel part of the village and as one woman told me once, I felt"same, same."

Through the cultural communication of dance, the student was invited into Indian culture. The women's invitation impacted both the women and student. Women experienced a genuine interest from a person outside the self-help group, fostering an opportunity to share their story and to become part of the student's life and reality. The student learned how to be part of another culture, meeting people"where they are," as she shared a few moments of the rural women's lives. The non-traditional learning experience inspired the student to seek additional learning about Indian culture.

The groups appeared to provide a close bond for expression of feelings, including worry and frustration:

- During self-help group meetings, women expressed problems that affect their livelihood. Initially, women responded with"no problems" to every question I asked. After further probing, the first and foremost issue …women expressed that there was no rain. [The women explained that] drought leads to shortage of drinking water, lower crop yields, and lower income. In S. village, wild animals were eating crops and lowering the production.

The self-help group participants said that migration of youth to the cities also affected agricultural production and cultural integrity:

- When families migrate to larger cities, the land is left barren and also looses percolation qualities. Not only could families in need of extra income use the land but it also affects the quality of the land around it, when it lies barren. Also, as families move to find better jobs, village traditions disperse and culture fades away.

In addition to rural youth drain, family distance, and cultural dissolution afforded by migration to urban areas, the rural women discussed gender role concerns and family issues. They complained of"hard labour from dawn to dusk and men do not recognize their labour as a source of income." The women said that,"Girls are required to drop education to learn domestic labour." Within the kinship-type networks of the self-help groups, the women shared information that is seldom discussed outside families:

- Alcoholism in men is overlooked in the villages, but families are affected especially when the ramifications include domestic violence. As a result [of domestic violence many] women do not appear to have a voice in the home or community.

Clearly the empowerment of women has far to go within rural northern Indian communities. However, the self-help group appears to be one way to begin.

Entrepreneurship Opportuntties for Women

One function of the self-help group is to promote new business developments for local women and their families. While this could logically be a sub theme of empowerment, the concept is sufficiently strong as to stand- alone. The student noted,"Women that understand the purpose of the group and participate in income-generating programmes are starting small businesses and earning their own incomes." Further, individual groups can elect to participate in monthly regional meetings to"contribute to the inter-loan fund, learn new income-generating skills, advocate for social change, and support one another." The student observed self-help group members in rural northern India villages provide financial support for entrepreneurial opportunities such as the purchase of a cow for selling milk, yarn for knitting scarves, bees for producing honey, and wax for making candles. Women from one village taught women from another village how to knit. The women developed their own wedding supply business. They loaned members money for family weddings and bartered goods amongst each other.

Sappenfield tells a story of entrepreneurship within one rural self-help group. This example demonstrates that developing financial capital leads to cultural capital. Further, women participants of self-help groups are active leaders of social change:

- When Phulbasin Yadav and 11 other women set aside $3 a month to start a business, skeptical elders turned the town against them. When Ms. Yadav learned to ride a bicycle, traveling between villages to set up a health clinic and offer hot meals for children, her husband threw her out of the house, saying she was ignoring her duties at home. And when she and her colleagues

> won the contract to run the local market, the businessman who lost the bid promised to kill them. Business in Suduldhain had always been a man's world. But today, Yadav is president of a districtwide network of women's groups with businesses ranging from mines to concrete works- totaling a half a million dollars in assets...Now in a position of power, these groups have begun to change the world one village at a time. They have saved 570 child marriages...offered dowries to poor families whose daughters would otherwise be shunned. They have paid for school uniforms and taken over fair-price stores that were once cheating villagers.

Women demonstrate leadership in owning Internet kiosks that connect villagers to the outside world, including information, health care services, and educational programmes. Another key financial function of the self-help group is allowing start up time for businesses with reasonable payment plans and lending rates of two to three per cent. This is in direct opposition to many predatory lenders in rural areas that have charged as much as"36 per cent to 3000 per cent per annum".

The self-help group support for developing business income does not just aid women. It supports their families, including men. Jobs with a living wage are scarce in rural areas. Government employment programmes are insufficient:

- All though the government seems to have social welfare programmes in place, I don't see them making a positive impact. In district A., men at village meetings discussed the 180-day work programme. They said that three months of work doesn't even support their family because wages are so low and sometimes they don't get paid fairly. My own country is no different.

Economic resources and power are invariably paired. The social work student noted that women self-help groups with collective financial assets participated as members of village councils called Panchayats. Self-help groups have directly influenced policy, including helping to influence decisions about which services receive government funding. The student learned of a woman leader that spearheaded the passage of the Indian Right to Information Act of 2005:

- The first day in India I was asked to attend a symposium, where Lady Irwin College students and staff were very excited and passionate to hear Ms. Aruna Roy speak. I started to realise that people in India are often trapped by government corruption. The Right to Information Act is an important tool for them to create change. Even though I did not actually meet her, Aruna Roy is one of the people in India who influenced me. She is one whom I would not have realised her importance until reflecting on her words. Looking back, I remember her and her message: keep promises, mobilize people to get together, and beat corruption.

Opportunities to generate new sources of family income such as entrepreneurial ventures of the women's self-help groups are a beginning step towards building stronger economic growth and social justice for women and families living in rural areas.

Access to Quality Education, Especially for Girls and Young Women

The student noted"nearly every self-help group member we talked to saw education as a need." Convincing exchanges about the importance of education to the women self-help group members took place as the student summarized responses of members about their needs across many self-help groups:

- *Student*: What changes do you want?
- *Women*: Education
- *Student*: What do you value?
- *Women*: Education
- *Student*: What do you want for your children?
- *Women*: Education
- *Student*: What problems do you see?
- *Women*: Education

Education was a reoccurring request of the women. One woman from village T. said,"We want to have awareness, read and write, like you. We want first education. It is most important for awareness and development." Most of the teachers, administrators, and parents echoed this sentiment with equalpassion. One teacher from B. said,"Children hold our country's future." Key informants noted that education generated"knowledge, understanding, ideas, opportunity, power, and the future." They said youth could benefit from formal and informal sources of education, books, trainings from people outside the village, knowledge about agriculture, and cultural learning from community members.

The observations of the social work student provide a glimpse of the current village educational systems:

- The NGO site was located next to a primary government school. Every day I came home, I saw the students sitting on the ground, repeating after one another and in unison,"A-a, B-b, C-c, D-d." Teachers sat in the shade watching the students for much of the day. After weeks of exactly the same exercise, I realise many sessions were similarly un-stimulating for the students. Each school was different; there was a lack of curriculum standardization. Other schools had inspired [enthusiastic] teachers but the facilities were bare. Many students had to walk into the woods to go to the bathroom. Colourful classroom pictures were rare. It did make me realise that all you REALLY need to teach students, or at least appear to be teaching, is an open field, one teacher, and a few young persons.

Key informants expressed concern that children have"unequal educational opportunities" as they stated that the quality of education depends on the family and village financial status. They noted a shortage of teachers, quality facilities, and teaching materials. Some key informants said that government teachers lacked"excitement" and"motivation" to teach." They said a quality education would avoid rote, repetitive learning and stifling of creativity. Teachers complained of government regulations, parental non-involvement, and heavy workloads.

The student observed that the children in the schools were engaged in passive learning. She said teachers appeared to have a"distant, uninvolved approach." The key informants, particularly women self-help participants, said they wanted"a new model of education" for their children. One said,"We are literate but we want our daughters and sons to have equal education. We want the best for them...to be intelligent, and have good character." The student suggested a plan for the development of an improved rural educational curriculum. It built on the community organization and group skills that the women demonstrated during the formation of the self-help groups. Additionally, the student created an example of a creative learning module focusing on child self-expression. She tested the learning module with one cohort of school children. Next, she presented her ideas and evidence of the children's learning to the leaders of the NGO programme.

The key informants expressed particular concern about the need to keep girls and young women in schools. Self-help group members noted that running entrepreneurial enterprises requires literacy and knowledge of business management. They recommended increased access of girls and young women to school midday meals, childcare, and assistance with paying for books and uniforms.

Not everyone in India is supportive of increasing female access to education. InfoChange describes state government cutbacks on literacy programmes after women's groups began to protest against the distribution and consumption of liquor. Liquor sales are a source of government revenue. Despite some national oppositional stakeholders, the rural northern Indian women, teachers, administrators, and parents stood clearly on the side of increased access to quality education for their children, particularly for girls and young women.

Worker Safetyin the Child Welfare System

The tragedy of a rural child welfare social worker meeting her death during the process of carrying out her job duties is an unfortunate reality. Recently a child welfare worker in rural Kentucky was killed as she was in the process of providing supervised visitation for a young child and her family. It is understood by those who decide on the pursuit of achild welfare social work career that interactions with angry and sometimes violent clientele can and often will happen.

While attempting to protect children and support families, child welfare social workers face a growing threat to their safety. Shields *et al.* maintained that child welfare social workers charged with the task of questioning clients about private family and personal matters are at greater risk of personal injury. In a discussion of child abuse risk assessment models, English and Pecora indicated that there is practical use for a tool to determine the severity, frequency, and prediction of child abuse by high risk parents. To date there is no tool to assist in the assessment of danger to child welfare workers who are intervening in the lives of high risk populations.

Scalera observed that factors contributing to increased concern for worker safety are a collapse of family structure; poor housing conditions or homelessness;

unemployment; lack of affordable health care; and substance abuse. These findings are in accord with the findings of English and Pecora who considered overall risk factors with regard to perpetrators of child abuse and found that economic status also had an independent effect on the urgency or"risk status" of child abuse cases.

RURAL POVERTY AND SUBSTANCE ABUSE

Almost 8 million Americans live in poverty in rural areas despite the economic growth of the last decade. Rural job growth and earnings continue to fall behind metro areas obstructing the ability to move welfare recipients into gainful employment. Rural families have culturally unique characteristics which include an isolationist mentality leading to a lack of understanding and utilization of formal resources. Because many rural social services clients are isolationist, they often reside in isolated areas affecting the child welfare social worker's emergency response times, and the client-professional relationship.

Templeman contended that rural client characteristics often impact child welfare social worker recruitment and retention rates. They expand on this trend by pointing out that decreased funding, high per-unit cost for services due to low population density, restricted mobility of families, and increased mileage cost contribute to the difficulty of transferring urban models normally taught in contemporary schools and departments of social work to rural models that are rarely taught. The lack of knowledge of rural models appears to lessen the retention rate of rural child welfare social workers due to a breakdown of understanding rural clientele. These barriers additionally contribute to increased worker safety concerns as child welfare social workers have more interaction with families outside of the agency than other social services professionals.

Studies performed by Burns give credence to an increase in substance abuse and mental health issues experienced by high risk parents in the rural social welfare system. The rise in methamphetamine use and production within rural settings has created further safety concerns for child welfare social workers. A study in a rural Midwest county found that nearly 25 per cent of daily child maltreatment reports involved parent methamphetamine abuse. Lowe reported that methamp-hetamine use and production is spreading throughout the rural Appalachia Ohio counties and that caseworkers need to ensure their own safety when conducting home visits. Caseworkers, who participated in the Statewide Training Assessment for the Ohio Child Welfare Training Programme, reported that they sought out training and educational materials on methamphetamine labs in an effort to protect themselves as well as their clients.

Child welfare caseworkers reported in an Ohio Statewide Training Assessment that they feel an increased sense of danger when they cannot take another worker into the field with them. They cited three reasons which prevented taking an additional worker into the field: small agencies in which two workers in the field led to inadequate coverage in the agency; agencies which would not approve overtime if two workers responded to a report after hours; and supervisors who were unaware of danger and would not approve for two workers to respond. Additionally, caseworkers cited a lack of cell phone coverage or lack of cell phone availability and an increased sense of danger.

Worker Perception of Safety in the Rural Workplace

One in every ten rural workers is pushed, shoved, or hit by one or more agency clients each year. While 97 per cent of the respondents of this study reported being screamed or cursed at on at least one occasion in the previous 12 months, one-third of the workers reported being threatened with death at least once in the year prior to the study. Macdonald *et al.* maintained that 84.4 per cent of the respondents who reported feeling unsafe with clients were the front-line staff. These authors observed that child welfare social workers felt just as intimidated by threats of violence as actual acts of violence. Newhill found an occurrence rate of 75 per cent for child welfare social workers, topped only by criminal justice workers and drug/alcohol workers. The results of these studies are echoed by Ringstad who found 86 per cent of social workers experienced some type of violence during their career. Despite the high rates of occurrence, Macdonald found that nearly 25 per cent of workers did not report an incident of violence.

Responses of Rural Child Welfare Social Workers

The annual conference of the National Association of Social Workers in West Virginia provided a venue for gathering information regarding the responses of child welfare social workers regarding the question of safety at work. The authors designed the workshop as a focus group from which information could be used to influence policy development at the agency, local, state, and national levels. There was no plan to meet the qualitative research definition of focus group as defined by Sherman and Reed in this workshop. Therefore the term focus group in this respect is a loose application. Information was collected in the form of summary notes rather than verbatim transcripts.

Participants were also asked to complete a questionnaire regarding their years of experience in child welfare, demographic information, and the types and numbers of child welfare social work safety trainings that they have participated in. They were also asked to rate the trainings that they attended and provide an estimate of the numbers of events that they had experienced in which they felt that their personal safety was threatened while performing their job duties. They were encouraged to expand on these events if they felt comfortable in doing so.

Of the 34 participants, 33 were women between the ages of 25-60. The mean number of years worked was 9.9 with a standard deviation of 7.4. With regard to threats to personal safety, 88.6 per cent indicated that they had experienced at least 1 situation where they felt compromised.

Information gained from the surveys and subsequent focus group summary notes revealed that participants had been: shot at with bows and arrows; hit by beer bottles; threatened with hand guns and knives; pushed and shoved; received death threats; beaten in front of the court house; the recipient of a bomb threat; and threatened with disembowelment upon the client's release from prison. Participants emphasized that they usually travel to remote locations often alone and do not have adequate assistance during their sessions.

Many participants voiced a concern about going alone on calls at night during their"on call" duties which all stated that they were required to engage in. Participants indicated that often their agencies are small and under funded. That, in tandem with their superiors' lack of understanding about the potential for violence from a particular family is often the recipe for a dangerous client encounter. Participants also discussed the potential for bodily harm from dogs, chickens, pigs, raccoons, rats, cat, possums, goats, snakes, and roosters which many rural families have on their property. Issues regarding general health concerns surfaced during the session with regard to having been spat on from a client reported to have HIV and issues with lice, fleas, and roaches in client homes as well as sitting in chairs where clients have urinated.

Several participants indicated that their clients had tried to get into their cars upon leaving a threatening scene, had lunged at them, run them off of the road, and had threatened to harm the worker's family members. Incidents involving physical violence towards family members are especially threatening in rural areas due to small population size which allows for more familiarity about family members and where they reside. Large urban populations often reside in areas that are condensed by high rise dwellings as opposed to the smaller rural populations residing in larger areas of land mass making criminal acts often easier to hide.

Regarding the vast miles that workers have to travel, participants stated that they had encountered issues in snow and ice storms, floods, mud and mudslides, and the hazard of having to cross a creek with no bridge to a client's home. Participants voiced a concern about discovering that some clients had a history of violence which was either downplayed or undisclosed by the client. Participants also discussed the possibility of injury from falling through wooden porches, holding onto rotten hand rails, and falling down steep stairs. Finally, participants indicated that they were often threatened by their clients in the form of the client threatening to file slander charges against them and calling the governor's and their supervisor's office to file complaints.

Rural Child Welfare Social Worker Trainings

With regard to safety training of the 34 participants, 31.4 per cent indicated that they had participated in safety trainings upon hire; 5.7 per cent indicated that they participated in safety trainings quarterly; 11.4 per cent indicated that they had participated in a safety training at least one time yearly; and 51.4 per cent maintained that they had never participated in safety trainings. Of the 49.6 per cent who did participate in safety trainings only 11.4 per cent felt that the trainings were"somewhat important to their work". With regard to the safety training being"feasible to use in their work", approximately 46 per cent of participants engaging in safety training believed the trainings to be a feasible component to their work responsibilities.

Regarding the"ease of learning the safety techniques" 40 per cent of participants who participated in safety trainings felt that the techniques were easy to learn. Participants were asked if the techniques that they learned were easily utilized in a threatening situation. Only 36 per cent of those who participated in training felt that the techniques would be useful in a threatening situation. Finally, participants were asked how"easily the trainings were worked into their work schedules". Approximately 35 per cent of participants felt that the trainings were practical with regard to their work schedules. These statistics reveal that these rural child welfare social work participants overwhelmingly never received any type of safety trainings related to their jobs. Although participants who were offered trainings felt that the information was important and easily learned, they appeared to be disenchanted with the feasibility of the techniques to work in a threatening situation. Clearly, participants felt that the trainings offered to them were not easily worked into their schedules. This finding could have ramifications for agencies with regard to making trainings an important if not mandated part of child welfare social worker orientation.

Safety Issues in Social Work Education Child Welfare Field Practicums

In a study conducted by Messinger gay and lesbian social work students reported the general feeling of lack of safety and anxiety during their field placements. The students related this feeling to working with clients and within the agency atmospheres in general. Gelman found 30 per cent of foundation- year MSW students were concerned about safety issues in the field practicum. Another 74 per cent of the students were concerned about the quality of supervision they would receive and that they might be put into situations without sufficient preparation or support. These results are congruent with the Delphi study, which found a strong consensus from respondents that safety issues needed attention in field settings.

In a national survey of field directors, 42 per cent of social work programmes reported having at least one student threatened by a client during the field experience. Yet only 12 per cent of the agencies had formal safety policies against assaults and threats.

The study found that nearly one-third of social work programmes provide safety training to students. The majority of programmes had mandatory safety training with half of the programmes integrating safety training into existing course curriculum. Two-thirds of the field directors did not feel that the safety training offered by their social work programmes was adequate. A study of violence with field placements in 1993, found that more than half of students reported their field sites did not have safety policies. Only half of the students in the study reported that their social work programmes provided safety information in relation to practice. In a similar study, students believed that field instructors are responsible for explaining safety concerns and risks concerning field placements. The study pointed out that students want field instructors to make them aware of safety procedures, formal or informal.

Current Solutions to Enhance Child Welfare Social Worker Safety

Scalera advocates for child welfare social workers to have a mandated buddy system when clients have a history of violence or a conviction involving the use of a weapon. He argues that the use of the buddy system demonstrates a commitment and a sense of entitlement that promotes worker safety. The participants at the annual National Association of Social Work conference in West Virginia also discussed safety options during the focus group session.

Their recommendations included: finding out when a client is to be released from prison; ask clients to remove barriers from exits or ask if this could be done by the worker; carry mace or pepper spray; try to stand in a client's home if possible; back your car up so that the front is facing an exit; leave purses and bags in the car if possible; carry a dog whistle; carry a regular whistle; carry dog biscuits; obtain prior information about the family and environment; do a risk assessment on violence before a home visit; use a buddy system; increase cooperation with law enforcement; leave an increasingly tense situation; build a good repairé with the client and family; obtain a concealed weapon permit for off duty times; leave the home before the client; make a call list of colleagues pertinent to a case and let them know your location before you leave; take off jewelry; put long hair into a clasp or rubber band; take a clipboard and if it is necessary to sit down it can be used; be respectful and ask the client's permission before taking any action; take few if any notes during a conversation, keep eye contact; use verbal de-escalation; take note of your instincts; use an interview room at the agency if possible; know when the client is frustrated; make sure that the agency lobby and interview rooms are secure; create alliances with family members; use flea collars in the cuffs of slacks and in car floor boards; use four wheel drive vehicles; use antennas designed to work in remote locations for cell phones; know where to find gas, food, and restrooms en route to a client's home; always keep an emergency cell phone charger in the car; have on hand disinfecting wipes; diaper wipes; lice spray; disinfectant spray; garbage bags; mentholated rub; extra clothes and shoes; flashlight and batteries; spare glasses or contact lenses; shovel; rock salt; and cat litter.

The participants also indicated that the worker should always lock their car doors, and if possible have an electronic opener and carry a spare set of keys in their pockets.

IMPLICATIONS FOR SOCIAL WORK

Clearly the literature over the past decade with regard to safety in field education and in the workplace although scant, continues to mound. However, it appears that little is being done to assist in child welfare social worker safety as a result of the literature. The studies highlighted here have important implications for agency planning, worker training, and resource allocation for child welfare agencies.

The recommendations are supported by the literature and implementation of the proposed recommendations is necessary. Students and employees continue to report a need for adequate safety training, yet the Counsel on Social Work Education and child welfare training programmes have not mandated safety training. As a result, child welfare social workers must advocate for their own safety and ask agencies to commitment to the safety of their workers. Workers must be educated on the potential for violence within the workforce. It is possible that if more individuals are educated on the risks and obtain the necessary skills to diffuse volatile situations as well as gain support from child welfare agencies the rates of violence will decrease. Child welfare social workers"cannot effectively protect children or help families if they themselves are not safe".

Teaching Social Work Research in two Formats

As mentioned previously, a BSW research course was taught in two course sections to meet the needs of a rural state's BSW students. The traditional class, was taught at the state university on Tuesdays and Thursdays from 9:30 to 11:00 a.m. This class was taught in a very traditional fashion with lecture, group exercises, written assignments, and examinations.

The Block Three Weekends class, was taught at an outreach site approximately 250 miles from the state university in order to offer the course to rural outreach students. Lecture, group exercises, written assignments, and examinations were used for this course also, but the instructor used strategies to maintain the best learning environment possible.

For instance, lectures never exceeded one hour, group activities were used more frequently, and students were required to leave the classroom during breaks. The same instructor, using the same textbook and the same assignments, taught the courses to maintain comparability between the two courses.

Bloom's taxonomy of learning was applied throughout both of these courses as well as the hybrid course. The taxonomy involves three types of knowledge dimensions including Factual, Conceptual, and Procedural knowledge. Factual knowledge involves students learning the basic elements to be acquainted with a subject, such as research. Conceptual knowledge means that students can understand the interaction of the basic elements and how they interact within the framework or structure of a subject. Finally, Procedural knowledge involves knowing how to do something or in the case of research, how to formulate a proposal for future research. Bloom's taxonomy also includes six different levels of learning.

The levels in ascending order are knowledge, comprehension, application, analysis, synthesis, and evaluation. Knowledge is level one on the taxonomy and is described as"being capable of recalling words, facts, dates, conventions, classifications, principles, and theories." Knowledge is a very concrete type of learning. Evaluation is level six and is described as"being capable of making a critical judgement based on internal and external critieria." Evaluation is an abstract type of learning when compared to Knowledge. The exams in all of the research courses involved measuring learning at the knowledge level. In contrast, written assignments required demonstration of"Analysis" as the minimum acceptable level of learning. Some assignments such as developing a research proposal or designing a single case research study required demonstration of the Evaluation level of learning.

Factual knowledge was measured using examinations containing multiple choice, true/false, and short answer items. Conceptual knowledge was measured through a written assignment. This assignment was an annotated bibliography of four research objects which required the student to identify each component of the object such as research question, methodology, and sampling.

The students were required to be able to articulate the relationship between components. For instance, if the study described in one of the objects used random sampling, the student was required to understand and articulate that the results of the study were generalizable. Procedural knowledge was measured by the student submitting another written assignment. This assignment was an outline for future research on the topic of her or his choice. The outline was required to demonstrate an understanding of the convergence of research regarding the topic, provide a rationale for choices such as method and sampling, and justify the feasibility of the proposed study.

Combination of Courses Intoahybrid Course

The combination of two sections of a BSW research course into a hybrid distance learning course will be presented in this object. Two sections of the same course were originally taught face-to-face at two sites that were 250 miles apart. One section was taught on the primary campus of the state university on Tuesdays and Thursdays. The second section was taught at an outreach site on three weekends. These two research courses were combined into one course that used compressed video and three intensive all day face-to-face Saturdays. Course evaluations and pretest/posttest research findings are presented. Strategies for teaching on compressed video and using other technology to supplement compressed video are discussed.

The rural social work programme was charged with delivering its BSW programme statewide. It was costly and time consuming for faculty to drive 250 miles to deliver the course over three weekends. The roads to the distance education site were in poor condition. Inclement weather including blizzards, ice storms, and thunderstorms often made travel dangerous. Instructors who taught courses in the three weekends format all agreed that by midmorning on Sunday morning the students were exhausted, overwhelmed with new content, and not likely to be able to learn any additional material. In addition to the problems with travel and pedagogical concerns the rural social work programme was not provided with any additional faculty to deliver the BSW programme statewide. The hybrid course emerged as a way to address the needs of both rural students and faculty.

Good distance education fits with the social work premise that one"begins where the client is." Rural areas have few if any public transportation options. For some rural students the use of compressed video and intensive Saturday face to face classes was more time and cost effective than coming to the university campus twice each week. The combination of compressed video and intensive Saturday face to face sessions eliminated the need for students to stay in a hotel over the weekend. It allowed students in geographically isolated rural areas to see their instructor every week instead of waiting several weeks between intensive weekend sessions. It also allowed the instructor to see the students every week. There was weekly contact without the need for weekly travel. Social work educators must reach out to students in rural areas to tap and develop the human resources which are present in communities. This is particularly important for rural communities because human resource pools may be smaller.

Compressed video involves one primary classroom from which the instructor teaches and several remote site classrooms. All of the classrooms have compressed video technology that allows students and instructors to see and communicate with each other in real time. Remote sites are seen and heard by the instructor on a large screen television. Unlike Interactive Television, there is no need to use a telephone to call in questions to the instructor.

When students have something to say they can hold up their hand and ask a question or make a comment. The video and audio are transmitted via digital transmission lines that make this real time interaction possible. It takes a moment for the communication to be broadcast across the digital lines so there is a slight delay that can result in students speaking at the same time or missing each others' comments. As students and instructors became familiar with the process, they quickly learned how to avoid these situations. Although digital transmission lines were available in this case, rural social work educators need to be aware of what resources are available in their area.

DEVELOPMENT OF HYBRID COURSE

Several factors including reduced resources, ensuring comparability across course sections, and attempting to better serve rural students led to the combination of the two course sections into a hybrid course. The hybrid course was offered on compressed video across the state at multiple sites on Thursdays from 5:30 to 7:00 p.m. and on three Saturdays from 8:00 a.m. to 5:00 p.m. The original plan for the course was to have the all day Saturday sessions in different locations, with the first and third Saturday sessions offered at the state university campus and the second Saturday session offered at the Outreach site. However, because of scheduling difficulties and lack of space at the Outreach site, all 3 Saturday sessions were offered at the state university campus.

STRATEGIES FOR THE RURAL HYBRID COURSE

The rural hybrid course was developed carefully. Assistance from the Center for Teaching Excellence at the university, collaboration with the university's Outreach school, and consultation with other faculty were a part of the process. Critical decisions made in developing a course that involved both intensive Saturday sessions and compressed video meetings were made thoughtfully and guided by Bloom's taxonomy of learning as explained earlier in the thesis. The strategies and some educational techniques are presented below.

INTENSIVE SATURDAY SESSION STRATEGIES

The Saturday sessions were used for interactive activities that would have been difficult to conduct on-line or through compressed video. These Saturday sessions also helped the students to get to know each other and the professor. In many rural settings people, including students, tend to distrust outsiders. Seeing the students in person was reassuring to both the students and the instructor for this reason.

Interactive group activities such as designing survey instruments, doing qualitative field observations, or selecting sampling and research methodologies for conducting needs assessments with populations at risk in rural areas were used to assist with developing Procedural knowledge as a group. Lunch was also provided for students in order to build a sense of community and to provide a respite from an all day class. The Saturday sessions were important for developing a sense of cohesiveness in the class and a bond between the students. Cohesiveness was based on the instructor's observations of the class. As the class members got to know each other questions and discussions tended to involve the entire class rather than small groups or clicks within the class.

The class members also referred to themselves as"we" in statements such as"we are very glad to have you hear to teach us on the weekend." Class members frequently spent breaks and lunch periods together rather than splitting into small groups and going their separate ways.

COMPRESSED VIDEO STRATEGIES

There were several strategies that were used to in an attempt to provide the best compressed video experience possible for the students and the professor in the hybrid course. In a compressed video course, Elmos or Power Point may be used for presentations. Elmos are like an overhead except that they broadcast across compressed video and have the capability of showing three-dimensional objects.

Elmos are easiest to read if they are printed on light blue paper and use a minimum font size of 32. Power Point presentations should use high contrast colours for text/background. For example, yellow text with a dark blue background works well. One strategy that was used during the rural hybrid course to make the compressed video portion of the class more student and professor friendly was having students introduce themselves the first day and tell a brief story about their experience with research.

This ensured that every student would use the compressed video technology to speak during the first class. Other strategies were to call on students by name and acknowledge their contributions to class. Yet another strategy is to invite them to respond to class comments and lecture material and be assertive in calling on students to help them learn to use the technology. As with any class, a good sense of humour helps ease tension regarding new material or in this case, a new way of teaching and learning.

QUANTITATIVE COURSE EVALUATION MEASURES

The course evaluations for the BSW Research class in the three different formats. The Traditional Tuesday and Thursday class from 9:30 to 11:00 and the Three Weekends class 8:00 to 5:00 were during the fall semester of one year. The hybrid course was taught during the fall semester of the following year. It consisted of compressed video 5:30 to 7:00 p.m. on Thursdays and three 8:00 a.m. to 5:00 p.m. Saturdays. The Course Evaluation forms were those the university used for all courses.

The quantitative portion used a Likert type scale with 1 indicating poor and 5 indicating excellent. Individual items included 1) Clarity and course purpose/ objective; 2) Distribution of course requirements; 3) Informational content of lectures; 4) Organization of lectures; 5) Presentation of lectures; 6) Varies the mode of presentation; and 7) Overall rating of the course. Mean scores and standard deviations are presented for each item. A One Way Analysis of Variance was conducted and showed no statistically significant differences between the three classes on the seven variables. Despite the lack of statistically significant differences the means show some differences between the classes that are worth discussing. Variables one and two, clarity and course purpose/objective and distribution of course requirements were both rated lower for the Three Weekends class.

Distribution of course requirement refers to the distribution of exams, written assignments, and assigned activities such as doing qualitative observation over the semester. Since the Three Weekends class only met for six days throughout the semester it was common to have a paper due, an exam to take, and an assigned research activity to do during one weekend. The time to meet with the students was in two 8 hour blocks on three weekends. The intensive weekend class format was paralleled by an intensive exam, papers, and research exercises schedule. Variables three and four, informational content of lectures and organization of lectures, were rated similarly for all three classes. Variable five, presentation of lectures was rated slightly lower for the hybrid class with a mean of 3.89. Variable six, varies the mode of presentation, was similar for all three classes. Variable seven, overall rating of the course, was rated the lowest for the hybrid class with a mean of 3.71 compared to a mean of 4.17 for the Traditional Tuesdays and Thursdays class and a mean of 4.07 for the Three Weekends class.

ANECDOTAL COMMENTS FROM HYBRID COURSE

Anecdotal comments on the course evaluations for the hybrid course varied. There were several negative comments regarding the compressed video technology such as:"compressed video is a really hard way to learn,""many times the compressed video was not working properly," and"a lot of technological difficulties with compressed video." The hybrid class also included three Saturdays of face-to-face teaching in a traditional classroom. There were some negative comments about the all day Saturday classes as well. These comments included"Saturday classes are tough, by 3 p.m. we have all had enough,""a Saturday class doesn't seem to give one a break," and"no more Saturday classes."

On a more positive note, some students showed enthusiasm for the hybrid course. Comments included"great class,""gets me fired up to do research,""I was pleased for a first time CV class," and"this class has provided me with life long skills for effective practice."

PRETEST POSTTEST RESULTS

A Pretest/Posttest instrument designed by Rubin and Babbie was administered at the beginning of the hybrid course on the first Saturday session and at the end of the course during the final Saturday session. It was a 100 item True/False questionnaire that had been tested for reliability and validity. The questions were taken directly from the test bank for the Rubin and Babbie textbook. One question was"If a purposive sample was used to select participants for a study the results of the study are generalizable." Another example is"Internal validity involves the relationship between the independent and dependent variables." The maximum possible score on the questionnaire was 100. The mean pretest score was 69.18. The mean posttest score was 75.76. Dependent sample t-tests indicated a significant difference between the pretest and posttest. This instrument measured both Factual and Conceptual knowledge on Bloom's taxonomy of learning. The Factual and Conceptual knowledge was measured by the Rubin and Babbie pretest posttest instrument for this object. Within the course the theory constructs were measured by exams, several small written assignments, and one primary written assignment.

DISCUSSION OF RESULTS

Teaching a hybrid course was a new experience for us as a rural social work educators. It was different teaching research over compressed video. In a traditional classroom, instructors can see the students' faces are able to tell if they aren't getting a particular concept. Over compressed video instructors only get to see the students' faces if one student asked a question and the video technician zoomed in on the person. Instructors could see one person's face clearly, but not the groups' faces. It was also difficult when there were problems with the video or audio portions of compressed video.

If only the video portion was working, instructors communicated via a white dry erase board. If only the audio was working, instructors communicated by voice and instructed the students to look at specific examples in their books. Sometimes it was a bit of a challenge but the challenges were solvable. The course evaluations confirmed that even though there were challenges the hybrid course and its technology were a viable way to deliver a BSW research class to students in isolated rural areas.

Although there were no statistically significant differences between the three classes, the data pose some areas of enquiry for future research. The scores for the hybrid class on variables one and two, clarity and course/purpose objective and distribution of course requirements, were similar to the traditional class scores. The similar scores for the hybrid course on quantitative course evaluation variables three and four, informational content of lectures and organization of lectures, were encouraging. The instructors attempted to deliver the same information and organized the lecture content in a similar fashion as in the previously offered courses.

The hybrid course score on quantitative variable six, varies the mode of presentation, was also encouraging as it was similar to the other two classes.

Teaching research to BSW students requires a substantial amount of lecture because for most BSW students the social work research course is the first research course they have taken. This is especially true for rural BSW students as many of them have no previous college experience and some of them are first generation college students. They are learning new content including the language of research, theories concerning research, research methodologies, and how research relates to social work as a discipline in evaluating practice and furthering social and economic justice.

Variable five, presentation of lectures, was rated lowest for the Hybrid class. This lower rating may be related to the compressed video technology and difficulties experienced with it, the all day Saturday classes, a combination of these variables or other variables not mentioned in the course evaluation. Social work educators should be mindful that a large range of attitudes towards technology, including computers and proficiency with them, still exists among social work students. However, this should not limit their use of technology in the classroom, but rather their approach to students.

Variable seven, overall rating of the course, was rated the lowest among the three classes for the hybrid class. While this is not encouraging, the mean of 3.72 is closer to a score of 5, or excellent, than it is to a score of 1, or poor. The significant difference on the pretest/posttest questionnaire was positive, indicating an increase in research knowledge occurred for the students in the Hybrid course.

LIMITATIONS

There are numerous limitations to this study. The greatest limitation was that this study used a non-randomized sample and had a low number of participants. The sample was one of convenience and the results from this hybrid course are not generalizable to other compressed video or mixed format courses. This study only involved the evaluation of one rural hybrid course that may have had unique qualities because it was the first time it was offered in the combined compressed video and intensive Saturday class meetings format.

Both the professor and the students may have become more familiar with the compressed video technology as it was used during the semester. The course evaluation instrument has not been tested for reliability and validity. The anecdotal comments on the course evaluations may not be representative of the entire class as students who took the time to write comments may have had stronger opinions than students who chose to not write comments. Finally, although the pretest/posttest scores showed a significant increase in research knowledge, the pre-experimental design did not control for any threats to internal validity. The increase in research knowledge cannot be attributed to the research class.

Workforce Participation by Socio-Economic Characteristics

The notion of work and employment, especially for women, is complex. The reasons why women work in gainful activity, or whether they work part time or full time, can be diverse and may be rooted in a complex interplay of economic, cultural, social, and personal factors. In developing economies, workers combine multiple activities over different parts of the year. The NSSO defines a person who is employed for a major part of the year as being"Principal Status" employed. If gainfully employed only for a part of the year, she is described as being employed in the"Subsidiary Status".

A person employed either in"Usual Principal Status" or"Usual Subsidiary Status" is enumerated as being employed in the"Usual Status". Unless otherwise stated, the reference is to UPSS employment throughout this thesis. The industry associated with her employment is the one which she is associated for a major part of the employment. We focus for the most part on rural employment, but also provide data on urban employment in order to highlight the contrasts.

As in most other parts of the world, fewer women participate in employment in India compared to men. In 2004-05, while in urban areas, 16.6 per cent women and 54.9 per cent men were employed, in rural areas, these percentages were 32.7 and 54.6 respectively. More women are employed only in the subsidiary status, than men, especially in rural areas. This can be explained by factors from the supply side as well as the demand side. Taking the former first, the rural economy has been largely stagnant over the years and employment opportunities have not grown.

Most women, therefore, are able to get work for only a few months in the year. This keeps them employed only in the'subsidiary status'. On the supply side, women's primary duties are supposed to be in the household. For economic reasons they have to work, but must do so in addition to their domestic responsibilities, and are therefore only able to enter the labour force as subsidiary workers. Over a thirty-two year span, the workforce participation rate of males and females shows no systematic variation despite a larger percentage of persons in the younger age groups joining education. The only notable changes appear to be a small increase in male WPR after 1987-88 and that urban females recorded a higher employment rate in 2004-05 over all preceding rounds of the survey. This also shows that globalisation appears to have enlarged work opportunities for women in urban areas, but has had no impact in rural areas.

Yet, there are large variations in women's participation in work across socio-economic groups and across regions and states in India which we shall presently discuss. While mainly economic factors determine a man's participation in employment, the forces that influence a woman's participation in work are many and diverse and include demographic, reproductive, social, religious and cultural factors. WPR is highest for scheduled tribe and scheduled caste women and lowest for women from the'other' caste. The SCs and STs are the most marginalised sections in the economy and the most impoverished. Women from these groups have higher WPRs because extreme poverty leaves them with little choice but to work, and because they do not face social taboos that disapprove of work.

The converse is true for women from'other' castes. When religious background is considered, Muslim women in rural areas have a significantly low WPR-nearly half the national rate for women of all religions. Once again it is social norms that restrict women's mobility and entry into the workforce that keep more Muslim women tied to hearth and home. Does education propel women into employment? The gender differences in this respect are interesting and stark. For male workers, higher levels of education are indeed associated with higher WPR, both in rural and urban areas.

But for women, WPR is higher for illiterate women than for women with higher levels of school education-a trend which reverses itself only for women with technical/ vocational education or graduates. This again is a pattern which reveals itself both in rural and urban areas. Thus 51 per cent of illiterate men are employed but this percentage goes up to 71 per cent among men who have passed their higher secondary.

On the other hand, 39 per cent illiterate women are employed, but this percentage declines to just 25 per cent among women who have passed higher secondary. Why? Multiple factors such as the compulsion for men to earn, the greater availability of jobs for men, and the restrictive social norms operating for women, appear to explain this pattern. It is interesting that in urban areas by contrast, women's employment goes up at higher educational levels and shows a pattern similar to that for men showing the narrowing of gender gaps in urban areas.

How does economic status of women influence their participation in work? Indeed, the relationship between workforce participation and economic status of the household is critical for policy and programme interventions. While the NSSO does not collect data on incomes, it provides data on monthly per capita consumption expenditure; a measure that is widely used as a proxy for the economic status of households.

The authors have computed participation in employment across MPCE deciles groups from NSS unit records. Workforce participation shows a consistently declining trend with rising economic status for rural women, clearly reflecting on the economic distress that compels poor women to work. In contrast, for urban women, work participation shows a skewed v-shape, declining as economic status improves, but rises again with the highest consumption decile. The latter reflects on higher educational attainments of women associated with higher incomes, and the greater availability of employment opportunities in urban areas.

To conclude, women's participation in gainful work is lower compared to men; it is higher for scheduled caste and scheduled tribe women who are less restricted by social norms; among religious groups, work participation is lowest for Muslim women; education impacts differentially for men and women, with level of participation increasing with educational levels for men, but declining for rural women; as economic status improves, work participation declines for rural women suggesting that when there are no compelling economic reasons to earn, social taboos on women's mobility and participation in work exercise a strong influence. In general, while the gaps in work participation between men and women are clear and well recognised, the gaps between different classes of women hailing from different social and economic backgrounds are less well known and need to be understood for effective policy measures.

Women's Employment in the Agricultural and Non-Agricultural Sectors

Within rural areas, work may be classified along two dimensions; a) by sector, *viz.*, agriculture or non-agriculture, and b) by employment status, that is whether a person is in regular employment, is self employed or is casually employed. An analysis of women's employment by sector and employment status can tell us a great deal about the outcomes for women and if the work they do promotes their well being or is low-end, low paying and driven by distress.

What is the significance of this classification and what does it tell us about the nature and disparities in women's employment? It illustrates vividly the more disadvantaged position of women in the rural labour market. Firstly, wages are higher for men in all categories of employment. The disparity is highest for regular workers in non-agriculture. Second, women are concentrated in agriculture where the wages are lowest. Thus 90 per cent women are in agriculture and only 10 per cent are in non-agriculture among casual labourers. Thirdly, there is a very low proportion of women in regular work where the wage rates are the highest, employment is more secure and working conditions are relatively better. This is the case both in agriculture and in non-agriculture.

How does economic status relate to the nature of work that men and women do? Along expected lines, the percentage of casual labourers among both male and female workers declines sharply with rising household MPCE deciles. The percentage of self-employed among workers shows an increasing trend with MPCE deciles, except for the highest deciles, where it dips. The share of regular workers is low throughout showing the scarcity of regular work; is negligible in the lower consumption deciles but rises in the highest deciles. For rural female workers, the share of the self-employed remains higher for each MPCE decile compared to male workers. On the other hand women remain disadvantaged when it comes to regular work. Although the structure of employment by employment status has been remarkably constant across the years, previous NSS surveys showed some increase in casual labour in the rural male and female workforce and a decline in the share of the selfemployed.

But during 1999/00-2004/05, there was a change in the trend; the share of selfemployed workers increased among both female and male workers, while the share of casual work declined. Why this has happened is difficult to say, but it is likely that the overall stagnation in agriculture and the rural economy may have led to this shift. The growth rate in agriculture and allied sectors was only little more than 2 per cent per annum in this period, registering a negative growth in some years. This may have led to shrinking availability of wage work and compelled workers to eke out subsistence from self employment. The next section discusses women's employment in agriculture, while the subsequent section takes up women's employment in non- agriculture. In each, the three broad status of employment are analysed.

AGRICULTURE

In rural areas, nearly 84 per cent women workers are engaged in agriculture, either as cultivators or labourers as compared to 67 per cent male workers. There has been a kind of'creeping feminisation' of agriculture; male workers have steadily moved out of agriculture while for women workers, this movement has been extremely tardy. Men have entered into more diversified occupations in non-agriculture, while women have largely tended to remain in agriculture that has been largely stagnant.

In 1972-93, 83.2 per cent male workers and 89.7 per cent female workers were engaged in agriculture. By 2004-05, only 66.5 per cent male workers were in agriculture compared to 83.3 per cent female workers. This has to be seen in the context of the fact that returns to labour are, on average, higher in non- agriculture than in agriculture, although the size of assets operated and type of employment, among other factors, are also relevant. One implication of the above slow change is that a significant proportion of the incremental female workforce gets engaged in agriculture. Between 1983 and 2004-05, nearly 72 per cent of the incremental rural female workforce was absorbed in agriculture, compared to 40 per cent for the male workforce.

Agriculture: Casual Workers

Compared to 23.2 per cent male rural workers, 29.2 per cent female rural workers were engaged as casual agricultural labourers in 2004-05. There is a disproportionate concentration of the most deprived social groups in this form of labour. Half of the female casual labourers and 43 per cent of male casual labourers in India belong to SCs and STs, nearly twice their share in population. Women agricultural casual workers form a distinct category: they are disadvantaged in many ways. There is significant gender segmentation of operations in agriculture.

While men predominate in activities such as ploughing and harvesting, women predominate in weeding, transplanting and inter-culture. The wages are uniformly lower in all female dominant operations. Overall women's wages are estimated at 69 per cent of male wages in 2004-05. Moreover, women also get fewer days of work. Further, women workers rarely get the minimum wages stipulated by the government: more than 95 per cent of female agricultural wage workers received wages lower than the minimum wage. The deprivation of casual workers is aggravated by the fact that not only are their lower than wages in non-agriculture; they have also grown at a lower rate in the recent period, thereby increasing the gap.

Moreover, as already pointed out, women workers who work as casual labourers are able to get work for only part of the year-their estimated employment days was only 184. Women agricultural labourers are also unemployed for more days a year than their male counterparts. The unemployment rate for agricultural labourers is quite high in rural areas by any standard; 16 per cent for men and 17 per cent for women for 2004-05 by the Current Daily Status criterion and this increased over 1993/94-2004/05.

Agriculture: Self Employed Workers

As noted earlier, women workers are increasingly engaged as self- employed in agriculture. There has been a steady increase in the numbers of both women and men farmers over all years since 1983 except 1999-00. The sharpest increase has taken place in the recent quinquennium when the share of women farmers increased to 41.8 per cent, the highest in 32 years. These results attest to the large role played by women farmers although they do not confirm a systematic trend towards feminization. Such a large presence of women farmers requires systematic public support to them, which is lacking mainly because women are not seen as principal producers in agriculture and because they do not have ownership or control over the assets on which they work.

The poor support to women farmers has been highlighted in several studies and reports, notably Planning Commission and NCEUS. Srivastava *et al.*, 2007, have shown that despite legislative changes few women have control over land. However, the Agricultural Census provides information on operational holdings, that is, agricultural holdings operated and controlled by men and women, whether or not they are owned by them. The Agricultural Census 2000-01, only 11.6 per cent of cultivated agricultural land holdings covering 9.1 per cent area were operated by women. There is a systematic decline in the percentage of land holdings and area controlled by women as the size of holding increases. In the smallest size class the percentage of land holdings operated by women was 13.4 whereas the area operated by them was 12 per cent. In large holdings, the corresponding percentages declined to 5.7 and 5.6 respectively. These figures could partly be explained by the pattern of outmigration since it is in smaller holdings where male outmigration is also likely to be higher. However, cultural and social factors are also very important in explaining the fact that a miniscule proportion of women have control on this critical resource.

This is brought out by the regional pattern of women's control over land holdings. The percentage of such holdings was much higher in the more progressive Southern states and in some of the North-eastern states. In Kerala women operated 21 per cent of the land holdings and 18 per cent of area. In Andhra Pradesh the corresponding figures were 20 per cent and 17 per cent respectively while in Tamil Nadu they were 18.1 per cent and 15.1 respectively. In the absence of land titles, women farmers have much smaller access to institutional credit compared to male farmers, and receive a much lower degree of institutional support.

NON-AGRICULTURE

Non-Agriculture: Casual Workers

Wages of casual workers estimated from the 2004-05 NSSO Survey show that female wages are lower than male wages across all industry groups. The relative male-female wage gap is larger in non-agriculture where female casual workers earn 65 per cent of male wages. In manufacturing, female wages are only 59 per cent of male wages. The low wages of female workers are principally due to the undervaluation of work and skills in activities in which women predominate. Thus the segmentation of women workers in certain types of activities largely determines the gender gap which exists.

A number of national and international studies have documented the sex- typing of occupations. In India, this has been noted in a number of industries such as knitwear and garments. These jobs provided limited opportunity for upward mobility. Such segregation can also be found in the services sector. In the health and education sectors, women are concentrated at the lower end as paramedics, teachers in lower grades, or support staff. The hierarchy of jobs within manufacturing or services is then used to value the jobs where women are concentrated as low skilled workers even if it involves exceptional talent and years of informal training.

Non-Agriculture: Self-Employed Workers

As we have noted earlier, the self-employed workers are not a homogeneous group. They fall into three sub-groups. The first are the'employers'. The second are the'own account workers', and the third group is constituted by the'helpers' who assisted the main family workers in an unpaid capacity. A significant percentage of self-employed women workers are classified as helpers *i.e.*, they are recognised only as auxiliary workers and this percentage is much larger than among male self-employed workers in non-agriculture among whom 15.2 per cent are classified as unpaid workers.

Further, while one of the stated advantages of self-employment for women is that this work can be done based at home and women can work at their pace and convenience, this results in multiple disadvantages in the form of limited opportunities, seclusion, and lower earnings.

Female Proprietary Enterprises

The NSSO informal enterprises survey, 1999-2000, provides a profile of female and male proprietary enterprises. The survey found that about 12 per cent of proprietary enterprises were operated by women and these were mainly own account enterprises. Approximately 10 per cent of the workers in proprietary enterprises were engaged in the female proprietary enterprises. A distinction is made between Own Account Enterprises employing no hired labour and Establishments which hire one or more labourers. In general, urban enterprises are larger in size, and for the same category, female proprietary enterprises are smaller than male proprietary enterprises.

In rural areas, female proprietary enterprises are very small in size, with an average fixed investment of less than '8000, while female establishments had a total fixed asset base of '123,786. The gross value added per worker was less than '7000 per annum, while in the latter it was slightly more than '26,000 per year. Among rural female OAEs, about 34 per cent of them have value of fixed assets of less than '1000, while only 7 per cent had value of assets greater than '25000.

Not only are few women involved in running non-agricultural enterprises of any kind, the scale of operation of women operated units is distinctly very tiny particularly in rural areas. Compared to the National Minimum Wage, 89 per cent of female OAEs and 42 per cent of male OAEs gave lower imputed daily returns.

Home Workers

Nearly 81 per cent of rural female enterprises and 39.5 per cent of male enterprises operated from home in 1999-00 *i.e.* they were home based enterprises. About 40 per cent of these enterprises in rural areas work on sub- contracted basis *i.e.* their workers were homeworkers as defined by the ILO. Home-workers work at the lowest end of a value chain, usually dealing with petty contractors, on whom they depend for supply of work, raw material and sale of finished goods. This dependence on the contractor together with the isolation undermines their ability to bargain for higher piece-rates, timely payments or overtime pay. The annual gross value addition of the rural female home-workers is, on average, '5270, much lower than even the '9000 that accrues in female OAEs.

The average value of fixed assets engaged by them is also very low at '3800. About 79 per cent of the women and 63 per cent of the male home workers were paid on a piece-rate basis. This wage has many hidden costs, including use of the house and electricity, delayed payments, and arbitrary cuts in wages on the pretext of poor quality.

Non-Agriculture: Regular Workers

Female regular workers in rural areas form a very small part of the female workforce as also of the total proportion of regular workers in rural areas. Outside of agriculture, they are mainly concentrated in education, manufacturing, private households, health and social work and public administration. Work in private household earns women the lowest wages of ' 39 per day, followed by employment in hotels and restaurants, manufacturing, and agriculture.

While the sectors with the highest daily remuneration, such as electricity gas and water, transport; financial intermediation; and real estate employ very few women on a regular basis, among the sectors where a larger proportion of women take up employment, education and health sectors afford reasonable daily earnings. The daily earnings of women regular/salaried workers are more than twice as high as women casual workers.

However, within regular work, as with casual work, there is a large gap in male-female earnings across most sectors, ranging from a female-male earning ratio of 0.3 in mining to 0.87 in construction. Even in the social sectors, there is a large gap in earnings, with this ratio being as low as 0.59 in education and 0.69 in health and social work. Women workers in these sectors tend to be concentrated in the lower segments-as paramedics, support staff, contract teachers or teachers in low grades.

Correlates of Poverty and Vulnerability for Women Workers

We now briefly draw attention to the characteristics of women workers and poverty levels in rural India. We have used the official poverty line as a benchmark, but have categorised the population into six groups following the methodology adopted by NCEUS. Consumption characteristics and social development levels, of households have been divided as follows:

- Extremely Poor: up to 0.75 PL;
- Poor: Between 0.75Pl and PL;
- Marginal Poor: Between PL and 1.25 PL;
- Vulnerable: between 1.25 PL and 2 PL;
- Middle: Between 2 PL and 4PL;
- Higher Income: Above 4 PL.

The four lower categories have together been characterised as"Poor and Vulnerable". The percentage of casual workers declines rapidly with improving economic status, the percentage of regular workers is only high in the last category. The Self-employed have a presence in all economic categories, but are more predominant as economic well being improves.

In terms of industrial composition, it can be seen that while agricultural workers are present in all categories in a large proportion, their weight declines in the highest while that of tertiary sector workers increases. It can also be seen that workers with higher levels of education are almost entirely present in the higher economic categories. One of the major attributes of women engaged in agriculture is their low level of educational attainment.

With the ongoing commercialisation of agriculture, crop diversification, introduction of new technologies and the imperative for better information processing, education has to be reckoned as a key input in any attempt at overall development and modernization of agriculture. However, the grim picture is that about 86 per cent of female agricultural labourers and 74 per cent of female farmers are either illiterate or have education below the primary level. Shocking as it may seem, the average education of a female agricultural labourer was less than one year in 2004-05.

Determinats of Women's Workforce Participation

In this section the determinants of participation of rural women in employment is analysed by use of regression analysis. In the absence of a single data set containing all the relevant variables, this thesis first does a Logistic Regression based on unit records of the NSS Employment- Unemployment Survey of 2004-05; this is followed by a similar analysis using the unit data records of another large-scale survey, *viz.* the National Family Health Survey of 2005-06 which also has information on women's autonomy using certain indicators. As both these analyses confirm significant differences across states/regions, an analysis using state level variables is also carried out.

DETERMINANTS OF PARTICIPATION IN EMPLOYMENT USING NSS DATA

The analysis attempts an explanation not only of why women participate in the workforce, but also why they participate in specific types of employment.The independent variables used are: age group, marital status, education status, caste group, religion, presence of children under 5 years, land holding size category, monthly per capita consumption quintile, and region. As mentioned earlier, Logistic Regression is used since the model does not make distributional assumptions on the predictors, which can be both continuous and discrete.

Agriculture: Determinants of Work Participation

As one would expect, possession of land has a very important influence on a woman's participation in employment. Controlling for land, the household's consumption level has a negative influence. Among the individual characteristics, it is seen that compared to women in the age group 15-29, older women have a higher probability of participating in work and women in the age group 30-44 have the highest odds ratio. Compared to never married women, married, divorced and separated women have a higher probability of participating in work, with divorced or separated women having the highest odds ratio. Compared to illiterate women, women with higher levels of education have a lower probability of being in the workforce. The odds ratio declines with rising levels of education, recouping somewhat only for women who are diploma holders or graduates. Compared to scheduled tribes, all other caste groups have lower probability of participating in work, with higher castes having the lowest probability. Muslim women have a much lower probability of being in the workforce compared to Hindu women. Finally women in all other regions have significantly higher probability are being in the workforce compared to those in the eastern region.

Agriculture: Casual Workers

In this case, younger women workers have the highest probability of working as casual agricultural labourers. The marital status variable is not significant. Scheduled caste women workers have a significantly higher odds ratio of being an agricultural labourer and this probability declines steeply with rising levels of education, for Muslims and for women workers with young children. Casual agriculture wage status for workers is much less probable for women workers possessing larger holdings and in higher consumption quintiles.

Agriculture: Self-Employed Workers

The highest proportion of women workers are engaged as self-employed in agriculture. The probability of a woman worker being self-employed in agriculture is highest for the high age group and for currently married women. The odds ratio are lower for divorced or separated women indicating that these women no longer have access to land. The odds ratio declines with increasing levels for education and is the lowest for women workers who are graduates or diploma holders. SC women workers who have the lowest access to land also have the lowest probability of being self-employed in agriculture. Muslim women workers again are less likely to be engaged in farming. As one may expect the probability of engaging in agriculture increases sharply with bigger landholdings and also with higher levels of household consumption. Women workers n the Northern region have the highest probability of being engaged in agriculture as self-employed, while women workers in the Southern region have the lowest probability of being so engaged.

Non-Agriculture: Determinants of Work Participation

Since female workers have largely remained confined to agriculture, the characteristics of workers who have moved out of agriculture are of great interest. Any type of worker in non-agriculture is taken up first. The probability of being a non-agricultural worker is highest for women in the age group 30-44 than for workers in the youngest age group and is lower for currently married women.

It rises sharply with increasing levels of education. Compared to illiterate women workers, those with secondary education have an odds ratio of 4.787 while those with graduate or vocational education have an odds ratio exceeding 30. Compared to ST women workers, all other social groups have significantly higher odds ratios, the highest being for"other" caste women. Muslim workers are more than twice as likely to participate in non-agricultural work. The odds ratio declines with increasing size of land holding and is significantly higher than one for women workers belonging to the highest consumption quintile.

Non-Agriculture: Wage Workers

Non- agricultural wage workers are younger and either unmarried or divorced women. The odds ratio is 0.58 for the highest age group and 0.61 for currently married women workers. The odds ratio steadily declines with higher levels of education. While there is no significant difference across social groups, Muslims have a significantly lower than 1 odds ratio. These ratios also decline dramatically with higher land holdings. The consumption level has a smaller influence on this variable but the odds ratio is significantly lower than one for the highest quintile. Compared to the reference region, the West and the North both have significantly lower odds ratios.

Non-Agriculture: Self Employed Workers

The probability of being self-employed is higher among young women workers and those who have never married. The odds ratio is significantly lower among currently married and widowed women workers. Education of the worker increases the probability of taking up self-employment, but the highest odds ratio are for those with secondary or higher secondary level of education. All social groups have higher odds ratio compared to the reference group and for the Muslim women workers, the odds ratio is more than twice as high as Hindu workers. This is principally due to the hereditary involvement of these workers' households in artisanal activities. Odds ratio declines steadily with increasing possession of land and is significantly higher than one only for the second quintile in terms of household MPCE. Women workers in the Eastern region have the highest probability of being so employed.

Non-Agriculture: Regular Workers

This is the smallest segment of workers among rural women. Compared to the reference groups, the odds ratio is higher for higher aged women and for widowed/ separated women. It increases dramatically with increasingly levels of education. Among social groups it is significantly lower than 1 for OBC and upper caste women workers. The odds ratio falls with increasing size of holding and is significantly higher than one for the highest quintile. The regressions bring out a number of interesting relationships between individual, household and regional characteristics in rural India.

First, possession of land is naturally a very strong determinant of the participation of women in work and particularly their employment as women farmers. Controlling for land, the household's consumption status raises the possibility of a woman worker being self-employed either in agriculture or non-agriculture, but reduces this possibility in all other cases. It may be noted that these cases would require the worker to be employed outside the home where cultural and social roles begin to play a bigger role.

Muslim women not only have a significantly lower than one odds ratio overall, this also holds for all types of employment except non-agricultural selfemployment. As far as social/caste groups are concerned, our reference is the Scheduled Tribes among whom access to land and common property resources is much higher than that for SCs which accounts for their high WPR, the odds ratio for this being the lowest among upper castes. For the same reason, SCs have the highest odds ratio for participating in agricultural wage employment, as one might expect. In non-agriculture, overall STs have the lowest probability of participation, followed by SCs, OBC and upper castes. The surprising result is that among workers, upper castes and OBCs have a lower likelihood of participation in regular work than SC/ST, controlling for all the other factors.

Considering the three demographic variables, the last has the smallest influence of participation in any/all type of work. Currently married women have a lower likelihood of working outside of homes, while single women are likelier to participate in self-employment. Other than this widowed and separated women have a higher likelihood of participating in most types of work. Other than land, education appears to be the most important determinant of employment status.

Participation in the workforce as well as participation in wage employment declines with level of education, while the likelihood of participation in non-agricultural work as a whole, as well in self-employment or regular work increases with rising levels of education. From these regressions, it is apparent that while the level of education may not positively influence a woman's participation in work, for women who are in the workforce, education is indicated as the most important determinant of better quality non-agricultural work. It must be emphasised again that we are examining the outcome of social, cultural and economic processes.

The potential availability of work is highest in rural areas for women whose households possess a measure of adequate landholdings. But even here, actual participation may be determined by socio-cultural factors as is evident from our results. The absence of education relegates women workers to wage work, whereas having education improves their chances of being in non- agricultural self-employment or regular work, with the latter mainly requiring higher education qualifications. Participation in wage work or non-agriculture also requires a greater measure of autonomy for women, confining the rest principally to self-employment in agriculture.

DETERMINANTS OF PARTICIPATION IN EMPLOYMENT USING NFHS, 2005-06 DATA

The National Family Health Survey has been carried out in India periodically since 1992-93. The latest round of results are available from the third round carried out in 2005-06. The NFHS collects detailed information on socioeconomic, reproductive and health characteristics of women in the age group 15-49, along with certain health and other characteristics of young children and the spouses of the women interviewed. Since the focus of the survey is on women in the reproductive age group, compared to the NSS, which covers the entire population, the NFHS gives the characteristics of a truncated age group of women.

The employment characteristics of these women are captured in the survey but not in the same manner or depth as the NSS. The survey enquires whether women are currently working or have worked in the last year. It also asks whether they work for family production or paid. The women workers are classified as per their occupational categories.

Logistic regression is used to estimate the influence of several variables on participation in employment, by status and industry so that the types of employment participation considered are similar to those in the NSS analysis. But it should be noted that the NFHS does not distinguish between paid casual stinguishing feature of the NFHS, because of which this data set has been analysed in this thesis, is that it collects information on women's autonomy using a number of indicators. Among these indicators, it used a set of three indicators to capture women's freedom of mobility which in our view is central to their participation in the labour market. The three indicators of women's mobility are if they are allowed to go alone to the market/health facility/or outside the village or community. The variables are similar to those used in earlier analysis, but with the following significant differences. First, this data has a younger age cohort. Second, as mentioned earlier, employment has been measured differently in this survey. Third, the NSS does not provide information on how many children a woman has, though it does give the number of children in a household.

With NFHS data it is possible to identify the mothers with young children. Fourthly, this thesis uses the synthetic wealth indicator given by NFHS which is built on a factor analytic score based on 33 assets. Finally, the NFHS does not allow us to estimate consumption expenditure as in the case of the NSSO and hence this variable has been dropped from the analysis. These results are similar to the earlier results in many basic ways and are not discussed here. Attention is drawn only to fresh findings.

Three main conclusions emerge sharply from the above analysis. First, the role of education is delineated more sharply among this age cohort of women. Increasing levels of education increases the possibility of women being in non-agricultural vocations. This result holds separately, both for self- employment as well as for paid work. Second, women's autonomy, proxied here by their ability to make mobility decisions autonomously, significantly increases the probability of their participation in all types of employment, except agricultural self-employment.

The reason for this is that whether it is in low paid work as casual labour or better paid work as regular workers, both take women out of the confines of the house and therefore require women to have freedom of mobility. However, where women do not have this freedom and are constrained by social norms to the home, but still need to work, self employment provides the answer. Third, women with young children are most likely to be working as self employed in agriculture and least likely to be employed as paid workers or in non-agriculture. This suggests the urgent need to provide early child care and crèche facilities for rural women.

DETERMINANTS OF STATE LEVEL VARIATIONS IN EMPLOYMENT PARTICIPATION

The large state-wise and regional difference in rural female employment participation in India has been alluded to earlier. The logit regressions confirm these differences but the NSSO data set gives very limited measures of socio- cultural differences. We therefore explore the impact of additional variables, gleaned from other data sources such as the National Family Health Survey, the Agricultural Census, the Central Statistical Organisation, and the National Bank for Rural Development on state-level variations in female employment. The WPRs by employment status and sector are also presented. Total WPRs are high in some of the Southern, Western and Hill states. They are the lowest in the Eastern states. There are important sectoral differences. For example, states such as Kerala, West Bengal and Orissa which have low total WPRs show a high participation of women in non-agriculture and the highest participation rate of women in regular work is in Kerala.

It is anticipated that these differences could be a result of supply related characteristics such as:

- The percentage of SC/ST households in a state;
- Mean years of education of women,
- Variables which could proxy women's autonomy to undertake conomic activity;
- Rural wages; or
- Employment demand.

Since our objective is to understand not only total work force participation rates, but also women's participation in specific types of work, especially in non-agriculture, these rates are regressed for 20 states across the variables, selecting only one variable. The'best' fits are presented below. Some of the independent variables that were considered were found to be highly correlated, in particular with Mean Years of Education and were dropped from the analysis. Fewer numbers of variables have therefore been tested and used in the regression analysis. These are briefly discussed below.

- *Total WPR*: The share of SC/ST in the total population is highly significant variable. A one per cent increase in the share of SC/ST in the population would increase total WPR by one per cent. Share of women operated holdings in total is also marginally significant. The Mean Years of education of the population is not significant.
- *WPR in non-agriculture*: The Mean Years of Education of the female population and the density of Self-help Groups are both significant variables. Increase in Mean Years of Education would increase the WPR of women in non-agricultural vocations by 1.35.
- *WPR in non-farm self-employment*: The only variable significant in this case is the state Density of Self-help groups. The Mean Educational attainment of women in a state is not a significant determinant of state level variation of WPR in non-farm self-employment.
- *WPR in non-agricultural wage work*: Mean Years of education and Share of area operated by women are both significant variables. A one level increase in education would increase the WPR in non- agricultural wage work by 0.81. The coefficient of share of area operated by women is 0.21.
- *WPR in non-agricultural regular/salaried work*: Mean Years of education is a highly significant variable; one level increase in education would increase the WPR in regular/salaried work by 0.82. The share of area in holdings operated by women is also significant but only at 10 per cent level of significance. The coefficient of this variable is quite low.
- *Discussion*: The share of SC/ST in the population emerges as the only significant variable in explaining inter-state variation in total rural female WPR. However, interstate variations in WPR in non- agriculture as a whole, as well as participation in non-agricultural wage labour are determined by the average educational level of the female population and by variables which reflect women's economic autonomy and control over resources. However, education is not a significant variable in explaining the inter-state variations in participation by women in nonagricultural self-employment, but here also their autonomous participation in self-help groups is an important determinant. It has already been noted that the above regression analysis has been able to incorporate demand side factors to a very limited extent. This probably accounts for the fact the adjusted Coefficient of Determinations are on the low side.

❑

3.

Rural Sociology in Information Technology

Introduction

It may seem paradoxical that modern information technology (IT), associated in our minds with developed country markets and capital-intensive methods of production, has any relevance for a country where many millions still lack basic needs. Nevertheless, there are many efforts underway in India and other developing countries to demonstrate the concrete benefits of IT for rural populations, and to do so in a manner that makes economic sense. This chapter outlines the conceptual and empirical case for the use of IT in India's rural development. A broad discussion of the potential role of IT in broad- based economic development. The conceptual issues from the perspective of demand for, and supply of IT-based services to rural populations in a developing country. The sessions of some of the efforts underway in India, including the work of Aksh, Drishtee, ITC, n-Logue and TARAhaat.

Ruralit: Issues and Conceptual Framework

We examine the potential for rural IT use, both from supply and demand perspectives. On the supply side, we examine the technical and organizational issues that arise for delivering IT-based services to rural populations in India. On the demand side, we examine the potential benefits that IT can bring to these populations, if the implementation is successful. We begin with the demand side, as a way of motivating the supply side issues.

Potential sources of demand for IT-based services can be framed in terms of a simple flow diagram representing the decisions of rural households. We will treat a typical household as engaged in farming, though this will not be true for all of them. Figure presents a simplified representation of the various economic decisions. Beginning from the left of Figure, input decisions include material inputs such as seeds, fertilizer and pesticides; and capital inputs such Rural Sociology in Information

Technology as tractors and land (whether through purchases or rentals); as well as the credit required for such purposes. The focus of analysis will be market transactions for inputs. In all cases, there is a potential for benefiting through improved information about prices, quality and availability. Labour is also an important input, but the labour market has special characteristics that reduce the importance of such information in rural contexts. Operations include decisions with respect to quantity and timing of inputs.

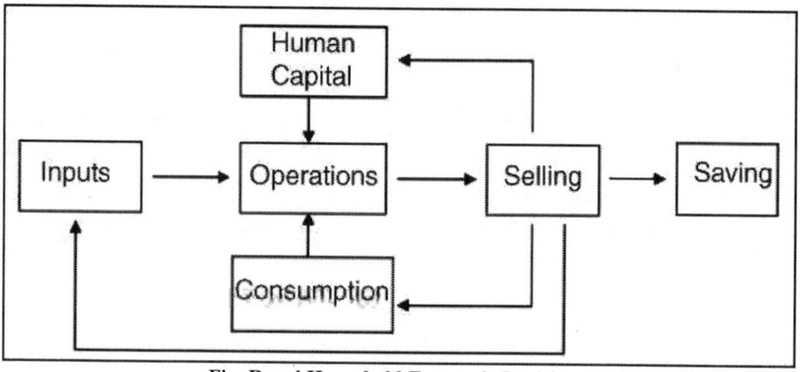

Fig. Rural Household Economic Decisions

A crucial aspect of agricultural operations is risk management, as both the weather and pest incidence are extremely variable. Ex ante decisions in the face of uncertainty, as well as ex post responses to realizations of uncertainty are both important. Predictive and technical information are both important for agricultural operations. Continuing to the right of Figure, marketing of outputs primarily requires price information. Increasingly, producing for sale also requires knowledge of quality requirements in different markets.

Selling of produce provides income for consumption, investment and inputs as well as generating information that affects input and production decisions. Non-production decisions of households can be roughly divided into pure consumption activities, as well as human capital investment in education and health. The boundary is fuzzy, since even basic food consumption has nutritional impacts and therefore a human capital component. These activities generate impacts on operations, since they affect the quality of decision-making, as well as household labour inputs: we indicate this with the vertical arrows.

While poorer households may be severely limited in their consumption, a significant proportion of rural households in India have incomes sufficient to support some discretionary consumption. In some cases, consumption may be only superficially discretionary–social norms may dictate spending on activities relating to marriage and other life cycle events.

Finally, the rightmost box captures household saving, again something that is not feasible for all rural households, but is an activity of growing importance. Saving may be for consumption smoothing, investment, or precautionary reasons. Even this simplified and summary picture of rural households' economic activity shows that they engage in a broad range of transactions and decisions with economic impacts. What is noteworthy besides this complexity is that many decisions are made with very limited information, and that market interactions are often subject to high transaction costs, due to imperfections in information, as well as high transportation costs, inefficient intermediation and time delays.

High transaction costs will always prevent marginal transactions from being undertaken; in extreme cases, the market may fail to function at all. Given this scenario, the role of IT can be understood in terms of reducing transaction costs, as well as improving the efficiency of decision making within households (both as producers and as consumers). Reductions in communication and transaction costs are particularly beneficial where they can allow new markets to develop, in the sense that existing goods and services, otherwise restricted to urban areas, or to a very limited segment of rural populations, now can be offered to broad cross-sections of the rural population. Examples include financial services, particular types of education, health services, long distance communications, and expertise on a range of production-related decisions.

IT-BASED RURAL SERVICES

Whether this can be done in a sustainable manner depends on the supply conditions for IT-based rural services. It must be further understood that the activities outlined, in Figure and the accompanying discussion, take place within a particular institutional environment. This includes private actors as well as governments.

For example, farmers may obtain credit and inputs, as well contract their output, to private 'commission agents,' even in the presence of government procurement and government-run local markets. Governments play a major role in subsidizing inputs, providing infrastructure, and enforcing property rights. To the extent that these activities are also subject to inefficiencies, it may be the case that, in order to be successful, IT-based interventions geared towards rural households will have to simultaneously alter the institutional environment, or else achieve sufficient scale and scope in order to impel changes in it. We will take this up later in the paper.

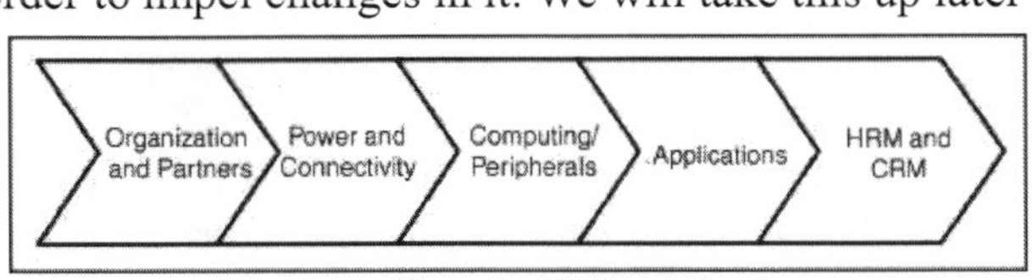

Fig. Value Chain for IT-Based Services

Turning to the supply side, we can show the various stages of decision- making and delivery of IT-based services in terms of a typical value chain, as Rural Sociology in Information Technology shown in Figure. At each stage of the chain, the IT components include a mix of hardware, software and services. In addition, the creation of an organizational structure and value network is a critical first step, while managing human resources and customers is vital for successful final implementation. We next discuss each of the components of the value chain in Figure. The organizational structure typically requires commercial goals of profitability to be built in.

This is easily done through a standard corporate structure. It is clear that, for scalability, some minimum size of the organization is required. In addition, there are fixed costs of innovation that can be spread more effectively across a larger organization. Social goals can be incorporated in two ways. For organizations that are dedicated specifically to rural IT-based services delivery, controlling ownership of the corporation by a non-profit entity provides the social focus. For existing corporations with broader businesses, social goals may enhance reputation, meet corporate social responsibility guidelines, or otherwise be consistent with the mission and values of the organization.

In other words, including social goals may make good bottom-line business sense. For both types of organizations, building the right capabilities requires some effort. Creating what amounts to a brand new infrastructure for rural IT service delivery requires a broad mix of skills, and finding talented and trained people who can be effective in a role that mixes entrepreneurial tasks with corporate line responsibilities, all in an unfamiliar rural environment, can be a challenge. One solution to the potentially insurmountable problem of collecting the necessary talent and skills is to enter into partnerships with other organizations that may provide specific pieces of the overall package that is needed: application software, content, maintenance services, technology, marketing, and so on. These partnerships can pose their own problems, particularly in goal alignment and consequent performance monitoring requirements. Of course all these organizational issues are well recognized in management writing and experience: what is important is to recognize their criticality in a setting that has more typically been the arena of pure 'social service' entities such as governments and NGOs.

It is also critical to recognize that the organizational innovation required in this case is an order of magnitude greater than the task of selling consumer goods in rural areas, something that is now accepted as a given in India. The greater complexity and variety of the services being delivered through IT is the root cause of this difference. The second stage of the supply chain in Figure concerns access to electric power and Internet connectivity.

In both cases, a major constraint is the failure of the public sector to deliver adequate power and telecommunications to rural India. Privatization has helped in the case of telecommunications, as has technological change. In fact, innovation in digital communications technologies is the foundation of all rural IT-based service delivery. While conventional telephone connectivity has often proved inadequate for Internet access in rural areas, because the quality of existing voice lines is too poor to sustain data transmission, several innovations provide alternatives that are likely to be cost effective. These include wireless in local loop (WLL), fibre optic cables, and highpowered versions of Wi-Fi (802.11 wireless standards). The Internet boom in the United States clearly played a role in pushing down costs and speeding innovation in fibre optics and wireless transmission. In some cases, VSAT satellite connectivity has been used for Internet access, but it is not very cost effective. The major challenges for connectivity are likely to be regulatory, having to do with interconnection to the main network, and with maintenance, rather than with the fundamental technological choices and implementation. Electric power is more of a problem, and this is true throughout India.

Battery backups are a very partial solution to the lack of reliable power supplies, and solar technologies may be more promising in the near future: they are already in use in existing rural IT efforts. The difficulty is that having to rely on these alternatives and backups unnecessarily raises costs of operation. Of course this is true for all of India's economy. It is well recognized that the power sector is the major bottleneck, with capacity well short of demand, and the quality of transmission and distribution remaining poor.

The third stage of the supply chain is the most straightforward, because of the standardization of components of desktop computing and peripherals, rapid technological improvements, falling costs of production, and, most recently, price reductions resulting from changes in tariffs on imported hardware. It is now possible to fully equip a singlecomputer rural Internet kiosk for less than '50,000, including CD drive, printer, scanner, power backup, and web cam. Potentially, the highest cost component is the operating system, since Windows enjoys a virtual monopoly on the desktop.

However, Microsoft seems to have concessional pricing for socially oriented developing country initiatives, and this helps to reduce costs. The operating system is still typically in English, but as long as simple drills can take kiosk operators to local language applications and content, this is not a substantial usage barrier. One can conclude that this stage of the supply chain is easiest to implement, with a highly standardized, almost cookie-cutter approach–although ongoing maintenance can be a challenge.

The major business decision is whether to have more than one computer per kiosk, but experience suggests that one is sufficient for almost all situations, at least in the beginning. The next stage of the supply chain, namely applications, presents more challenges. The range of possible applications is vast. Many IT-based services require non-IT logistics or processes as complements. Availability of local language software becomes more of a constraint. There is much more variation across localities, not just regions.

Delivery of services or development of content often stretch the resources and expertise of the primary provider, and require varied partnerships or other contractual relationships. Deciding the sequencing, scope and sophistication of various applications can be a major challenge, since many of the services are being offered for the first time, or are being delivered in novel ways that challenge existing institutional frameworks and relationships. Pricing for low income markets, where market penetration is limited in any case, and where some services may be perceived as public goods that are traditionally unpriced, presents another major challenge. In the case of financial services or government records or services, substantial government cooperation may be required, raising political and bureaucratic hurdles.

In some ways, of course, the essence of the success of the rural IT-based-service business model depends on the selection, quality and pricing of the services being offered. What is interesting is that a substantial amount of learning has occurred in this arena, in just a few years. The final stage of the value chain in Figure refers to human resource management (HRM) and customer relationship management (CRM). In this context, these more general terms take on specific focuses.

Training of rural kiosk operators, whether they are formal franchisees or independent farmer operators, becomes a key aspect of the delivery model. Training the field personnel at various levels (village and district hub) is also critical.

Gathering customer information on usage patterns (nature and timing of use), revenue streams, responsiveness to pricing, social acceptance, and so on is also vital, as these are brand new markets in terms of the nature of service delivery. Furthermore, being able to respond to this information with appropriate and timely changes in strategy is also necessary for successful implementation.

One might expect that a 'labour surplus' developing economy such as India's would not have a problem with the more labour-intensive tasks at either end of the value chain as it has been mapped in Figure. However, it seems that these value chain activities are the most difficult to carry out successfully, because those with the requisite skills are more likely to be taken up by more traditional corporate organizations, in urban environments.

This does not minimize the challenges associated with technical implementations and adaptations for rural areas, whether in software, hardware and maintenance. However, solutions in these cases are often one- time and replicable, whereas building organizational expertise involves much more of a situation-specific or local approach. We have so far provided a general and abstract discussion of the various aspects of supply and demand of rural IT-based services. This discussion is made more concrete and specific, through an assessment of several initiatives in India.

It, Economics and Development

In abstract, there are two types of potential economic gains from the use of IT. First, there are both static and dynamic efficiency gains. Static gains are one-time, and come from more efficient use of scarce resources, allowing higher consumption in the present. It is useful to distinguish two kinds of static efficiency gains.

One kind pertains to increases in operating efficiency, while the other comes from reduced transaction costs. In both cases, the channel for gains is through more effective and lower cost information storage, processing and communication. Dynamic gains come from higher growth, potentially raising the entire future stream of consumption. The second type of potential benefit comes from reductions in economic inequality, to the extent that such reductions are an agreed-upon social goal, and therefore a social benefit.

The two types of gains may conflict, if growth requires increased inequality, or they may be mutually reinforcing, where broad sharing of the benefits of growth enhances the rate of growth. We can discuss the role of IT in achieving greater economic gains along both dimensions, without having to commit to a particular position on the relationship between inequality and growth. However, a focus on using IT for rural development is, at least on the surface, supportive of reduced inequality along with increased efficiency and growth. Of course, benefits that are measurable as increased market-based economic activity, and hence show up in national accounts statistics, are not the only component of development.

Development can also include improvements in the capabilities of the population, such as education, health and nutrition, independently of any direct or indirect economic impact. The ability to participate in democratic decision-making also falls into this category. Broad-based improvements in capabilities can also have positive impacts on long-run economic well being, but this is not a necessary condition for desiring such improvements. The role of IT in effecting improvements along non-economic dimensions. Turning to specific impacts, note that IT involves the electronic processing, storage and communication of information, where anything that can be represented in digital form is included in the term 'information'.

Thus news, entertainment, personal communications, educational material, blank and filled-out forms, announcements, schedules, and so on are all information. Software programmes that process data (searching, tabulating, and calculating, for example) are also information in this sense, representing a particular kind of intermediate good. We can use standard economic characterizations to classify the different kinds of information. For example, entertainment, personal communications, and sometimes news, are final goods. Educational material, job announcements, or some kinds of news (weather news for farmers, for example) are intermediate goods, typically used for improving income-earning opportunities. Information goods typically have the characteristic that one person's use does not reduce their availability for another person. Thus, a message or weather news can be viewed by many people, simultaneously or sequentially. Depending on the content of the news or message, different people may place different valuations on the information. Only friends and relatives may be interested in a personal message, all farmers in a district may be interested in local weather news, and so on. The ability to share information among users can impact the feasibility of providing it on a commercial basis.

IT dramatically increases shareability of information, and this affects the economics of private provision of information goods and services. The government may provide information goods because they are shareable and non-excludable (pure public goods). The classic example of a pure public good is national defence, but such goods may also be local in nature, such as public parks or law and order. Of course many local shareable goods can be provided exclusively, in which case private provision is a feasible alternative, in a club- like arrangement.

Here, government provision may be justified more on equity grounds than on the basis of failure of private provision. In some cases, government financing through taxes or statutory user charges can be combined with outsourcing of delivery to private providers to achieve both equity and efficiency goals. Often, private provision is feasible, but neglects the spillover benefits that it creates, in which case government subsidization may be socially beneficial. For example, primary education has private economic benefits that people are willing to pay for, but it can also have substantial non-economic benefits to the individual and to others in the society (improved understanding, ability to make sound judgements, political decisionmaking capacity, and so on). Additional roles of government that are important to bring out are in redistribution to achieve equity objectives, and in regulation of private activities through licensing and certification.

In both cases, the government also uses economic resources, and IT has a potential role in increasing the efficiency of government. For both government and private provision, one of IT's main direct benefits is in increasing efficiency by economizing on resource use in the operations of firms as well as in market transactions. Information that would otherwise be conveyed through face- toface contact, post, courier, print delivery, telegraph or telephone may instead be communicated in digital electronic form via the Internet. Efficiency gains from Internet use are not automatic: the telephone, in particular, is an efficient means of communication for many types of information.

IT also requires new investment, so the benefits of trips, time and paper saved must be weighed against the costs of installing and maintaining the new infrastructure. Efficiency benefits of IT are not restricted to thecommunication itself. IT can improve the efficiency of the telephone network, and it can make it possible to track and analyse communications. Word processing, maintaining accounts, inventory management, and other such activities that may not require longdistance communications are also made more efficient by IT. Experience with Internet use in developed countries suggests that information exchange related to the completion of market transactions is especially valuable.

The ability of IT-based communications (combined with storage and processing) to bring together buyers and sellers more effectively represents major potential gains. These gains can come about through lower search costs, better matching of buyers and sellers, and even the creation of new markets. The successes of auction and employment web sites in the US show these gains. In the rural Indian context, farmers selling their crops and buying inputs, parents seeking matrimonial alliances for their children, and job seekers are all potential users of Internet-based matching services. Efficiency gains of IT can also come about through the enabling of new goods and services. In many cases, the new good is related to something available earlier, but is presented in a form that reduces costs and expands the size of the market. For example, recorded music is a mass-consumption item, whereas only a small minority of the population could afford or have access to live performances by the highest quality musicians.

Educational material is another example where recording and duplication can replace more expensive, skilled-labour-intensive alternatives for delivery. The possibilities for interactivity with IT-based educational materials show the advantages of IT over older technologies based only on recording and duplication. Interactivity also implies personalization, in that an individual can select the precise content that he or she wishes to see. This feature also distinguishes IT-based content from what was available through previous technologies.

Finally, the sheer volume of information that is accessible through IT is much greater than before: this also allows new kinds of services to be provided at a cost that is affordable to larger segments of the population. We have outlined the potential static efficiency benefits of IT, but the direct dynamic benefits in terms of higher growth are harder to identify. Of course, if IT economizes on current resources, more is available for investment, which can increase growth. If IT increases the efficiency of education delivery to the broader population, this investment in people (human capital acquisition) is also likely to lead to higher growth.

IT may also have positive impacts through impacts on the innovation process. For example, IT can make innovation easier by allowing simulation and low-cost testing of new designs or searching through possible chemical compounds for beneficial drugs. Finally, IT may speed the diffusion of innovations through better communications, which may stimulate further innovation–though this last channel is speculative. An important barrier to realizing the economic benefits of IT is the oftensubstantial up-front cost of investment in new infrastructure–both hardware and software. In developed countries such as the US, large potential customer bases and efficient capital markets help overcome this barrier. Hardware and software designed for developed country markets can easily be adapted to serve higher income consumers in developing countries, but this leaves out the majority of the population in developing countries.

Thus, one potential consequence of IT is an exacerbation of inequality, as only higher income groups enjoy its benefits–this is the so-called 'digital divide'. On the other hand, because government-provided goods and services, including redistributive transfer payments, are often aimed at lower income groups, to the extent that IT can increase the efficiency and effectiveness of government, the benefits of IT will be more widely spread, partly reducing 'digital divide' concerns. However, achieving these benefits requires more than just internal use of IT: beneficiaries of government services (particularly the economically disadvantaged) must be able to access IT resources also. While governments may invest in such front-end interfaces with citizens (and have done so in developed countries), the cost of doing so for governments in developing countries may be prohibitive.

Such governments typically already have difficulties in raising sufficient resources through taxes and user charges. While successful examples of implementation of 'e-governance' initiatives exist, there is a conceptual alternative. This comes from recognizing the fact that citizens typically incur private costs (often substantial) in availing of government-provided services.

If the use of IT can reduce such costs, even low-income individuals may be willing to pay at least some fraction of the cost savings, and there is scope for private provision of intermediate services that reduce the cost of access to government. Of course, this idea is not specific to IT: private intermediaries already help in filling out forms, getting access, and so on. One difference that IT can make is in reducing costs even further, often by an order of magnitude. In broad terms (as is also the case with electronic marketplaces and job- matching boards), IT changes the scope and nature of intermediation. Private providers may therefore have a role in delivering IT-based information services that are complementary to government services, as well as in providing conventional private goods and services. However, the private individual benefits that determine the prices charged by private providers may not reflect the overall social benefits of provision.

As discussed earlier, these may include benefits such as greater awareness and participation in the political process. In such cases, there may be a role for government subsidization of private provision. This assumes that government provision is likely to be less efficient than private provision, which seems to be true in some cases in developing as well as developed countries. In either case, richer information flows increase the transparency with which the government operates, thereby promoting better monitoring, and potentially– depending on whether electoral and legal institutions are effective–greater accountability.

The ultimate payoff is more efficient delivery of government services. Looking at the case of India, in cities and larger towns, cyber kiosks have already begun to proliferate. Urban population densities, income levels, cultural attitudes and telecom infrastructure all seem to be sufficient for the commercial success of these enterprises. The falling cost of hardware and the availability of a variety of English language software have also supported this trend.

Finally, the government's belated opening up of Internet service provision to competitive entrants has been a crucial supporting development. In non- Internet IT-related services, IT education has clearly taken off in cities as well, inspired by India's success in software exports. In rural areas and smaller towns, however, the various demographic and socioeconomic factors such as income levels, cultural attitudes, and geographic and social fragmentation may not be present in configurations that would easily enable the diffusion of commercial access to various IT-enabled services. Furthermore, the market power of traditional rural intermediaries may act as a barrier to partial innovations in how matching of buyers and sellers is conducted. Finally, vernacular language requirements and different demand patterns imply the need for software that is tailored for fragmented rural markets. We examine the technical and organizational issues in implementing widespread rural IT use in India.

Implementation: Cases, Impacts and Lessons

The discussion of several rural-IT initiatives is based on field visits conducted over a two-year period, from December 2001 to December 2003, as well as discussions with various members of each organization. The goal is not to provide an exhaustive description or analysis of any single organizational effort, but to use the conceptual framework of the previous part to bring out common features as well as differences. Nevertheless, it is useful to describe each initiative separately, rather than organize the discussion according to value chain components or demand-side factors, as this provides a better sense of each overall effort.

DRISHTEE

Drishtee.com had its origins in , a government project in Dhar district of Madhya Pradesh, in central India. Gyandoot provided an intranet for 33 village information kiosks, offering a range of mainly e-governance-related services. The most prominent of these is land record certificates, which are needed by landowners for transactions such as sale or leasing of land.

While Gyandoot was a specific local initiative, involving heavy support from the District Collector, Drishtee has attempted to take that model and rapidly replicate it across the country. Currently, Drishtee has over 100 rural Internet kiosks in several states, run by franchisees according to a revenue sharing arrangement. In Drishtee's case, a kiosk has, at least initially, just one computer. The set-up cost is in the range of '50,000. Drishtee is a commercial organization, with specific social objectives of targeting benefits to the rural poor built into its vision and strategy. Drishtee has developed some software on its own, but also relies on various partners for software development, as well as, in some cases, other partners for management of district hubs, from which kiosks in a district are managed.

Thus Drishtee's model involves not only franchising individual kiosks, but also potentially franchising district hubs. Partnering with local district hub 'channel partners' allows Drishtee to expand faster without creating a bulky organization, spreads risks, and also insulates Drishtee from some of the commercial pressures that might conflict with social objectives. At the same time, it reduces Drishtee's ability to monitor and implement the achievement of social objectives. This tension between commercial success and meeting social objectives is a general challenge for all the rural IT initiatives examined here.

Despite some challenges, Drishtee appears to have built a capable but lean organization, with learning having been systematized in a manner that makes it transferable across locations, permitting more effective scaling up. Electric power and telecom connectivity have posed challenges for Drishtee, since it is a pure startup, without resources for heavy investments in infrastructure. It uses standard battery backup for power interruptions, and has relied mainly on dial-up Internet access, though it is experimenting with Wi-Fi for district-level intranets. In some cases, it has set up kiosks even without phone connectivity, relying on physical delivery of information. Software has also been developed that economizes on bandwidth for information exchange, making the constraint of dial-up access less severe.

As we have noted, the software and hardware for basic kiosk operations are quite standardized, and their cost has been falling. Drishtee was able to get concessional terms for using the Windows operating system. Various local language software applications have been developed, for e-governance, market price information, buying and selling, and so on. With the origins in Gyandoot playing a role, simple e-governance, such as making government forms available and allowing a variety of complaints to be relayed to the district level government, has typically been the lead service in setting up operations in a new district.

In this context, informal partnerships with district level government officials (both state and local) have been very significant. For example, in Sirsa and Jaipur districts, Drishtee has been able to act as a significant intermediary for information exchange between the district government and constituents. It obviously remains limited in its ability to improve the internal functioning of government.

Nevertheless, Drishtee's approach can be viewed as achieving the right kind of 'embedded autonomy' at the local level, to use Peter Evans' term, meaning a societal structure with coherent institutions that are autonomous, but nevertheless connected through institutionalized channels for continual negotiation of goals and policies. Expanding the range of services has meant tying up with content partners, particularly organizations such as Agriwatch, which provides a substantial quantity and range of agricultural information to farmers.

Agriwatch is essentially developing into a large-scale Internet portal for farmers, and Drishtee's role can be seen as providing lastmile access to this rich information, through its kiosks.

It is difficult to quantify the benefits of this service, but its popularity with farmers suggests that it is valuable. Related examples from the cases of ITC and n-Logue will provide a more definite assessment of these benefits. Drishtee's pricing scheme for e-governance services follows a set model.

The full cost of a transaction such as obtaining, filling out and submitting a government form is estimated, including imputing the value of time spent in travel. The kiosk owner's fee for this is then set at about 10 per cent of the estimated transaction cost, also taking into account possible willingness-to- pay considerations in choosing "pricing points" such as `5, 10 or 20. Assuming that these fees can cover the full cost of the kiosk owner and Drishtee (which depends largely on generating sufficient volume) the saving in transaction costs is substantial.

The savings in such cases are generated by reductions in travel and time costs. There may also be benefits in terms of improving the effectiveness of transactions (*e.g.*, if a complaint through this channel s more likely to be addressed), but these are harder to quantify. In the case of other services, such as matching buyers and sellers, or providing horoscopes or matrimonial advertising, additional services require partners who can provide software, maintenance, content or other components of the complete service. Education has played a limited role in Drishtee's offerings, though kiosk owners have often used the presence of a computer and peripherals to offer computer training, as well as other offline services such as printing and games.

The benefits in these examples are reductions in transaction costs for existing transactions, improved quality of successful matches, and potentially most significant, completion of activities (*e.g.*, training, entertainment, communications) that would otherwise not take place because of high transaction costs. Finally, Drishtee has appeared to learn rapidly with respect to the selection and training of kiosk owners, and eliciting the preferences of rural Internet kiosk users. This partly reflects the organization's own structure and character. As a lean start-up, it seems to have attracted people who are relatively in tune with rural market environments. The process has not been painless, and there are still challenges in managing operations that are spread across several states, but Drishtee's ability to manage its own human resources and the end users of its services has grown over time. In sum, Drishtee has emerged as a typical start-up.

Without very substantial financial resources, it has still managed to expand, and it has built an organization with strong competencies in what may be broadly termed 'rural IT-based service delivery.' This judgement holds despite Drishtee's lack of any clear strength in technology, applications, partnerships or ability to scale. In all these dimensions, it is 'good enough,' but it appears to have built a strong, low-cost organization from scratch, one that may be well suited to delivering at least some components of the overall service. This competence is discussed further in the context of Aksh, a former Drishtee partner.

AKSH

Aksh is essentially a fibre optic cable company, with its core competence in laying and maintaining cable. Its revenue model is driven by the content and data that can be delivered over this cable. Therefore it has an interest in increasing such content delivery. While urban areas in India have seen substantial penetration of cable TV, through a model (now in transition) of largely unregulated local operators, the rural market remains largely unserved. The bottleneck has been the lack of last mile infrastructure, since there is a significant percentage of rural households (especially in richer districts) that can afford cable TV.

Aksh, along with other companies such as Reliance, has received licenses for laying a new fibre optic network in rural areas. In the case in point, Aksh rapidly laid a large fibre optic network in rural Jaipur district (excluding the city itself).

It initially partnered with Drishtee for the development and maintenance of kiosks that would act as distribution points for cable TV access, as well as Internet kiosks. The Drishtee franchise model, interface and services were adopted, but with the brand name of "Gramdoot." Aksh therefore appeared in the value chain as the provider of connectivity, with Drishtee handling all the other value chain stages illustrated in Figure. However, this asymmetry between Drishtee and Aksh was fairly quickly reversed, and now Aksh stands as the main service provider, with Drishtee reduced to the role of providing software and related services. There are several reasons for this shift in the business relationship.

Most obviously, Aksh's far greater size, resources and hardware capabilities give it an advantage in setting up and maintaining the hardware aspects of the kiosks. The rapid expansion of kiosks in Jaipur, with over 100 being set up within six months, stretched Drishtee's human resources beyond their limits. It was also not feasible to hire and train large numbers of people for servicing the kiosks. Second, the needs of the cable TV business, and some degree of competition that emerged with another cable TV provider in the same district created additional problems of maintenance (*e.g.*, Aksh's cables were cut by the competitor) and conflicts in terms of priorities for bringing Internet-based services online–essentially, Internet services were the tail of the cable TV dog. Finally, Aksh's incentive was to control and brand the effort to score points for corporate social responsibility. In any case, the model of rural IT-kiosks managed by a large company with incentives to provide access to large numbers of rural households appears to be scalable and sustainable. Cable TV over fibre optic networks provides a strong revenue base, and a range of Internet-based services and content can be provided through partnerships.

As companies such as Drishtee also scale up, they may be more effective in providing the necessary scale for ongoing management of the kiosks, including training services and customer relationship management. For now, providing software is easier for start-ups in such cases. The history of Aksh's initiative means that the range of services provided in their kiosks, the revenue model, and pricing structures currently follow the Drishtee model. Hence the earlier discussion of benefits transfers over to this case. The importance of cable TV revenues, however, suggests that these kiosks may emphasize a range of entertainment services more than utility services such as agriculture-related information or e-governance. It is conceivable, however, that kiosk operators will be able to span the entire range of services. The bandwidth available will certainly support a full range of offerings, and the issues will be managerial attention and the perceptions of rural users.

One important implication of greater bandwidth is that video interactions are possible, and Drishtee and Aksh have been able to test several communication services based on this. The power of video over text is in increasing the richness of information exchange, as well as greatly increasing the attractiveness and acceptance of all the services offered by the kiosks.

N-LOGUE

While Aksh and Drishtee are mostly active in north India, n-Logue has its origin and chief presence in the south. It is a for-profit corporation, with majority ownership residing with a non-profit organization. The main impetus for n-Logue came from the IIT Chennai research group headed by professor Ashok Jhunjhunwala. This group has been responsible for a stream of hardware and software innovations that enable rural IT-based service delivery, through connectivity and applications.

The core innovation at the heart of n-Logue's operations is a WLL technology, Cordect, which provides joint wireless Internet and voice connectivity. The kiosk-level hardware is relatively inexpensive, and adds only marginally to the overall cost of a kiosk. However, the construction of WLL towers and maintenance of the WLL hub is relatively costly, and this fixed cost requires a substantial density of kiosks within a particular radius of the tower.

The n-Logue model is designed to achieve this density, with kiosks generating returns from fairly small user populations (somewhat smaller than in the case of Drishtee and Aksh). Another constraint on this connectivity model is the requirement of clear lines of sight, and therefore relatively flat topography. Nevertheless, large parts of India are still suitable for this implementation. Furthermore, n-Logue has progressed well beyond being simply a connectivity provider, to delivering a range of services–these can be adapted to different connectivity technologies. N-Logue is the second largest organization in this field, supporting over 500 rural-IT kiosks. The WLL technology does provide several strengths.

It overcomes lack of dial-up connectivity, and provides an extra revenue stream for kiosk operators, through voice calls. Furthermore, it has greater bandwidth than traditional fixed line dial-up, which allows a wide range of applications to be delivered. In particular, the IIT Chennai group has been able to develop video applications that are sufficiently compressed to work within the constraints of the WLL. In general, the close links with the IIT Chennai group have given n-Logue access to a range of software innovations for delivery and implementation of various applications in the fields of education, health and agriculture.

For example, web cams have been used for remote diagnostics for diseases of people, animals and plants. A considerable amount of local language software has been created quite rapidly and effectively. The university connection is important, and stands out as a model for other providers to emulate. N-Logue has also been able to leverage its university connections to build strong partnerships across the board. The Tamil Nadu government has been strongly supportive of n-Logue's operations in Madurai district, where numerous innovations have been piloted and showcased.

MIT's Media Lab has also been involved in the initial stages, and ICICI Bank is piloting various financial services products in kiosks in Madurai. IN Nellikuppam district, n-Logue has partnered with EID-Parry to improve sugar farmers' access to information, and reduce their transactions costs in dealing with Parry's large sugar factory in the district, through improved tracking and settlements of payments. In this case, the factory chimney has also served as a base for the tower, and the control hub is housed in the factory, substantially reducing fixed costs. Parry plans to use those kiosks that are under its own brand (several dozen in total) to offer processed foods to farmers.

N-Logue also appears to have developed a very capable organization, and has expanded beyond Tamil Nadu into other southern states, as well as the west and north of India. One advantage that emerged in discussions was the relative ease of establishing organizational capabilities, training kiosk operators, and serving rural communities in the south relative to the north of India. This reflects higher proportions of the population with basic education, greater population densities, and, in general, a more structured and stable civil society. A factor that seemed to emerge in all cases was the greater average success of women kiosk operators, possibly reflecting the fact that there is greater untapped potential for rural women, given their otherwise more restricted employment opportunities.

Overall, n-Logue has several strengths compared to Drishtee, in terms of access technology, software applications and partnerships. Nevertheless, the two organizations are quite similar in terms of the range of services offered, and their ability to deliver close to an 'end-to-end' solution. Their social goals are more salient than those of Aksh, and each has achieved a substantial geographic reach and partnership capability. There are some differences in emphasis in terms of applications, services, and revenue models (Drishtee relies more on overall revenue sharing, whereas n-Logue charges mainly for connectivity).

In each case, however, there has been a demonstration that rural IT-based services are commercially feasible, and as a corollary, provide quantifiable economic benefits. Since estimates of the overall market size suggest that it can support at least 50,000 kiosks (roughly one per 10,000 people), and these two organizations, plus Aksh, have less than 1,000 kiosks, there appears to be substantial room for further growth.

ITC

ITC stands out as a large Indian corporation serving global markets. Its kiosks are called e-choupals, and they have several differentiating features. The key distinguishing factor is that the e-choupals are totally designed to support ITC's agricultural products supply chain. This gives them a focus that is not present even in EID-Parry's kiosks in Nellikuppam. In addition, the e-choupals are totally owned and set up by ITC, with the operators not having any investment or risk of their own. Furthermore, e-choupal operators are, because of the focus, always substantial farmers, and therefore always male. All these features make the e-choupals different from the previous three initiatives.

The e-choupal initiative has involved a clear focus and strong direction from the head of ITC's International Business Division. ITC has been able to turn its substantial organizational and managerial capabilities towards this initiative. Management trainees are heavily immersed in the e-choupal model as part of their inculcation into ITC's workings. There are four kinds of e- choupals, tailored very specifically for four different products: shrimp, coffee, wheat and soybeans. The first two of these involve large commercial farmers, and the focus is on creating Internet access to global market information to guide production and supply decisions.

There are a few dozen of these e-choupals. In the case of wheat and soybeans, there are many small farmers, and over 2,000 e-choupals have been set up, in several states of India. The description here is based on soy-choupals. Wheat-choupals are somewhat similar, with the final market and products being somewhat different. Soybeans are pressed to extract oil, which is sold domestically, while the remainder is exported as animal feed.

Thus they are a cash crop, without the regulated market conditions or subsistence consumption associated with a food grain such as wheat. Soy- choupals are used as registry points for procurement of soybeans. Actual procurement is done at factories and warehouse hubs, but the initial logging in is done through the e-choupal, which provides price information and therefore price certainty. In fact, the e-choupal price acts as a floor price for procurement–the factory or warehouse price can be higher. E-choupals also provide access to local market (mandi) prices and global market price information on soybeans and derivative products, to allow farmers to compare prices. They give access to operational information, developed by ITC experts, pertaining to cropping, seeds, fertilizer, and so on. E-choupals are set up by ITC, with solar power backup and VSAT connectivity.

The equipment cost for the e-choupal is borne by ITC, with the selected farmer providing the location. In addition to the adoption advantages that come from using a farmer with high social status as the operator, the house should be spacious and sturdy enough to house all the required equipment, including the VSAT and solar panel on the roof. Echoupal farmers take an oath to serve the village, and they are trained by ITC.

While there is an important element of social pressure and pride of work, the operators also receive commissions on soybean shipments booked through the e-choupals. This provides substantial revenue to the e-choupal operator. The narrow (at least initial) focus of the e-choupals and the substantial commitment of financial and human resources by ITC has made rapid expansion possible, as well as quick acceptance by farmers. The narrow range of applications has limited software requirements, and operators bear no risk in the ITC model. The longer-term goal is, however, to use e-choupals and warehouse hubs as sales points for soybean oil, tractor rentals, and eventually a range of ITC-produced consumer goods.

The initial benefits of the ITC effort include a substantial reduction in transaction costs, from 8 per cent of a transaction, down to 2 per cent, approximately. It is estimated that these gains are shared roughly equally between ITC and individual farmers. Some of this gain may be at the expense of traditional intermediaries, who operate in mandis, but much of it comes from genuine efficiency gains, including clearer quality guidelines and measurement, greater timeliness and reduced waits, quicker payments, and reduced uncertainties. To some extent, traditional intermediaries are co-opted in the new process, by being hired to perform tasks such as handling payments at ITC's receiving points. Clearly the use of information technology is just a part of ITC's overhaul of its supply chain, but speedy delivery of complex information pertaining to market conditions makes IT essential. It might be asked what acts as a check on ITC's market power in this process. Clearly, the traditional mandi system, with its accompanying government regulation and oversight, acts as continuing competition. More significantly, ITC's concern with its reputation acts as a disciplining device.

Finally, the long term goal of selling back to farmers as customers also gives ITC an incentive to cultivate relationships with individual farmers. In fact, farmers view ITC as treating with greater respect and dignity than is the case in traditional mandi interactions. It is quite conceivable that the ITC model will not broaden significantly beyond the two-way flow of agricultural produce from farmers to ITC, and processed foods, consumer goods and inputs from ITC to farmers, without extending to e-governance, entertainment, health or education-related services. Instead, other firms may provide these services in similar locations to ITC e-choupals.

TARAHAAT

TARAhaat has evolved in a somewhat unusual manner. It achieved wellpublicized success with Internet kiosks in Bundelkhand in Uttar Pradesh. These kiosks were very much along the lines of those implemented by Drishtee and n-Logue, with a mix of e-governance services, market price information, and so on. TARAhaat's longrange plans include a comprehensive portal for rural information services and an extended vision of its 'TARAkendras' as community centers.

However, in its expansion into Punjab, at the invitation of the administrator of Bathinda district, its model evolved quite differently. While the Bundelkhand model had used VSAT connectivity, this was not economical for a commercially sustainable expansion. While Punjab is a high-income state with relatively good infrastructure, the level of telephone connectivity turned out to be too poor for practical Internet use. Other issues arose with the substantially greater investment required by TARAkendra operators, since the model assumed that each kiosk with have three or four computers. Perhaps the greatest problem was in building an organization for implementation. While TARAhaat is a subsidiary of Development Alternatives, an established NGO, it is set up as a corporation, with social goals meant to be enforced through ownership by the non-profit parent. The expansion of TARAhaat required building an organization from scratch, and this turned out to be a slow process.

There were also problems with establishing effective partnerships with local and state government, and TARAhaat has mostly gone it alone. TARAhaat does have an educational content partner, called TARAgyan. In association with various partners, TARAgyan is developing local language content and software for use in TARAkendras. Basic IT education is an important part of TARAgyan's actual and potential offerings, but it is not the exclusive focus. In fact, there has been a substantial diversification into developing materials for English language instruction, rural marketing, personality development, and so on.

This development was initially very slow, though it may be picking up steam. The constraints faced by TARAhaat pushed its Punjab effort in the direction of locating in mandi towns rather than villages, and focusing on offering offline education rather than a full array of IT- and Internet-based services. Thus, the few dozen TARAkendras in Punjab have emerged as quite distinct from the Internet kiosks of the other organizations. It is conceivable that TARAhaat will end up occupying a very distinct niche in small town India, quite different from a direct impact on the rural, agricultural part of the country. Interestingly, Punjab may have been the wrong place to try to create efficiency improvements in agriculture, since there are relatively strong market and related institutions for existing crops such as wheat, rice, cotton and sugar cane.

Efficiency gains in Punjab agriculture are more likely to come about through the intervention of the government to create a new infrastructure to support alternative, higher value-added crops, or through concerted efforts by large agribusiness firms such as ITC.

❐

4.

Importance of the Study of Rural Sociology

Rural sociology is a field of sociology traditionally associated with the study of social structure and conflict rural areas although topical areas such as food and agriculture or natural resource access transcend traditional rural spatial boundaries. It is an active field in much of the world, and in the United States originated in the 1910s with close ties to the national Department of Agriculture and land-grant university colleges of agriculture.

The sociology of food and agriculture is one focus of rural sociology and much of the field is dedicated to the economics of farm production. Other areas of study include rural migration and other demographic patterns, environmental sociology, amenity-led development, public lands policies, so- called "boomtown" development, social disruption, the sociology of natural resources (including forests, mining, fishing and other areas), rural cultures and identities, rural health care and educational policies. Many rural sociologists work in the areas of development studies, community studies, community development and in environmental studies. Much of the research involves the Third World.

The Meaning and Scope of Rural Sociology

The nomenclature 'Rural Sociology' indicates that it is the scientific study of Rural Society. Broadly speaking, it deals with the systematic study of Rural Society, its institutions, activities interactions, social change etc. It not only deals with the social relationship of man in rural environment but also takes urban surroundings into considerations for a comparative study. So Rural Sociology primarily deals with the description and analysis of groups of various kinds as they exist in rural environment.

Different sociologists have defined Rural Sociology in different ways. The tone of these different thinkers varies but the whole essence is same.

According to A.R. Desai, "The prime objective of Rural Sociology should be to make a systematic, scientific and comprehensive study of the rural social organisation, of its structure function and objective tendencies of development and on the basis of such a study to discover the laws of is development. Since every science social or natural, has for its aim the discovery of the hither to hidden laws of development of a domain of nature or society, the basic task of Rural Sociology, they unanimously declare, is to discover the law of development of Rural Society."

T.L. Smith has defined Rural Sociology as some investigators study social phenomena that are present only in or largely confined to the rural environment, to persons engages in agricultural occupation. Such sociological aspects and principles as one derived from the study of rural social relationship may be referred to as Rural Sociology.

According to F. Stuart Chapin Rural Sociology is "the sociology of rural life, a study of rural population, rural social organisation and the social process."

Bertrand has defined Rural Sociology. In the broadest definition Rural Sociology is the study of human relationship in rural environment.

From the above definitions, it is revealed that Rural Sociology deals with the study of rural environment, rural social facts and interactions, rural populations, rural social organisation, rural social processes etc. It studies the whole structure and functions of rural social organisation and institutions.

It is a holistic study of rural social setting. It provides us valuable knowledge about the rural social phenomena and social problems which helps us in understanding Rural Society and making prescription for its all round progress and prosperity.

SCOPE OF RURAL SOCIOLOGY

Rural Sociology is comparatively a new branch of Sociology which is of recent origin. It is a separate science having its own subject matter and method of study. The scope or Rural Sociology refers to what it studies. To draw attention on the scope, N.L. Sims says, "The field of Rural Sociology is the study of association among people living by or immediately dependent upon agriculture. Open country and village groupings and groups behaviour are its concern."

According to Lowry Nelson, "The scope of Rural Sociology is the description and analysis of progress of various groups as they exist in the rural environment. In the words of Bertrand and his associates: "In its broadest definition Rural Sociology is the study of human relationship in rural environment." On account of the opinions given by Sims, Nelson and Bertrand, it is observed that the scope of Rural Sociology covers rural people, their livelihood and social relationship in rural environment. It studies society from the rural standpoint. But its main aim is concentrated on rural lives. The subjects that are included within the scope are very comprehensive in nature and we can blindly say that its boundary is varying large. The scope of Rural Sociology may be clear from the analysis of the following subjects.

Rural Society

Rural Sociology, as is clear by the nomenclature, is the sociology of Rural Society. As sun is the centre of solar system, in Rural Sociology, Rural Society is the centre. Rural Sociology, basically studies Rural society, its nature and basic ingredients from the structural and functional standpoints. Its main aim is to study of rural social life. Rural social life covers the behaviour patterns, web of relationship, social interactions, standard of living and socio-economic conditions of the rural people. The scope of Rural Sociology, therefore, expands where the boundary of Rural Society is expanded.

Rural Population

Rural population is the basic essence of Rural Sociology. It studies the nature, characteristics, size, density and distribution of rural population from different angles. Rural Sociology aims at the study of the factors of growth of population, its evil effects of Rural Society, rural –urban migration for the greater interest of the country at large.

Rural Community

Rural community is the oldest organisation of mankind. Rural Sociology, therefore, is mainly concerned with the divine origin, nature characteristics, social attributes and human ecology of rural community. It also studies the homogenous rigid and conservative nature of hither to existing customs, traditions, folkways, mores, norms, values and so on in rural community.

Rural Social Organisation

Social organisation is the most fundamental basis of every society as well as social life. The most important function of Rural Sociology, therefore, is to provide basic knowledge about rural social organisation. Rural Social organisation covers the spiritual lives, religious activities sacred relationship and divine notion of rebirth, Karmaphala etc. Of rural folk which deeply affect the entire rural social life. Rural sociology, thus, for the betterment of rural life, studies the future prospectus of rural social organisation and governing laws for its development.

Rural Social Institution governing the relations between the rural people. Rural sociology, thus, studies the structure, characteristics and functions of rural social institutions. Rural social institutions include family, marriage, kinship, religion, caste and Rural Sociology studies the sociological importance of these institutions in the rural context.

Rural Economy

Rural economy is basically known as agricultural economy. Agriculture is the backbone of rural economic life. Rural people directly depend on agriculture for their livelihood. Rural Sociology therefore studies the factors responsible for the failure of agriculture and suggests various measures for the improvement of agriculture in rural areas. Besides, the adoption of new agricultural technology among the farming centers, modernisation of old farming methods, creation of open markets and providing agricultural training to the farmers are the important areas of the study or Rural Society.

Rural social Process

Rural Sociology mainly studies the two process of rural social interaction, namely, conjunctive and disjunctive. Rural conjunctive process includes co- operation, accommodation and assimilation. Rural disjunctive process, on the other hand, includes competition and conflict. Thus, the nature, characteristics and social importance of these processes are to be properly studied by the scope of Rural Sociology.

Rural Religion

Rural Society is basically a religion oriented society. Religion is the soul of rural people and it is regarded as the chief essence of rural life. Religion, therefore, plays a vital role in Rural Society. Rural Sociology, in this context, and studies the concept and social importance of rural religion and its impact on Rural Society.

Rural Culture

Culture, as we mean, is that complex whole which includes knowledge, belief, moral law, art, custom and any other capabilities acquired by man as a member of society. Rural culture is strictly based on rigid and conservative dogmas and it is very static in nature. It includes old customs, tradition, folkways, mores, norms, values and so on. Rural Sociology studies the complexities of rural culture, its different structural organisations, cultural patterns, cultural traits and cultural lag in the rural contexts.

Rural Social Problems

Rural Society is a hell of social evils. It is basically called a hot bed of rural social problems. Its major problems are poverty, unemployment, population growth, illiteracy, casteism, untouchability and so on. Rural Sociology, therefore, studies the causes and evil effects of these problems and also suggests measures for their eradication for the greater interests of the country at large.

Rural Social Control

Social control as we mean, is the control of society over individual. In Rural Society, social control is in formal and rigid in nature. Rural Sociology significantly studies the informal means and agencies such as religions, customs, folkways, mores, norms etc., of social control. In Rural Society, the important primary groups like family and neighbourhood play a vital role in social control.

Rural Social Change

Social change is meant only such alterations as occur in social organisation, that is, structure and functions of society, Rural Society, now-a-days, is on the way of social change. Due to the impact of money modernising forces, Rural Society is undergoing tremendous changes in the twentieth century. For a better account of the speed of social change in Rural Society, Rural Sociology undertakes necessary steps. Rural Sociology also studies the various factors responsible for social changes in a systematic way.

Rural Urban Contrast

The study of Rural Society shall not be completed unless the study of rural urban contrast is done in a proper and scientific manner. Both village and city, hypothetically, are the two contrasting modes of community life. Rural Sociology studies the rural-urban contrast on the basis of social, economic, religious and cultural point of view. Besides, Rural Sociology also draws attention on the comparative study of these two societies. As a result, the concept of Rural Society and social institutions can be clear by this contrasting analysis.

Rural Planning and Reconstruction

Rural planning and reconstruction are very much essential for under developed societies. In this context, the poor and backward condition of Indian Rural Society needs rural planning and reconstruction in a systematic and planned manner.

Rural Society is full of social problems. For the eradication of these problems and for the betterment of rural life, the proper planning and reconstruction should be made by the state as well Central Government. A.R. Desai says, Rural Sociology studies all these subjects and provides proper guidelines in this direction.

It is evident from the above analysis that the scope or subject matter or Rural Sociology, no doubt is very vast. Though, it is the youngest and progressive science, yet it studies the various aspects of Rural Society as well as rural life to a great extent.

IMPORTANCE OF THE STUDY OF RURAL SOCIOLOGY

The importance of rural sociology can be evaluated properly when it realize the importance of rural society. Rural society presents a scientific picture of rural life. Villages are important because they are the springs to feed urban areas. The importance of rural sociology can be put under following heads. Man has an urge to know human relationship and this can be satisfied through rural sociology.

RURAL POPULATION IS IN A MAJORITY

In almost all the Countries of the world majority or the world resides in villages in villages. It is more true that over 80 per cent population of India resides in villages.

IT GIVES COM PLETE KNOWLEDGE OF VILLAGE LIFE

Rural sociology gives us complete knowledge of village life. Village is the first unit of development in country. It is a centre of culture of any country.

RURAL REFORMATION

Rural reformation is the primary aim of rural sociology. In this context it helps in following works.

Organization

Village unit which are disorganized and can be organized through rural sociology. It improved in the co-ordination of various units and helps in bringing an improvement in economic, social and health conditions.

Economic Betterment

Through detailed study of village problems and observation rural sociology gives stress on the importance of increasing the quantity and quality of production. This results in to raising the standard of living.

Provide Technology and Systematic Knowledge and reforms in Farm Production

Main occupation of 80 per cent population of village is agriculture. In order to improving this main occupation of rural people. The earlier researches in rural sociology was made in agricultural college.

Rural sociology examines the social pathological problems and it suggests ways for the improving these problem.

Education

The improvement t, the development of any community depends on its education. Rural sociology lays stress on education in rural problems.

Planning for Development

Rural sociology encourages the development of various plans for any rural development programme. The work must be carried out according to these plans for the progress in rural society.

Rural Sociology is Most Important in Agricultural Countries

About 90 per cent of world progress is based on agriculture. It is only in agricultural countries that people realize the importance of rural sociology. India is mainly agricultural country. For its all sided development the development of rural sociology is very important.

NATURE OF RURAL SOCIOLOGY

There is a controversy whether the sociology can be regards as science with his own subject matter. Science may be defined as body of systematized knowledge or synthesized body of knowledge. In the collection of facts for any knowledge, when we apply a scientific method it is called as a science. Science goes with the method and not with the subject matter. Scientific method consists of systematic observation, classification and interpretation of data. It is believed that rural sociology employs the scientific method. The nature of rural sociology as a science can determine on the basis of following facts:

1. *Use of Scientific Method:* It is uniform fact that rural sociology employs the scientific method. Almost all the methods of scientific study *viz.* observations, interview schedule, questionnaire method, case study, statistical methods etc. are employed in the study of rural sociology. In the absence of scientific approach the village problems can not be studied. On such studies we formulate generalized principles and laws on which we forecast future trends.
2. *Factual Study:* It studies the social events, social relationship and process in a factual manner. It also studies and analyzes the facts and the underlying general principles and theories.
3. *Discovery of Cause and Effect:* Rural sociology formulates its theories and laws on the basis of cause and effect relationship.
4. *Universal Laws:* The laws formulated by rural sociology are universal in nature. Because under normal or similar condition they prove to be correct and produce the same result.
5. *Predictions:* Since the laws formulated by rural sociology by rural sociology are based on cause and effect relationship. It is possible to predict the result.

   On the basis of conditions enumerated above, it is said that rural sociology is by nature a science. However, there are some factors which limits the scientific sociology is by nature a scientific nature of the subject.

THE NATURE OF RURAL SOCIOLOGY AS A SCIENCE

By the nature of Rural Sociology, as we generally mean, it is not clear whether it is a science or not. Augusta Comte, the father of Sociology, called Sociology as the queen of sciences. Some sociologists have come to view Sociology in terms of natural sciences. Most of the sociologists opine that Sociology possesses all the characteristics of science and it is, no doubt, a science. Since Rural Sociology is a specialised branch of Sociology, therefore it is also a science.

Before we proceed to elaborate Rural Sociology as a science, it is essential to know what science is. Science is a method and way of looking at things consisting of systematic steps like observation, collection and classification of data, hypothesis, testing, theory and conclusion. Science possesses six basic ingredients. Firstly, science employs the scientific method. Secondly; it is a study of facts. Thirdly scientific principles are universal. Fourthly, scientific laws are vertical. Its validity can be examined at any time and it proves true in every place. Fifthly, science discovers the cause-effect relationship in its subject- matter and in this connection provides universal and valid laws. Finally, science can make predictions on the basis of universal and valid laws relating to the cause-effect relationship in any subject. The function of science is based upon a faith in causality.

The nature or Rural Sociology as a science can be examined on the following grounds.

Use of Scientific Method

Rural Sociology employs scientific method. All the methods used in Rural Sociology are scientific in nature. These methods are observation, interview, case study, schedule, and questionnaire and so on. In these methods, the first step is collection of data through observation. Then the date is classified and finally the results are brought out on the basis of accepted data. The validity of these results is verified.

Factual study

Rural Sociology is always based on factual study. It studies relationship and activities in a factual way. It makes a scientific study of facts, general principles and theories involved in them.

Universal Principles

The laws and principles of Rural Sociology are universal in nature. Because they prove true at all times and at all places and produce the same results. For example, the principles of family disorganisation and social disorganisation are correlated, it true every where.

Vertical Principles

The principles of Rural Sociology prove true at every verification and re verification. Their validity can be examined by any one. For example one can consider the law that and increase in the rate of divorces indicates acceleration of family disorganisation. This principles can be examined any where by anyone.

Discovery of cause-effect relationship

Like Sociology, Rural Sociology also discovers a cause effect relationship between the phenomena. For example, in the modern society, the rate of divorce increases rapidly due to the family disorganisation. Similarly, due to the rapid growth of population the rate of poverty and unemployment increase in the Rural Society. In these illustrations, family disorganisation and population growth are two causes and divorce as well as poverty and unemployment are their effects. Rural Sociology has discovered a cause effect relation between the phenomena and population growth and divorce. Thus Rural Sociology traces cause-effect relationship in social disorganization and other incidents, activities and relationship in Rural Society and then formulates laws concerning them.

Predictions

Finally, on the basis of cause-effect relationship. Rural Sociology can anticipate the future and make predictions concerning social relationship, activities, incidents and so on. For example, if disorganisation in the families becomes pronounced, it can make predictions concerning the number of divorces and many other things. Knowing the cause-effect relationship, Rural Sociology can determine 'what will be' on the basis of 'what is'.

Thus, it is evident from the above analysis that Rural Sociology, by nature, is a science. It possesses all the essential characteristics of science.

But a lot of objections against the scientific nature or Rural Sociology are found. Some sociologists have raised their views against the nature of Rural Sociology as a science. They have strongly objected to the scientific nature Rural Sociology on the basis of the following grounds.

Lack or Objectivity

The first objection rose against the nature of Rural Sociology being called a science is that, an unbiased and objective study cannot be made in it. The main cause of this is that the sociologists have to play dual role of both the doctor and the patient in society. They are the members of that very society which they studies. From this point of view, they have established a very close relation with the contents, very beginning of society.

The sociologists study religion, family, marriage, economic system etc. But they possess their observation lacks the ingredient of objectivity, which is so much essential to science. The sociologist being a member society can study it just like a teacher can teach himself.

Lack of experiment

The second objection against the scientific nature of Rural in it. Rural Sociology is not a science just because of the term, science used in it. If science is used for physical sciences, then Rural Sociology cannot claim to be a science. The term science is used for physical sciences includes the twin process of experimentation and prediction.

Rural Sociology, in this context, is not a science because its subject matter, the human relationship and behaviour and they are abstract in nature. We can neither see nor touch, neither weighs nor analyse in the test tube of the laboratory. It does not possess the instruments like the microscope and the thermometer to measure the human behaviour as science does. It is not possible to verify and test the theory and the principles of Rural Sociology like science.

Lack of measurement

The third argument against the nature of Rural Sociology as a science is that it lacks measurement. In natural sciences, definite and standard measurement is used to measure and weigh. The different measurements like units, grams, meters, centimetres etc., by which the subject matter of natural sciences can be measured the units or Rural Sociology. Due to the lack of measurement, the results of Rural Sociology vary from time to time which is no possible in the case of natural sciences.

Lack of Exactness

The fourth objection is. Rural Sociology lacks exactness. It is not possible to follow the laws and principles or Rural Sociology universally as the principles of natural science can be followed. Its law and principles vary on the basis of time and place concerned. For example, the rural social problems of one country may be different from the other country. In India untouchability is a serious rural problem but in America it is not so.

Lack of Prediction

The fifth and final objection against the nature or Rural Sociology being called a science is that it lacks prediction. Observation and hypothesis are the two basic ingredients of science. On the basis of observation and hypothesis, science has formulated many laws and through which any prediction can be possible about any experiment. But due to the lack of objectivity and electivity, the principles that are formulated by Rural Sociology are not always correct.

As a result, nay prediction cannot be possible about the laws and principles of Rural Sociology. For instance according to the standing principles of natural science we can predict that the combination of two hydrogen molecules and one oxygen molecule produces water. But such type of prediction is almost impossible in the field of Rural Sociology.

It is evident from the above analysis regarding the nature of Rural Sociology, that it is very difficult to determine whether, by nature it is science or not. Because there are dual opinions both in favour and against the scientific nature of Rural Sociology. The laws and principles of natural sciences so far as the ex activity, laboratory experimentation and prediction are concerned, Rural Sociology is day-to-day handing towards that.

There can be no doubt over the question that rural Sociology use scientific technique like observation, experimentation, classification and tabulation in the collection and interpolation of data systematically. The conclusion drawn by the Rural Sociology is based upon empirical realities. The sociologists are prospects of Rural Sociology. Therefore Rural Sociology, no doubt can definitely be a novel branch of science having the subject-matter and methodology of its own.

RURAL SOCIOLOGY: NATURE, SUBJECT, METHODS

NATURE OF RURAL SOCIOLOGY

Sociology is considered as a social science. Though, there are debates on the nature of sociology in international social sciences. By and large, sociology is a science. There are scholars like C. Wright Mills, Peter Berger and others who consider sociology as an 'imagination' only as an art. The debate is not new. It starts from the period when social sciences parted their company with philosophy. In its earlier period, sociology was considered as positivistic science. At a later stage, it was realised that sociology could not be like any natural sciences because of its subject matter. Without entering into the debatable nature of sociology it could be observed that the nature of sociology is scientific.

Pierre Bourdieu, in one of his discourses, observes that: Sociology seems to me to have all the properties that define as science....All sociologists worthy of the name agree on a common heritage of concepts, ethods and verification procedures. What characterises a science is that it has certain concepts, methods and verification.

Sociology as certain theoretical formulations, it has logic of enquiry and above all it is subjected to verification. Despite this common agreement on the scientific nature of sociology it must be agreed that sociology is a diversified discipline. It is because of this nature that it is being divided into different realms.

It studies different aspects of human society, such as demography, education, family, caste, tribe, village and a number of other segments of a society. Essentially, however, despite having a large number of 'specialities' it continues to remain a social science.

Some of the reasons advanced for sociology being a science are as under:

Empiricism

Biology or physics had laboratory for precise experiments, measurement and verification. To some extent, the empirical method, *i.e.*, fieldwork in sociology provides opportunity for experimentation, observation and verification. The research material available in the body of sociology clearly shows that many of its theoretical formulations have emerged out of the data generated from fieldwork.

Accumulated Facts

Science grows on the data accumulated from the field. Robert Merton very rightly observes that a sociologist stands on the shoulders of other sociologists. Whatever Talcott Parsons or for that matter, Marx, Durkheim or Weber did, was carried forward by the next generations.

Objectivity

Yet another characteristic of science is its objectivity. It means the willingness and ability to see things as they really are—to study facts in a given field of investigation as they exist—without personal bias, prejudices or feelings as to their desirability or undesirability. Personal values and desires are not involved in a scientific endeavour.

The objective nature of science is difficult to be applied in social sciences. The status of researcher in empirical investigation has been debatable in sociology and social anthropology right from the 18th century. Pareto argued that when subjectivity and objectivity coincide it becomes objectivity. Max Weber, however, did not agree to this hypothesis.

He said that in any activity the role of actor is decisive. He gave due place to subjectivity. In one of his recent works Bourdieu has taken up the issue of subjectivity and objectivity. Bourdieu takes up issues of epistemology and methodology for wider scrutiny. He says that subjectivity is important so that individual has his own consciousness but beyond that there is an objective social reality also. He observes:

There is, therefore, more to social life than the subjective consciousness of the actors who move within it and produce it. There is, if you like, an objective social reality beyond the immediate interactional sphere and the self-conscious awareness of individuals.

What goes on in sociology about objectivity is that there should be a healthy negotiation between the subjective consciousness and the objective reality. The social scientist, therefore, in his research endeavour, should make a fine combination of his subjectivity, objective reality and the prevailing ideology.

Precision and Accuracy

Science is also characterised by accurate and precise observations. "When scientific observations are made it is extremely important that these describe situations or persons as they actually do exist at the time of observation—this is accuracy."

Methodology

Science must have a valid methodology. It should be valid in sense that other scientists could also employ the same method and reach to their findings. Such a rigourous methodology can yield dependable theoretical constructs.

Reciprocity in Theory and Empirical Research

Theory in science is constructed out of the experiments made in the laboratory. But approach to laboratory is through the media of theoretical constructs and hypotheses. Generally, in scientific research, we move from theory to empiricism or from empiricism to theory.

In any case there is both-way interaction between theory and empirical research. There is a healthy interaction in the domain of science between laboratory investigation and theoretical formulation. C. Wright Mills very emphatically observed that theory without data is empty, but data without theory are blind.

Almost all the social anthropologists including the rural sociologists have done hard fieldwork. Malinowski, Radcliffe-Brown and others have done tremendous field- work before constructing their theories. Rural sociology precisely is a specialised field of sociology and social anthropology.

Its nature is scientific as it borrows heavily from these social sciences. Those who have conducted rural studies in the field of caste, family, agrarian relations and land reforms have under-gone fieldwork in the villages.

Whatever, theoretical constructs which we have in the field of rural sociology have grown out of the intensive fieldwork done by social scientists.

SUBJECT MATTER OF RURAL SOCIOLOGY:

The subject matter of rural sociology has never been static. In the earlier days of its development, during 18th and 19th centuries, it studied the society of aboriginals and primitive people. The colonial countries of south and central Africa along with India were the target countries for the study of primitive people.

The British Raj along with its anthropologists approached these countries for discovering new markets and spreading Christianity. The British administrators turned to the study of primitive people. We have in our country administrators-turned sociologists and anthropologists who studied the primitive people and the indigenous institutions of village, caste and culture.

The initial subject matter of study for social anthropology and in this respect rural sociology was the life of village people and the forest dwellers. In fact, rural sociology remained restricted to the small places of the type of villages or clusters of neighbourhood.

Henry Maine, the British administrator, was perhaps the first person to study an Indian village. He characterised an Indian village as a republic in itself. Theoretically, such a kind of portrait of village life can be criticised vehemently.

Yogendra Singh (1986) provides a critique to such an understanding of village life because here Maine's emphasis was "on showing how each of these social entities (villages) affirmed the principles of segmentation and autonomy rather than being parts of an organic whole".

Despite the criticism made on the republic character of village India, the fact remains that each village was self-sufficient and independent. At a later stage, Gandhiji also observed that our villages were self-reliant and had their local rule.

Thus, the subject matter of rural sociology during the colonial period in India remained confined to the study of hill and forest people the tribals, the villages and a few of the traditional institutions such as family and caste which were pervasive in the small places.

Soon after independence there was a sudden shift and emphasis in the subject matter of rural sociology. It was unhistorical for India to prepare a constitutional agenda for the development of more than its 5 lakh villages.

The Constitution of India made it obligatory that the state shall spare no efforts for the development of villages. The Constitution also laid emphasis on the development of Panchayati Raj. It was in the year 1950 that the Constitution of India was promulgated. And then came in 1952 the five year plans and subsequently the community development and extension programmes.

Now, in the real sense, the idiom of our development became the development of village. The government policy, thus implemented, created the need for the study of village life.

With this context historically created in village development, there came a flood of village studies by the middle of 1950 to the end of 1960. The subject matter of rural sociology, thus, consisted of the study of tribal people, caste and village communities.

M.N. Srinivas (1955), in his edited work, India's Villages makes the point that in the context of development planning it was necessary to provide a portrait to the layman about the social life lived by village people. The subject matter of rural sociology, according to Srinivas, consisted to the unity of village, caste and other village institutions.

The contributors to this work argued that the Indian village had a traditional unity. The villagers who lived in a restricted area at some distance from other similar groups, with extremely poor roads between them, a majority of them were engaged in agricultural activities. They closely depended upon each other economically and otherwise. They shared a vast body of common experience and this fostered what is called as the unity of the village. It was the dominant caste in the village which supported and maintained the total village system.

However, the development programmes and the forces of technology, industrialisation, urbanisation, market, and a host of other factors brought about tremendous change in the community. This provided a new set of subject matter to the body of rural sociology.

Land reforms, land ceiling, land tenure, and above all agrarian relations constituted new issues for intensive study. The process of democratisation, along with the emphasis on Panchayati Raj, created a new awakening among the people.

Agricultural capitalism, as is manifest in green revolution, provided a new stratification pattern to the village society. The village peasantry witnessed widening social differentiation in the form of big or kulak farmers, small farmers, marginal farmers and landless labourers. The peasant struggles became more than frequent. There emerged rural leadership and rural conflicts. All these areas constituted a new discourse on subject matter of rural sociology.

Beyond the new subject matter, rural sociology has begun to study the role of village people at the state and national level politics. There is a distinct village lobby working in national politics. The village politics is yet another theme forming part of rural sociology.

To conclude this section on the subject matter of rural sociology, one could put down the following themes as the substantial areas for the study of rural sociology:

1. Rural sociology consists of the study of tribal, forest and village people. It provides a discourse on the study of the social life of these people.
2. Rural sociology is concerned with the problems and structure related to land and agriculture. In other words, it dwells heavily on the themes related to agrarian relations.
3. Village development programmes have been new additions to the subject matter of rural sociology. The objective of these programmes, on one hand, is to improve the life-standard of the people and, on the other hand, make them participants in the task of nation- building.
4. Rural sociology also studies the stratification pattern which has emerged from the working of developmental programmes.
5. It also analyses the impact of technology on the rural life.
6. And finally, the subject matter of rural sociology also includes environmental decay and erosion of ecology.

METHODS AND TOOLS OF RURAL SOCIOLOGY:

Methods

There is a fundamental difference in methods and tools of study. Method is the basic of enquiry whereas tools are the instruments by means of which data are generated from the field. In social sciences, when we talk about methodology, we include both the logic and the tools of data collection.

The methods of structural-functional, structural, structural-historical and historical-materialist or Marxist, broadly, constitute the logic of enquiry. Fieldwork, comparison, observation, administration of schedule and case studies form the tools of data generation.

In the case of the methodology of rural sociology, one could ask the question:

From whom does rural sociology borrow its methodological kit? Obviously, it borrows its approaches to the study of rural communities primarily from social anthropology and sociology. It also draws heavily from economics and political science so far the village economy and Panchayati Raj are concerned.

At the outset, it must be observed that it is the need of the rural society which constitutes its subject matter and finally it is the subject matter which determines its methodology. Yogendra Singh, in the Survey of Research in Sociology and Social Anthropology (1969-1979) (1985), observes that "during the fifties there was dominance of the structural-functional theory" as a major theoretical orientation in sociology and social anthropology. Towards the end of this decade structuralist, structural-historical and historical-materialist or Marxist approaches came to be employed by sociologists and social anthropologists.

However, during 1970s and onwards, village studies became infrequent or out of academic endeavour. Structuralists, structural-historical and Marxist orientations became out of vogue in rural studies. Though, conflict became a method of study. In these studies, the emphasis was to consider conflict as adaptive tensions resulting from the structures outside of it.

Yet another method employed for village studies has been comparative method. This method has remained popular with the social anthropologists since 18th century. The comparative method employed in village studies has been based on systemic comparison. The third method, generally used by rural sociologists, has been intensive fieldwork.

In the following section we discuss all the three methods or approaches employed in the study of rural life:

1. Structural-functional method
2. Systemic comparison
3. Fieldwork

Structural-functional method

The structural-functional studies of village India implied a systemic 'teleology' based on the Brahminic or hierarchical model of caste society, assumption of harmony or consensus as the system state from which status of mobility, differentiation or roles of power structure and of factional ties, and processes of fusion and fission in the caste structure, were studied. The village studies, thus, were microstructural. In these studies, the expressions of conflict in the affairs of the village or for that matter in polity and economy were considered as deviant but manageable expressions. Mobility within the caste was interpreted often through a reference group theory which itself was deeply anchored in consensual ideology.

A stock-taking of village studies undertaken by Indian and foreign sociologists show that the villages are considered as small and self-sufficient. In the paraphrase of Robert Redfield, the villages are, in fact, little communities. M.N. Srinivas argues that a social anthropologist selects a small community as he wants to obtain an idea of the way in which all the parts of a society hang together. The structural-functional method is appropriate for the holistic study of village life.

The Marxist approach, however, has not been employed in the rural studies conducted during 1950s to 1970s. The weaknesses, which are found instructural-functional method, are also found in these studies. The method suffers from the fact that it does not take into consideration the mode of production, production relations and, in fact, the total kit of Marxian terminology.

Systemic Comparison

Rural sociology is quite ambitious in its study. It has the whole of human society as its field of interests, and tries to understand the connections between the various aspects of our existence. For instance, when we study the economic system of a village, say, Rampura or Kishangarhi, we simultaneously try to find out, how their economy is connected with other aspects of their society and finally compare it with other village studies.

If comparative method had not been the mainstay of rural studies, there was no need to study only one tiny village or tribe. When the mankind is concerned with the study of vast masses of people, the knowledge gained by the study of one village can hardly be a reliable guide. It is in this context that M.N. Srinivas (1962) lays emphasis on systematic comparison.

- *He observes:* But then, systematic comparison is considered to be of the essence of the method of social anthropology. For instance, no anthropologist would dare to speak of Indian villages as a whole until a sufficient number of villages in the different cultural areas had been studied...In addition it provides the anthropologist with some insight into rural social life all over the country. Of course, such insight is not knowledge, and once this distinction is clearly made, even a single village study enables the anthropologist to say a good deal about rural social life in India as a whole.

There are several illustrations of the application of comparative method in rural studies. T.S. Epstein, in her study on Economic Development and Social Change (1962) in two of the villages of south India, makes a comparative study of dry and wet communities. She comes out with the finding that the villagers belonging to wet village, *i.e.*, village having irrigation from canal water, are progressive and forward- looking compared to the villagers from dry village.

Comparative method of study has been a reliable logic of enquiry in rural studies. The concepts of dominant caste, sanskritisation and great and little traditions have stood the taste of comparative method. There is sufficient evidence of the usefulness of dominant caste in a variety of village studies.

Fieldwork

It may be reiterated that the methods employed in rural sociology are largely those which are in vogue in social anthropology. It is because of the fact that social anthropology is concerned with the study of tribal groups and villages. In the field of methodology, sociology has little to impart to rural studies. In India, sociology is concerned with the complex communities or groups. Because of this, its methods are not considered to be useful for the study of village life.

Among all the social sciences, social anthropology distinguishes itself from the other social sciences through the great emphasis on the fieldwork as the most important source of new knowledge about society and culture.

- *Describing the importance of fieldwork in anthropological studies T.H. Eriksen (1995) observes:* A field study may last far between a few mon hs to two years or longer, and it aims at developing as intimate and understanding as possible of the phenomena investigated. Although, there are differences in field methods between different anthropological schools, it is generally agreed that the anthropologist ought to stay in the field long enough for his or her presence to be considered more or less 'natural' by the permanent residents, although he or she will always to some extent remain stranger.

Most of the valuable theoretical formulations in social anthropology have been constructed out of fieldwork carried on for a protracted period. For instance, Malinowski worked among the Trobriand islanders for years together. Similarly, Radcliffe-Brown worked among the Andaman islanders and Australian tribes. Recently, Pierre Bourdeau, who is known for his contribution to habitus and structuralism (Richard Jenkins, 1992), worked in Algeria for a long period and conducted fieldwork.

It is certain that a sociologist who is trained in fieldwork carries to his credit substantial work in social anthropology. As a matter of fact, fieldwork is very demanding, much time-consuming, in terms of professional expertise and human relationships. Eriksen very rightly observes that fieldwork is highly troublesome for an anthropologist when he writes:

The tidy, systematic and well-rounded texts written by anthropologists are more often than not the end-product of long periods in the field characterised by boredom, illness, personnel privations, disappointments and frustrations….

M.N. Srinivas who is credited to have worked in Rampura village and among the Coorgs of south India has considerable experience of working in the villages. In his book The Remembered Village (1976), Srinivas gives vivid description about his familiarity with the people of Rampura.

- *He describes the appropriate time for conducting field- work:* The field worker records practically everything he sees even when, for instance, his aim is only to make an analysis of the kinship system of the people he is studying. He will try to collect as much information as he can. In the 12-18 months at his disposal, about the other activities of people, such as agriculture, house building, commercial activities, manners, morals, law and religion.

In Indian context, thus, a social anthropologist should devote a year for conducting fieldwork even for a tiny village. Many of the village studies included in Srinivas' India's Villages and Mackim Marriot's Village India show that the field work for a single study took about six months to more than a year.

Requirements in fieldwork: It is expected of a researcher to take part in local life of the village in as much as possible way. When he is in the field, looking to the kind of fieldwork, he applies several tools of data generation. The tools include structured interviews, observation, case study, statistical sampling and other techniques. Most of the fieldwork depends on a combination of formal techniques and unstructured participant observation. We shall have detailed description about the field techniques or tools employed in the field.

While in the field, the researcher keeps with his person a note book or diary as it is called for regarding what he observes in the field in all possible details. He would even note down the things for which he is not concerned.

It is due to his overdeveloped sense of curiosity, and partly to his awareness that the various aspects of a society form a closely woven mesh, and that the particular aspect he is studying might influence and be influenced by every other aspects of social life. The field worker will have obtained, by the time he has completed his study, an intimate and all-round knowledge of the village or tribe he has been with.

The social anthropologist when in the field actually takes the role of a clown. He speaks strangely with a flawed local dialect; he asks surprising and sometimes tactless questions, and tends to break many rules regarding how things ought to be done.

He would not hesitate to dress in the style of the people of his village putting on a turban or taking food on leaves. Such a role of a researcher is essential to establish rapport and proximity with the people. The beginning of fieldwork in such a way is an excellent starting point.

The field researcher has to move very cautiously in his village of study. A little flaw on his part might defeat his objective of enquiry. He might run the risk of encountering suspicion and the hospitality. Andre Beteille had to encounter hostility from the village of a study, Sripuram of Tanjore district in south India. In his book, Caste, Class and Power (1971), he gives details of his fieldwork experiences. What happened with him is that in the beginning of his visit to the village he stayed with a Brahmin family. It was really a privilege given to him. Actually he was "the only non-Brahmin ever to have sat and eaten with the Brahmin in Sripuram on ceremonial occasions. I was identified with the Brahmin by my dress, my appearance and the fact that I lived in one of their houses". Beteille recollects his field experiences further and says that his identification with the Brahmin caste made him suspect in the eyes of the non-Brahmins and Adi-Dravidas, who at first regarded him as just another Brahmin from north India. Such a suspicious social environment of the field, according to Beteille, influenced the quality of his fieldwork.

- *He writes:* Consequently my data for the Adi-Dravidas and also, to some extent for the non-Brahmins are of a poorer quality than for the Brahmins. But it has to be realised that there was, in fact, very little choice. It is also required of a researcher for rural studies that he should employ informal field methods for generating data, whether or not it is supplemented with other techniques.

  The objective of employing informal field method is to enter as deeply as possible into the social and cultural field to the village life. In such situations, the researcher neither belongs to the host community nor to his parent community.
- *Evans-Pritchard makes a very remarkable observation on this account:* The researcher in practice becomes doubly marginal person, in a sense suspended between one's own society and the society under investigation.

  A recipe for doing fieldwork: I have many ways of conducting fieldwork, and it is impossible to provide a clear recipe for how to carry it out. For one thing it is certain that the researcher studying the rural life is himself the most important 'scientific instrument'. He invests a great deal of his/ her owns personality in the process. He must tailor his methods to fill the requirements of the particular village where he is doing fieldwork.

Evans-Pritchard once recalled his first attempts to learn about field- work in the early 1920 (1983, 1937). “He had asked a number of renowned anthropologists how to do it and he received various answers. First, he asked the famous Finnish ethnologist Westermark, who said: “Don’t converse with an informant for more than twenty minutes because if you aren’t bored by that time he will be.” Evans-Pritchard comments: “Very good advice, if somewhat inadequate.” Alfred Haddon said: “…that it was really all quite simple; one should always behave as a gentleman.” Evans Pritchard’s teacher, Charles Saligman told: “…to take 10 grams of quinine every night and to keep off women.” Finally, Malinowski himself told the new researcher, “not to be a bloody fool”.

Evans-Pritchard himself emphasises, later in the same account, that facts are themselves meaningless; in other words, one must know precisely what one wants to know,” and then fashion a suitable methodology from the available techniques. There is alas no simple recipe for fieldwork. It is a method where the researcher’s most important “scientific instrument is him”.

Fieldwork does not have to be capital-intensive or labour- intensive. As a research process, it is cheap, since the only scientific instruments involved are the fieldworkers themselves and possibly a few assistants. Eriksen has the following to observe in this regard:

However, and this is perhaps the main point about fieldwork as a scientific method, it is time-intensive. Ideally, one should stay in the field long enough to be able to see the world as the local see it. Even if this may be impossible, among other reasons because one cannot entirely get rid of one’s own cultural background, it can be a worth-while aim to pursue.

The strength of the anthropologist’s knowledge can thus be said to lie in his or her mastery of both the local culture and a different culture (his or her own), and of tools of analysis, making it possible to give an analytical, comparative account of both.

It may be recalled that any rural study large or small village is ultimately related to theory. Empirical material is fundamental in all empirical sciences including sociology, social anthropology and rural sociology. No science can rely on theory alone, and if it does so it becomes pure mathematics or philosophy. In other words, research has an inductive and a deductive dimension.

“Induction consists of going out there, watching and wandering, collecting information about what people say and do. Deduction consists of attempts to account for facts by means of a general hypothesis or theory. Suppose I work to explore the hypothesis that the position of women in society is proportional to their contribution to the economy, working deductively, I would develop an argument showing why this made sense. In the actual research process, however, I would have to shift to an inductive mode, exploring the relationship between the position of women and the economy in a number of existing societies. As soon as I came across one or several societies where there was no apparent relationship between the contribution to the economy and the relative rank of women, I would have to modify my initial hypothesis."

Actually, the researcher has to develop a general insight through the processes of observation of facts and theoretical reasoning. Where new facts modify the theory and modified theory accounts for the fact, the research exercise is worthwhile. Each time one shifts from theory to description of empirical process and back, one's insight has become a little bit mare accurate.

In social anthropology and sociology, fieldwork has become much more common since the 1950s. However, one argument sometimes used against fieldwork in one's own society is that the overall aim of the discipline is to account for cultural variation.

It is in this context that when we take up rural studies one should study people who seem culturally remote. What is particular about our villages in India is that they are increasingly coming closer to the urban life. Communication facilities including the forces of market and consumerism have made amazing changes in the rural life. Despite all this, there is a marked cultural variation in the rural life. So far this continues fieldwork is a reliable method of enquiry in the rural life.

Tools of Data Generation

Data in the field are generated through the administration of a wide variety of tools. The Survey of Research in Sociology and Social Anthropology enumerates a few of the tools employed by government development agencies, social science research institutions, census and sociologists and anthropologists.

A catalogue of such tools is given as under:

Rural Survey

Surveys are holistic in naturc. Thc totality of village life in all its dimensions is presented through the tool of social survey. The Ministry of Agriculture of the Government of India financed many surveys since independence through the agroeconomic research centres, associated with various universities in the country. Its objectives were to conduct village studies to monitor changes in the structure and functioning of the village economy due to external stimulus, government plans or other inputs. These studies were thus problem-oriented.

Village Monographs

The Department of Census, Government of India has regularly every decade brought out village monographs. These monographs present an overall picture of the village life. In these monographs a casual observation of the village life is made. The fieldwork in these monographs has always been casual non-intensive. The researcher just steps in the village, meets knowledgeable people and goes out with a battery of data.

Observation

Observation is the fundamental method employed in village studies. Though, it is a vaguely defined research technique, it serves as a convenient blanket term to cancel both ethical and methodological shortcomings in the actual research process. Observation is two-fold: participant observation and non- participant observation. Participant observation refers to the informal field methods which form the basis for most fieldwork. It provides opportunity for coming closer to the subject of study.

Most of the village studies conducted after 1950s have used participant method for enquiry. The non-participant method is one wherein the researcher does not participate in the activities of the villagers. He only becomes a bystander.

The difference in participant and non-participant observation is that, in the former, the researcher identifies himself with the village people. In his study of Rampura, M.N. Srinivas identified himself with the village people. He was even involved in setting the disputes of the village people.

Interview

It is difficult for village people to spell out about the activities which take place in their community. They also do not want to reveal the caste relations among the members. In such a situation protracted interviews reveal a lot of information. At the time of report writing, whatever is revealed through interviews is analyzed by the researcher and put in the form of conceptual formulations.

Structured Schedule

Illiteracy is a common phenomenon in India's villages. Though, the people have their moderate earnings, and levels of consumption, they do not have accounts for this. Such a life has been a way of living for them for centuries.

The exploitation of the villagers for their illiteracy has become proverbial in India. Much of their indebtedness is due largely to their illiteracy. Such a situation denies the administration of questionnaires to the people. For factual data, however, structured schedule is administered by the researcher. Even the schedule is sometimes taken with suspicion by the people. It, therefore, has to be administered with caution.

Case Studies

Case study is a deep study. Some of the authors of village studies have profitably employed the technique of case studies. Generally, it is the supplementary data generated through case studies to provide insight to the main study. F.G. Bailey, in his work, Cast and the Economic Frontier- (1958), has made some case studies to throw insight in the study of his field.

LIMITATIONS OF RURAL SOCIOLOGY

Lack of Objectivity

It is not possible to have objectivity in the study of rural sociology as in case of natural science. While in the study of rural sociology and its problems the investigator continues to remain as a part of the society he is studying. He has own ideas and are influenced by the subject matter.

Lack of Laboratory

Rural sociology is not studied in laborites as a natural science. Because of this it is not possible to verify and test the theory and principles of rural sociology.

Lack of Measurement

There is no definite and standard measurement for measuring units of rural sociology.

Lack of Exactness

It is lack of objectivity and different to follow its laws and principles universally. They are not acceptable at every point.

Lack of Prediction

Because of lacks objectivity and exactness the principles formulated by the rural sociology are not always correct. As such predictions are not possible.

It is not possible to draw a line between the rural and urban areas. There is no sharp demarcation to tell where rural area ends and urban area begins. The science of rural sociology is not fully developed.

IMPORTANCE OF RURAL SOCIOLOGY IN INDIA

India is predominantly an agricultural and rural Country from ancient times. Village is the basic and important unit in the organization of Indian Society.

After independence the process of reconstruction of the country has been started and the importance of rural sociology was recognized. If India is to achieve the progress, the villages are to be improved and education has to be spread in these villages. In order to this every attempt is being made to improve the villages of this country in community development programme. This object can be achieved only when the administrators and planners have the correct knowledge of the rural life.

The importance of the Study of Rural Society in India can be Evaluated Under the Following Heads:

1. The village is the basic source of Indian culture. India lives in villages. The birth and development of its culture took place from the villages. India's progress is based on the progress of villages. Thus it is necessary to develop the villages.

2. India is an agricultural country and poverty of this country can only be removed when the agriculture is improved.
3. Solution of rural problems can bring about change in rural society.
4. The country and its society can be reconstructed only through rural reconstruction.
5. In the interest of democratic decentralization, village community is to be studied in a totality.
6. Rural sociology can helps in organizing the disorganized Indian rural structure.

SCOPE OF RURAL SOCIOLOGY IN INDIA

India is an agricultural country and village is a basic and important unit of the society. After independence the process of rural reconstruction was started and importance of the rural sociology was recognized. The need of development of the villages and speed of education in the villages were understood and to achieve this community development programme was started. It can be achieved when the planners and administrator correct knowledge of the rural life.

1. It is very essential to develop village because India's development depends upon the progress of the villages.
2. India is agriculture country and poverty can be removed through improvement in agriculture.
3. Solutions of rural problems can bring the change in the rural society.
4. The country and its society can be reconstructed only through rural developments.
5. For successful implementation of democratic decentralization the village community is to be studied in detail.
6. Rural sociology can help to organize the disorganized Indian in detail.
7. The extension worker must know the rural culture, rural institutions, problems, resources etc. for successful transfer of technology for improvement of agriculture. It can be achieved through the study of rural sociology.
8. Through the technology and communication methods are known to the extension workers. The study of rural sociology helps the extension worker to transfer the technology.
9. For successful implementation of the community development programmes the knowledge of rural sociology is very essential.

ORIGIN AND DEVELOPMENT OF RURAL SOCIOLOGY

Rural sociology is a new branch of sociology with studies being carried out from 19th century. The prominent scholars engaged in rural sociology during this period were- Sir Henry Maine, Etton, Stemann, Baden Powell, Slater and Pallock etc. The period of 1890-1920 in America saw the rural societies facing many socio-economic problems which attracted the attention of the intelligentsia thus establishing study of rural society as an academic discipline. The appointment of Country life Commission by Theodore Roosevelt was an important landmark in the history of rural sociology. In 1916 the first text book on sociology was published by J.N Gillettee.

The Second World War caused heavy destruction and damage to human society which needed reconstruction. As a result rural sociology got an impetus in USA. The main concern of rural sociology came to be the understanding and diagnosing of the social and economic problems of farmers. More emphasis was placed on issues such as the internal structures of community life and the changing composition of rural populations than on their relationships with land or the social aspects of agricultural production. Theoretically rural sociology remained caught up in bipolar notions of social change whereas rural often got defined as the opposite of urban. Rurality was conceptualized as an autonomous sociological reality. The identification of rural sociology with rural society has also raised questions about its relevance in the western context where no rural areas were left anymore and almost the entire population had become urbanized.

In response to these critiques of rural sociology a new sub-discipline of sociology emerged that operated largely within the functionalist paradigm and was preoccupied with the study of the community life of rural people. This sub-discipline known as sociology of agriculture focused its attention on understanding and analysing the social framework of agricultural production and the structures of relations centred on land. It raised questions about how and on what terms the agrarian sector was being integrated into the system of commodity production and about the unequal distribution of agricultural incomes and food among the different social categories of people.

The sociology of agriculture also distinguished itself from peasant studies on the grounds that its focus was on capitalist farming where the production was primarily for the market, not on peasants producing for their own consumption by using family labour. Thus it claimed more kinship with the tradition of the political economy of agriculture or agrarian studies. At the methodological level, historical enquiries became as relevant as ethnographic/ empirical studies. This conceptual shift during the early 1970s also helped in bringing sociologists working on agrarian issues in the western countries closer to those concerned with agrarian transformations in the third world.

Rural Sociology, relatively a new branch of Sociology, originated in the U.S.A nearly in 1820. From that period a good deal of literature had been produced about the new knowledge or Rural Sociology. But, actually a deep scientific study about Rural Society was started in the middle of the nineteenth century.

In that period, a new knowledge about modernisation was emerged and it was regarded as the 'Age of Modernisation 'in the history of mankind. Due to the deep influence of modernisation, a radical change took place in the different aspects of Rural Society. As a result some eminent personalities like Charles Henderson of

Chicago University, Butler Field of Michigan University, Earnest Burnholme of Michigan State College, John Moris Gillin of North Decota University, Martin H. Giddings of Columbia University, Themas Ninon Carver of Harvard University and so on have made their original contribution regarding the study and development of Rural Society.

But as a separate discipline of study Rural Sociology had not achieved its target till the beginning of the twentieth century. Roosevelt, then the President of United States of America was appointed the Country Life Commission in 1970. It was the landmark in the history of Rural Sociology.

The President was influenced in his decision to set up the Commission by Sir Horace Plunkett, who had observed the deterioration of rural life in Ireland. The main aim of the Country Life Commission was to study rural social problems and make recommendation for the development of rural life.

The report of this Commission was brought to the attention of sociologists and therefore a critical analysis was brought to the attention of sociologists and therefore a critical analysis was done on the attention of sociologists and therefore, a critical analysis was done on the topic "Rural Life" in the annual meeting of the American Sociological Society in 1912. G.M. Gillatee published his first book on Rural Society in 1916.

The first research studies on the rural community were probably certain Doctoral Dissertations at Columbia University under Professor Franklin Giddings. The Department of Rural Sociology was first set up by the American Sociology Society in 1917. Two years later, in 1919, a Rural Sociology Department was established under the Bureau of Agricultural Economics and Dr. Charles J. Galpin of the University of Wisconsin was appointed as its head.

Its name later on was changed to Rural Population and Rural Life, Rural Sociological research develop still further with the encouragement of grants form the United States Department of Agriculture after 1919, when Galpin was appointed as the chief of the Division of From Population and Rural life.

A systematic source book on Rural Sociology was published in 1930 which opened the new face of the subject. A quarterly magazine titled Rural Sociology was published in 1936. In 1937, the Rural Sociological society was formed in America.

But the outbreak of Second World War and its devastative nature and adversely affected the human society to great extent. For the protection of human civilization and reconstruction of social life a wife effort had been made on world basis which resulted in the popularity or Rural Sociology in the whole world.

Particularly after the Second World War Rural Sociology extended beyond the boundaries of U.S.A. into Europe and the East Under the "Point Four Programme", America sent rural sociologists to work in underdeveloped countries. A European Society of Rural Sociology was formed in 1957.

In under-developed countries, the main role of the Rural Sociologists was and in primarily in the applied field of more effective planning the operation of rural community development programme.

Since India is a country of villages, therefore, the study of Rural Sociology is very indispensable in our country. After independence, it was felt that the development of country, to some extent, depends on the progress of rural life. Therefore, certain governmental and non-Governmental efforts have been made for the all round development of Rural Society Different sociologists have made their original contribution in the field or Rural Sociology in India.

Dr. D.N. Mazumdar, Prof. N.K. Bose, S.C. Dube and Prof. M.N. Srinivas are the pioneers among them. Besides, Planning Commission has introduced several projects for Rural Development-Community Development Project, Land Reforms, Co-Operative Movement, Five Year Plans, Panchayati Raj, National Extension Service and so on have contributed a lot of the Development of Rural Sociology in India.

Now a days Rural Sociology is a compulsory subject at the undergraduate level for B.Sc.(Agricultural Engineering),B.Sc.(Home Economics or Home Science), B.Sc.(Veterinary Science) and B.Sc.(Agriculture)students in all agricultural colleges and universities and it is occupied as a major field of specialisation of Post-Graduate level in some of the universities in India. Though, the Development of Rural Sociology of India. Though, the Development of Rural Sociology of India has not yet attained a scientific level. It is to be hoped that there will be development in this direction in the future.

THE INDIAN CONTEXT OF RURAL SOCIOLOGY

In India the importance of rural sociology gained recognition after independence. The agrarian context occupies special status both in the social scientific literature on India and in the literature on agrarian societies in general. However unlike studies on caste, kinship, village community, gender, study of agrarian relations did not occupy a central position in Indian sociology. The first systematic study of rural India was done by D.N Majumdar followed by N.K Bose, S.C Dubey,M.N Shrinivas. However it was with the publication of Andre'Be'teille's Studies in Agrarian Social Structure in 1974 that agrarian sociology gained professional respectability within the two disciplines.

Peasant studies in a way arrived in India with village studies. The collection of essays, Village India, edited by Marriot with its emphasis on little communities and great communities was brought out under the direct supervision of Robert Redfield. By defining little communities not in relation to land but through other social institutions such as kinship, religion and the social organization of caste there was a shift away from looking at the rural population in relation to agriculture and land. Caste hierarchy came to be defined in terms of ritual or social interaction over institutions of commensality and marriage.

According to Nelson up to the comparatively recent times the story of man is largely the story of rural man. So rural society is the basic foundation of human life, the keystone of the developmental process and the basic unit of social structure. Villages have been in existence since time immemorial unlike cities which are of more recent origin. In the Indian context rural sociology is of greater significance of the following reasons.

According to S.C Dubey from time immemorial village has been a basic and important unit in the organization of Indian social life. Unique nature of transformation of Indian society where elements of traditional and modern cultures have been juxtaposed. For rural development and solution of rural problems according to A.R Desai this systematic study of rural organization of its structure; function and evolution has not only become necessary but also urgent after the advent of independence. Growing influence of industrialization and urbanization. Village as the basic unit of study. Scientific study of village community is a prerequisite for democratic decentralization.

In modern India, the need of rural sociology is very urgent and it is progressive social science gaining importance.

MAIN FEATURES OF RURAL SOCIETY

Village is a community

The village satisfies all their needs in the village. They have a sense of unity and a feeling of amiability towards each other.

Village is a institution

The development of villages is influenced considerably by the life of the village. In this way village is a primary institution.

Religiosity

Faith in religion and universal power is found in the life of the villages. The major occupation is agriculture which involves dependence on nature.

Farmers worship forces of nature. The life of the village is the joint family system.

Family has a strict control and administrative powers over the individual. All the members of the family share the burden of the family occupation. In this way of working together the villagers maintain sense of cooperation among themselves. In the life of the villagers group feeling occupies an important place. They respect the judgement and obey the orders of their elders and the panchayats. Society, caste and panchayat have control over the individual.

CASTE STRUCTURE IN RURAL SET UP

The institution of caste represents the entire system by which the whole society is organized into different groups their interrelationships are determined, division of labour and exchange of goods and services are carried on the social roles and obligations of the individuals are prescribed.

Risley defined caste as a collection of families or group of families bearing a common name claiming a common descent from a mythical ancestor, human or divine, professing to follow the same hereditary calling and forming a single homogeneous community.

According to M.N Srinivas the features of caste prevailing through the past centuries may be described under 9 heads: hierarchy, restriction on food, drink and smoking; distinction in custom, dress and speech; pollution, ritual and other privileges and disabilities; caste organization and caste mobility.

a. Hierarchical division of society- Caste brings an element of hierarchy in society by dividing it into different strata, Brahmin, Kshatriya, Vaisya and Sudra on the basis of relative ritual purity. These major groups are again subdivided into a number of small groups which are also graded into various positions in terms of high or low. According to Bottomore in modern India there are perhaps some

   2500 jatis in each major region. Ghurye also finds that in each linguistic region there are about 200 caste groups which are further subdivided into about 3000 smaller units each of which is endogamous and constitutes the area of effective social life for the individual.
b. Hereditary-Each caste is a hereditary group. The membership of the caste is confined to those who are born into it by an endogamous marriage relation. The status of an individual is determined by virtue of his birth. Each caste has a traditional occupation and all the members strictly follow this occupation to earn their livelihood.
c. Endogamy-Every caste is an endogamous group. This endogamous character is maintained by the rules and regulation of marriage. However gotra exogamy is maintained in each caste. Every caste is subdivided into different small units on the basis of gotra. The members of one gotra are believed to be successors of a common ancestor-hence prohibition of marriage within the same gotra.
d. Unique culture- Ghurye says that castes are small and complete social worlds in themselves marked differently from one another though subsisting within the larger society. Every caste has a distinct culture, traditions and customs which distinguish it from those of the other groups. The behavioural pattern, food habits etc. is prescribed by the caste rules.
e. Closed group- Endogamy, unique culture and heredity combined together to make caste a closed group. No person can enter into a particular caste except by birth. Srinivas talks about process of Sanskritisation which takes place with in Indian society.
f. Organization- Every caste has its own organizational structure known as caste panchayat which lays down rules and regulations that have to be obeyed by the members of that caste. The internal differences and conflicts are

settled in the caste panchayat which serves as a judicial system. Socially every caste group is an autonomous body having judiciary, executive and financial power of its own which it exercises over the members of that caste in the interests of the caste as a whole.

g. Rights and Privileges-These vary from caste to caste. Generally the Brahmins enjoy the most privileged position and have extensive rights which they can exercise over the members of other castes. They have a dominant position in social, political and economic fields of rural life. Such rights and privileges decrease as one descends the caste hierarchy.

ROLE OF CASTE IN RURAL SOCIETY

Caste stands as a pivot of rural social structure. It acts as the most powerful determinant of individual behaviour and social order in rural unity. Caste is the determinant of individual status and role. It determines the status of the individual as soon as he takes birth. Hutton says that the system provides him from birth a fixed social milieu from which neither wealth nor property, success nor disaster can remove him unless of course he so violates standards of behaviour lay down by the caste.

Caste also guides the behaviour of an individual in his conduct, his association and interaction. It has helped maintain the continuity of social order by preserving its pattern of culture and traditions. It plays a vital role in the process of socialization by teaching individuals the culture and traditions, values and norms of their society. It unifies society in a chain by assigning different places and positions to different groups. It works as the basis of division of labour in society which keeps society away from tensions and conflicts arising out of competition for occupation, power and prestige. Caste also has a deep influence in the religious lives of rural people. The notion of karma and dharma kept social and economic system intact. Performance of rituals, worshipping of different kinds of Gods and Goddesses and celebration of festivals are determined by the caste system.

There are some negative aspects according to P.N Bose the caste system has acted essentially to impose that attitude of mind, needed to raise men from savagery but to stop them half way on progress. Caste acts as a barrier to modernization. Modernization essentially needs a change in outlook and mentality along with socio-economic development. It has hindered development as it imposes strict rules regarding occupation of different people. The society characterized by the caste system is a closed one permitting very little or no social mobility. It acts as a perpetuating force of social inequality and untouchability. It is based on inequality of status and opportunities which often creates conflict and tension in the society.

JAJMANI SYSTEM IN RURAL SOCIETY

The notion of the jajmani system was popularized by colonial ethnography. It tended to conceptualize agrarian social structure in the framework of exchange relations. In its classical construct, different caste groups specialized in specific occupations and exchanged their services through an elaborate system of division of labour. Though asymmetry in position of various caste groups was recognized what it emphasized was not inequality in rights over land but the spirit of community. Wiser argued, each served the other. Each in turn was master. Each in turn was servant. This system of inter relatedness in service within Hindu community was called the Jajmani system. Central to such a construction of exchange is the idea of reciprocity (Gouldner) with the assumption that it was a non-exploitative system where mutual gratification was supposed to be the outcome of the reciprocal exchange.

The concept of Jajmani system

Inter-caste relations at the village level constitute vertical ties. They may be classified into economic, ritual, political and civic ties. The castes living in a village are bound together by economic ties. Generally peasant castes are numerically preponderant in villages and they need the carpenter, blacksmith and leather worker castes to perform agricultural work. Servicing castes such as priest, barber, and washerman and water carrier cater to the needs of everyone except the Harijans. Artisan castes produce goods which are wanted by every one. Most Indian villages do not have more than a few of the essential castes and depend on neighbouring villages for certain services, skills and goods.

In rural India with its largely subsistence and not fully monetized economy the relationship between the different caste groups in a village takes a particular form. The essential artisan and servicing castes are paid annually in grain at harvest time. In some parts of India the artisan and servicing castes are also provided with free food, clothing, fodder and residential site. On such occasions as birth, marriage and death, these castes perform extra duties for which they are paid customary money and some gifts in kind. This type of relationship is found all over India and is called by different names-jajmani in north, bara batute in Maharashtra, mirasi in Tamil Nadu and adade in

Karnataka.

Oscar Lewis defined jajmani system as that under which each caste group within a village is expected to give certain standardized services to the families of other castes. Jajmani is more than a relationship between families than between castes. Jajmani is sort of mutual give and take form of relationship in which one family is hereditarily entitled to supply goods and render services to the other in exchange of the same. The person rendering the services or supplying the goods is known as kameen or prajan and the person to whom the services are rendered is called a jajman. Thus under jajmani system a permanent informal bond is made between jajman and kameen to meet each other's need for good and services.

Main features of Jajmani System

The jajmani system is characterized by the following features:

- Unbroken relationship- Under the jajmani system the kameen remains obliged to render the services throughout his life to a particular jajman and the jajman in turn has the responsibility of hiring services of a kameen.
- Hereditary relationship- Jajmani rights are enjoyed hereditarily. After the death of a man his son is entitled to work as kameen for the same jajman family of families. The son of a jajman also accepts the son of the kameen as his kameen.
- Multidimensional relationship- Due to the permanency of relationship both the jajman and kameen families become mutually dependent on each other. The relationship becomes very deep. They often take part in the personal and family affairs, family rituals and ceremonies.
- Barter exchange-Under jajmani system the payments are made mainly in terms of goods and commodities. The kameen gets his necessities from the jajman in return of his services.

The jajmani system has gradually decayed in modern society. There are many reasons responsible for it. Modern economic system that measures everything in terms of its monetary value. The decline of belief in caste system and hereditary occupation has given a strong blow to the system. Growth of better employment opportunities outside the village and introduction of new transport options.

AGRARIAN CHANGES AFTER INDEPENDENCE IN RURAL SOCIETY

In many ways independence from colonial rule in 1947 marked the beginning of a new phase in the history of Indian agriculture. Having evolved out of a long struggle against colonial rule with the participation of the people from various social categories, the Indian state also took over the task of supervising the transformation of its stagnant and backward economy to make sure that the benefits of economic growth were not monopolized entirely by a particular section of society. It is with this background that development emerged as a strategy of economic change and an ideology of the new regime.

However at the micro-level the structures that evolved during colonial rule still continued to exist. The local interests that had emerged over a long period of time continued to be powerful in the Indian countryside even after the political climate had changed. According to Daniel Thorner the earlier structure of land relations and debt dependencies where a small section consisting of few landlords and money lenders were dominant continued to prevail in the Indian countryside. The nature of property relations, the local values that related social prestige negatively to physical labour and the absence of any surplus with the actual cultivator for investment on land ultimately perpetuated stagnation. This complex of legal, economic and social relations typical of Indian countryside served to produce an effect that Thorner described as a built -in depressor.

LAND REFORMS IN RURAL SOCIETY

The agrarian question had been an important topic of discussions for Indian freedom struggle leaders as well who wrote extensively and debated on how Indian society and economy should be reorganized. Land reforms became a question of considerable academic interest and debate in the discourse about planning and development. They were viewed as necessary for initiating modernization in agriculture. While there was a general agreement that the prevailing agrarian structures marked by absentee landlordism and semi-feudal relations of production, needed to be reorganized, two extreme positions were taken on the crucial questions-what kind of agrarian reforms were required and which would work the best? Is there an economic logic behind land reforms?

The first view was that of the institutionalists who argued that the way out for Indian agriculture lay in a radical reorganization of land ownership patterns that would not only democratize the village and revive the independent peasant economy but also increase the productivity of land. Thus the slogan came up-land to the tiler. They also argued that smaller-sized holdings gave higher productivity.

The second viewpoint argued against the redistribution of land on the grounds that it was both unviable as not enough land was available for everyone and that it worked against the logic of economics. The modernization of agriculture required landlords' reorientation. They needed to be motivated to cultivate their own land with wage labour and using modern technology. The land reforms would only divide the land into unviable holdings rendering them unfeasible for the use of modern technology. However the process of agrarian reforms is inherently a political question. The choices made by the Indian state and the actual implementation of land reforms were determined by the politics of the new regime rather than by the theoretical superiority of a particular position.

The Indian state chose to reorganize agrarian relations through redistribution of land but not in a comprehensive and radical manner. Joshi described it as sectorial or sectional reforms. The Government of India directed its states to abolish intermediary tenures, regulate rent and tenancy rights, confer ownership rights on tenants, impose ceilings on holdings, distribute the surplus land among the rural poor and facilitate consolidation of holdings. A large number of legislations were passed by the state government over a short period of time.

However most of the legislations provided loopholes that allowed the dominant landowners to tamper with land records by redistributing land among relatives, evicting their tenants and using other means to escape the legislations. In the absence of concerted political will land reforms could succeed only in regions where the peasantry was politically mobilized and could exert pressure from below.

Despite overall failure, land reforms succeeded in weakening the hold of absentee landlords over rural society and assisted in the emergence of a class of substantial peasants and petty landlords as the dominant political and economic group. For example in Rajasthan though the abolition of jagirs was far from satisfactory it made considerable difference to the overall land ownership patterns and to the local and regional power structures. The Rajputs possessed much less land after the land reforms than they did before, Most of the village land had moved into the hands of those who could be called small and medium landowners. In qualitative terms most of the land begins to be self-cultivated and the incidence of tenancy declined considerably. The fear of losing land induced many potential losers to sell or rearrange their lands in a manner that escaped legislations.

However in few cases the landless laborers living in the countryside most of whom belonged to the extouchable castes received land. The beneficiaries by and large belonged to middle level caste groups who traditionally cultivated land as a part of the calling of their castes. While land reforms were supposed to deal with the problem of landlordism, the hold of moneylenders over the peasantry was to be weakened by providing credit through institutional sources initially by credit societies and later by the nationalized commercial banks.

According to the findings of an official survey carried out immediately after Independence from colonial rule up to approximately 91 per cent of the credit needs of cultivators were being met by informal sources of credit. Much of this came from moneylenders. Indian state planned to expand the network of cooperative credit societies. With the imposition of social control and later their nationalization, commercial banks were also asked to lend to the agricultural sector on priority basis. Over the years the dependence of rural households on informal sources has come down significantly. The assessment studies on the cooperative credit societies showed that much of their credit went to the relatively better of sections of rural society and the poor continued to depend on the more expensive informal sources. This was explained as a consequence of the prevailing structure of land tenures. The state response was to bureaucratize the cooperative societies. Though in some regions this helped in releasing credit societies from the hold of big landowners, bureaucratization also led to rampant corruption and increasing apathy among those whom they were supposed to serve.

Yet despite inherent bias of institutional credit against the rural poor, its availability played an important role in making the green revolution a success and definitely helped to marginalize the professional moneylender in the rural power structure.

RURAL SOCIOLOGY IN INDIA AFTER INDEPENDENCE

Rural background of India

For Indian Rural Sociology is more important than in any other country. India as we have already seen is basically a country of the villages. After independence, the process of reconstruction of the country has been started and therefore, the importance of Rural Sociology was recognised in India is to active progress, the villages have to be improved and education has to be spread in these villages.

This is way, in community development programme, every attempts is being made to improve the villages of this country. This object can be achieved only when the administrators and the planners have correct knowledge of the rural life and that knowledge can be proved only by Rural Sociology. That was the reason why is acquired greater importance for this country after independence. 82 per cent of the Indian population lives in villagers and that is why they are the centers of Indian culture and life. Dr. Dubey has rightly remarked.

In India our ways of life and thought are changing very fast who are required a large number of community studies both. In rural and urban areas on the different cultural regions of the country.

Importance of Rural Sociology for India Rural Sociology is very important for India. It is more important for a modern India.

Its importance can be evaluated is the following heads:-

1. India lives in villages and villages are the centers of Indian culture.
2. India is an agricultural country and the poverty of this country can be removed only when the agricultural is improved.
3. Solution of rural problems can being absent the changes in Rural Society.
4. The country and its society can be reconstructed only through rural reconstruction.
5. In the interest of democratic decentralisation the village's community is to be studied in totality.

India lives in villages and the villages are the centers of Indian culture India is basically a country of the villages over 80 per cent of the population still live in villages. Since 1822, up to the present age, the rural population of the country has been over 80 per cent and that is why villages are the centers of Indian Culture. Unless we know these villages, we shall not be able to know what the India actually is that is why Desai has remarked.

Village is the omit of the Rural Society. It is the theater where the quantum of rural life unfolds itself and functions like ovary social phenomena, village is a historical category".

Dr. Dubey has marked, "From times immemorial village has been basic and important omit in the organisation or Indian social polity".

Mayer has something similar to say.

Village is on the one hand, a unit like in nuclear settlement which is by definition spatially separate from other units and on the other hand an essential unit based on a unit policy which makes use of this spatial separation; for the enforcement of law and order, tax collection etc.

- *India is an agricultural country and the poverty of this country can only be removed when the agriculture is improved:* India is not only a country of villages but its economy is also mainly agriculture. Through the study of the Rural Sociology, we are able to know about various programmes for improvement and carrying out of agriculture. This country can become rich only when its agriculture.

This country can become rich only when its agriculture is improved with the improvement of agriculture and rural economy of this country, the backwardness of this country can also be removed. Desai has very correctly pointed the book of rural life in this country.

India rural life provides a spectacle actual misery, social disintegration cultural backwardness and above all enveloping crises.

If the half marked people of this country have to be clothed properly and fed adequately, the rural economy and agriculture has to be improved. This can be done only when we have correct ideas of the poverty of the country which Mrs. Goodwill has rightly pointed as given below. 'The name of India conjures up a vision of the people, poor fragile, half fed and half marked, trading on in life journey in the vast number of 5,58,000 villages.

Solution of rural problem can bring about charge in Rural Society:

Through the study of the Rural Sociology, we can know about problems of the village society in his country. Through this knowledge, the problems can be solved and the Rural Society charged. If after independence, the rural society is charging at a pace, the responsibility lies with the greater study of the Rural Sociology. Once the problems of rural life are solved the face of the country shall be greatly changed. It is here that the Rural Sociology can play an important part.

- *The country and its society can be reconstructed only through Rural Reconstruction:* Rural Sociology provides us knowledge about the Rural Society and also helps us to solve these problems and thereby re-contract the Indian Rural Society. With the construction and change in the Rural Society, the whole of the Indian Society shall be changed. The formers of India Constitution realised the importance of the rural life and society and that is why in Article 40.43 and 48 they laid down this note on the form of directive principles of state action. Desai has clarified this point further, in the following words.

  "This systematic study of rural, social organisation of its structure, function and evolution, has not only become necessary but also urgent after the advent of Independent.
- *In the interest of democratic decentralisation, village community as to be studied in totality:* India can really improve economically and politically only when decentralisation of economical and political powers take place. Village Panchayats and other units of community development programme and also other programmes integrated in the Five Year Plan are the efforts in this direction knowledge about them can be secured, through the study of Rural Sociology.

The village has various aspects and all the aspect are to be studied as a totality. For this propose, the village may be treated as a microscopic unit study. They could help the understanding of various problems of villages as Dr. Srinivasan has pointed out:-

May study have convinced all the enormous value of studying all Indian Sociological problems on single village? It does not say all sociological problems can be studied in the villages but only many of the most important ones.

❐

5.

Women's Empowerment in Rural India

INTRODUCTION

Since the 1990's women have been identified as key agents of sustainable development and women's equality and empowerment are seen as central to a more holistic approach towards establishing new patterns and processes of development that are sustainable.

The World Bank has suggested that empowerment of women should be a key aspect of all social development programmes. Although a considerable debate on what constitutes empowerment exists, in this document we find it useful to rely on Kabeer's definition: "The expansion in people's ability to make strategic life choices in a context where this ability was previously denied to them." For women in India, this suggests empowerment in several realms: personal, familial, economic and political.

Since the 1980's the Government of India has shown increasing concern for women's issues through a variety of legislation promoting the education and political participation of women. International organizations like the World Bank and United Nations have focused on women's issues especially the empowerment of poor women in rural areas. In the late 1980s and early

1990s, non-governmental organizations have also taken on an increased role in the area of women's empowerment.

NGO's, previously catering to women's health and educational needs, have moved beyond this traditional focus to addressing the underlying causes of deprivations through promoting the economic and social empowerment of women.. There are many challenges that face NGOs who make it their goal to empower women. This document addresses one specific challenge that is faced by NGOs located in rural areas that wish to promote women's empowerment. These NGOs have little or no access to skilled social workers. They must often depend on the local population for their employees, employees who may be vulnerable to the similar social pressures and are often equally marginalised as their clients. For rural NGOs to be successful they must attract employees who must at some level be relatively more empowered than the clients. They must have certain credibility to be able to effectively persuade their marginalised clients to alter their ways of thinking on many long-standing traditional issues, such as dowries, child labour, and patriarchal subjugation.

The literature of behaviour change in the health field suggests that self- efficacy is one of the four most commonly cited constructs for behavioural change 1. Although stated for different purposes and from different perspectives, the literature on self-efficacy can be brought to bear on issues of empowerment. Self-efficacy determines when an individual will undertake new behaviours such as self-empowerment. Low self-efficacy beliefs of women in rural India often stem from the limited and disadvantaged positions women have in society.

This makes any behaviour change towards self-empowerment difficult if it merely relies on verbal persuasion. The best way by which self-efficacy is acquired is by combining persuasion with role modeling in a supportive and appreciative environment. NGO employees must model empowered behaviours in order to evoke sustained behaviour modification for the empowerment of women they serve. Rural NGOs, who have to often depend on the same local pool for clients and employees, find it difficult to promote empowerment effectively. Despite the training given to employees to promote empowerment among their clients, there may still be a gap between what the employees 'preach' and what they may 'practice' in their own lives. This, in turn, may make them less effective and impede the NGO from achieving its goals. In this document we seek to explore how a relatively small and isolated rural NGO in the foothills of the Himalayas has been successful in the empowerment of rural women living in highly patriarchal and traditional societies

BACKGROUND

Chinmaya Rural Training Centre is a successful rural NGO in India that has received accolades for its success in empowering the women of the region and drawing them out of the cycle of dependency. CRTC is located in an impoverished village of Sidhbari, in Himachal Pradesh, nestled in the foothills of the Himalayas. The vast majority of the population is made up of landless poor and unskilled people who have few opportunities for full-time employment. Villagers work the land, owned by a handful of upper caste families. As agricultural activity is seasonal and ceases in the winter months the employees are underemployed.

Hence many of them eke out a living through subsistence farming around their homes and are involved in local trade that is generally not profitable.

They belong to many of the lower castes and tribes that are categorized by the Indian Government as 'Other Backward Classes'. CRTC was the founded by Swami

Chinmayananda, a revered Hindu spiritual leader, who chose one of the most depressed areas of the Himachal Pradesh to start a religious centre to practice his beliefs as well as an NGO that would empower local women. Sustainable development of the region, he believed, was only possible if the women were uplifted and could contribute to the success of their family and community.

Dr. Kshama Metre, a follower in his religious centre and a practicing pediatrician in New Delhi, took on the leadership of this NGO in 1985. Starting in relatively small way with a donation of a few sewing machines, Dr. Metre, single-mindedly pursued the vision of empowering the women of the dismal rural area.

From this humble beginning she infused energy and vision to make this organization into a large well funded NGO currently serving over 27,000 clients spanning 900 villages offering a variety of programmes that included literacy and health services to sanitation, micro-finance and legal aid.3 Though women are regarded as the primary focus, by extending their services to include the families of these women where relevant, CRTC ends up serving the entire village community. The effect of empowerment of women creates a powerful influence on the norms, values and finally the laws that govern these communities.

RESEARCH QUESTION

In this document we seek to explore how CRTC, a relatively small and isolated rural NGO in the foothills of the Himalayas, has been successful in the empowerment of rural women living in highly patriarchal and traditional societies.

The Indian Government as well as CIDA profiles CRTC as a model NGO in the arena of women's empowerment. In particular we investigate the employees at CRTC, who come from the same villages as the clientele, and examine whether they are significantly different in their levels of empowerment than those they help.

Is a gap between the rhetoric and reality of empowerment among the employees? Are employees whose aim is to empower women, empowered themselves? Do they practice what they preach? We seek to uncover the reasons for their success. We organize this document as follows: a literature review on behaviour change and empowerment of women and concludes with empowerment measures we use in this research. This is followed by restates our research question and sets out the methodology. Our findings, quantitative and qualitative, are presented and discussed. In the conclusion, we offer some policy implications and some final comments.

BEHAVIOUR CHANGE

We first start with a review of the self-efficacy literature and focus on the criteria for successful behaviour change. Bandura suggests that a person's self-expectations determine whether or not certain behaviour will be undertaken, the extent of effort expended by the individual, and whether the individual can persist in the face of challenges encountered. This notion of self-efficacy is mediated by a person's beliefs or expectations about his/her ability to achieve certain tasks effectively or exhibit certain behaviours. For example, individuals with low self-efficacy regarding their behaviour limit their participation when making difficult behaviour changes and are more likely to give up when faced with obstacles.

Their efficacy beliefs about themselves serve as barriers to change, and in this case, their own empowerment. Furthermore, these authors state that self- efficacy is not necessarily an in-born trait and can be acquired and nurtured. This fact makes these concepts particularly relevant to our study. Bandura identifies four ways in which self-efficacy and self-efficacy expectations are acquired: performance accomplishments, vicarious learning, verbal persuasion and physical/affective status. Performance accomplishments are beliefs that stem from the reactions with which individual accomplishments are greeted. A negative assessment can lower confidence and self-efficacy beliefs; conversely a positive assessment encourages self-efficacy beliefs and the self- efficacy expectations that similar behaviours will be well received in the future.

Vicarious learning results in beliefs that are acquired by observing modeling behaviours. When the modeling behaviour is undertaken within similar contexts5 such as gender, economic and social class it presents a realistic option.

Thus, one of the most effective strategies for enhancing self-efficacy beliefs and self-efficacy expectations is that modeling behaviour is context specific. It is of little use for a woman of low social class to observe the success of an entrepreneurial woman born to a family of high social standing with access to resources that are unavailable to the poor woman. Other ways such as 'verbal persuasion' and 'affective status6' encourage selfefficacy. Persuading women to attempt positive behaviour change and providing a supportive environment in which women can attempt change, further enhances self-efficacy. Changes based on verbal persuasion, affective status and modeling behaviour can lead to significant changes in self–beliefs and self-expectation.

These 'personal factors' according to Bandura and Pajares, from an integral part of a triadic relationship necessary for change. They suggest that there is a reciprocal relationship between 'personal factors', 'behaviour' and

'environmental factors', which result in social change. Changes in personal factors can affect an individuals' behaviour, which can impact on environmental factors. These relationships are reciprocal and reinforce each other. This suggests that strategies purposefully introduced in order to enhance women's personal factors can lead to reinforcing behaviours which in turn can impact and reinforce environmental factors. The interaction and reciprocity of the triadic relationship can result in a positive and significant change for women.

Womens Empowerment

Although the notion of women's empowerment has long been legitimized by international development agencies7, what actually comprises empowerment, and how it is measured, is debated in the development literature. Malhotra, Schuler and

Boender, 2002 provide an excellent review of this debate. They review the many ways that empowerment can be measured and suggest that researchers pay attention to the process in which empowerment occurs.

The frequently used Gender Empowerment Measure is a composite measure of gender inequality in three key areas: Political participation and decision-making, economic participation and decision-making and power over economic resources. It is an aggregate index for a population and does not measure Empowerment on an individual basis. It is made up of two dimensions: Economic participation and decision-making and political participation and decision-making.

For our purposes GEM is limited and does not capture the multidimensional view of women's empowerment. It cannot be assumed that if a development intervention promotes women's empowerment along a particular dimension that empowerment in other areas will necessarily follow. A number of studies have shown that women may be empowered in one area of life while not in others. While we do not attempt to resolve this debate, we take the position, that women's empowerment can be measured by factors contributing to each of the following: their personal, economic, familial, and political empowerment.

We make a point to include household and interfamilial relations as we believe is a central locus of women's disempowerment in India. And by including the political, we posit that women's empowerment measures should include women's participation in systemic transformation by engaging in political action.

Amin, Becker and Bayes split the concept of women's empowerment into three components each measured separately: Inter-spouse consultation index, which seeks to represent the extent to which husbands consult their wives in household affairs; Individual autonomy indexes which represents women's self-reported autonomy of physical movement outside the house and in matters of spending money; and the Authority index, which reports on actual decision- making power.

These indices are similar to those of used by Balk in her 1994 study. Comparable components of empowerment are included in the eight indicators by Hashemi: mobility, economic security, ability to make a small purchases, ability to make larger purchases, involvement in major decisions, relative freedom from domination by the family, political and legal awareness, and involvement in political campaigning and protests.

Several different efforts have been made in recent years to develop comprehensive frameworks delineating the various dimensions along which women can be empowered. We construct four separate components of empowerment in Table that draw from many of the authors revealed earlier and especially rely on Hashemi and Amin Becker and Bayes, as their work seems most relevant for rural women in India.

These measures in Table reflect our belief that to measure women's empowerment more fully and in the broadest sense, it is necessary to add an individualised component representing her political autonomy to the autonomy within the family. Given that the legislation in India reserves special seats for women in elected bodies, even at the village level, an empowerment index for rural women should include her awareness of political issues and participation in the political process.

Research Methods

Ethnographic and survey research was undertaken at CRTC. Face to face interviews were conducted with CRTC's employees, and participant observation of the meetings and activities that took place at CRTC during two weeks in January in 2003 followed by visit in March 2004 to present our findings and tie up some loose ends. We also observed and documented the various programmes at the village level where the women gathered at a prearranged time to participated in a variety of programmes. To document the levels of empowerment among women in the NGO we drew our data from the employees who were responsible for the services that were designed to empower the rural village women.

At the leadership level we interviewed nearly all of the '``Supervisors''' of the various programmes. These ``Supervisors'' administered the `Field workers' who went into the villages and worked directly with the village women. We interviewed 32 of the 57 ```Fieldworkers''' who assisted the "'Supervisors'''.

We also chose to interview 25 local women living the area that the NGO served. They represented women who were eligible to be among the'Recipients' of the services of the NGO, by the fact they lived in the areas the NGO served. Although these are potential recipients we call them 'Recipients' for convenience. We chose not to interview current recipients of services, as we wanted to establish a baseline of empowerment among the village women from whom the employees were drawn. As all of the employees lived in the neighbouring villages before seeking employment the findings on the empowerment indices of the 'Recipients' may also be seen to reflect the those of the employees before coming to the NGO We chose to interview women employees and eligible women 'Recipients' to ascertain the main research question, of whether the employees were 'walking the talk' and if the employees were significantly different from the recipients. In other words did the women employees who intervened to help promote the empowerment of women were themselves empowered. We were seeking to establish whether the employees own individual levels of empowerment were significantly different from the recipients of the services. Furthermore, we interviewed individuals at both levels of hierarchies in the organization to ascertain if all employees had same or differing levels of empowerment.

We decided to interview half of the 'Fieldworkers'. We ended up with a sample of 32/57 of 'Fieldworkers'. The latter was an opportunistic sample, in that we simply interviewed all the employees who happened to be present in the CRTC headquarters on the days we visited. During the period we visited the NGO, there was a rotation of the 'Fieldworkers' assigned to duties at villages coming in to meet with the 'Supervisors'.

We were thus able to interview 32 of the 'Fieldworkers'. The sample of women eligible to be recipients was done by employing two of the NGO employees to visit every third house in the village and identify women who would be likely potential recipients. We were able to get a sample of 25 women who were willing to be interviewed. Two 'Supervisors' helped us fine tune and translate our instrument for the 'Recipients', which included the measures of women's empowerment used for the employees.

Additionally, we trained one local woman to undertake the interviews due to their fluency in the language12. To get a better understanding of how the NGO worked, and how the employees were selected and trained, we conducted several interviews conducted with the Director, Dr. Kshama Metre, over the course of two weeks.

These interviews ranged from short half an hour discussions to longer two-hour conversations. Dr Metre also invited us to visit the weekly meetings held with all staff so we could observe first hand the training and interactions. We also attended six meetings in the villages held by staff with the clients to observe their interactions as well.

Demographic and Socio Economic Data

The women in our study are all from the district of Sidhbari, Himachal Pradesh. There is a wide age spread in the total number of respondents. They range in age from 21 to 65; most women are married and lived with their husbands and have an average of 2.74 children.

Only five women in our study did not live with a spouse, 3 of the women are divorced and two are widowed. Divorce is not common in the rural areas and the general tradition is to put up with an abusive spouse or a bad marriage. With reference to caste 89 per cent of the women categorize themselves as low caste or 'OBC' or Other Backward Classes. This is a 'catch all' category developed by the Government of India census to include some of the most marginalised caste segments of Indian society.

Four of the 'Supervisors' belong to the higher castes, as do two of the 'Fieldworkers' and one from the group of 'Recipients'. Family structure is relevant to discussion of empowerment. As many of the questions relate to domestic decisions making to establish empowerment levels family structures can influence the responses.

The traditional family structure in India is not a nuclear family, it a joint family. In this system, when a son marries, he continues to reside with his parents with his wife and their children. The daughter on the other hand goes to her husband's home and lives with his parents, unmarried siblings, and the families of his married brothers. The parents of the husband, in a joint family, tend to hold decision-making authority that often overrides the authority of any of the married sons or their wives. Twenty-nine of the seventy two women in our study live in traditional joint families, whereas the rest lived in a nuclear family setting, which is far less than the norm in Himachal Pradesh of over 50 per cent.

The women had an average of 6.13 years of education (The literacy rate in Himachal Pradesh is 77.13 per cent which is much above the national average of 65.38 per cent; Male literacy is 86 per cent and female literacy is 68 per cent (The Tribune, Chandigarh, India, Saturday, March 31, 2001) In this area where alcoholism is rampant, we asked our respondents if they had problems related to alcohol consumption.

We find that half of the women suggested that they had experienced problems related to the alcohol consumption by their husbands. This ranged from beatings and the use of household money for alcohol to unemployment. The differences between the groups were striking, in that the least amount of alcoholism was present in the families of 'Fieldworkers' and the most in the

'Recipients', where as the half the 'Supervisors' experienced alcohol related problems.

We then compared the differences of the means of several socio demographic variables and the means of the empowerment index between the three groups: 'Supervisors', 'Fieldworkers' and 'Recipients', to see if they differed significantly on any of the socio demographic variables and empowerment levels. While they appeared significantly different on the number of all counts with the exception of age, the Scheffe Post Hoc test showed that not all the differences were significant.

Table. Comparison of Means of Socio Economic Data and Empowerment Index for 'Supervisors', 'Fieldworkers' and 'Recipients'

Mean	Superv-isors	Fieldwo-rkers	Recip- ients 3 groups	ANOVAF F TestS and F	T-Test for2 groups Sig 2-tailed
Age	40	38.94	36.64	.818	.669
No. of Kids	3	2	3	5.117*	.048*
Income class	1.79	1.65	1.32	5.348*	.357
Years of Education	10.27	8.00	1.40	51.380*	*.032*
Years in NGO	10.53	6.40	N/a	N/a	.008**
Empower-ment Index	21.72	17.47	9.40	37.815*	*.007**

***Note*:**

*Correlation is significant at the 0.05 level

** Correlation is significant at the 0.01 level

Scheffe Post Hoc tests reveals that for the variables Education and Income class there were no significant differences between the 'Supervisors' and 'Fieldworkers', but both groups of employees were significantly different from the 'Recipients'.

This is not surprising, as NGO employees need to be literate and have education to be hired as professional employees. The (income) class variable asked respondents to choose between three classes income: high, middle or low. The results show that respondents only chose either low or middle. This is expected given the poverty level in this area.

We find that there were no significant differences between the 'Supervisors' and 'Fieldworkers', but both groups of employees were significantly different from the 'Recipient' group. This may be explained by the fact that NGO employees earn a steady income while the 'Recipient' group do not have a steady income and are dependent on the local economy, Only six of the 'Recipient' group worked outside the home as compared to all the 'Fieldworkers' and 'Supervisors'.

Finally the Scheffe Post Hoc test shows significant differences between all three groups on the empowerment index. Each group was significantly different from the other.

Empowerment Levels of Respondents

There is a clear downward slide in rates of empowerment as one descends the ranks of 'Supervisors', 'Fieldworkers' and 'Recipients'.

Table gives the individual and aggregate scores on the Empowerment index (E-Index) for the three groups. Comparing the E-index between these groups, we find that it is significantly different between these three groups14

Table. Empowerment Indexes for 'Supervisors', 'Fieldworkers' and 'Recipients'.

Group	Personal Autonomy Index	Family Decision-Making Index	Economic Consultation Index	Political Autonomy Index	AggregateE -index
'Supervisors'	5.73	5.27	5.23	5.49	21.72
'Fieldworkers'	4.33	4.33	4.36	4.45	17.47
'Recipients'	3.02	3.02	2.54	0.82	9.40
All groups	4.17	4.07	3.91	3.41	15.55

Furthermore, the Scheffe Post Hoc test reveals significant differences in the E-Index between the 'Recipients' and the two employee groups of the NGO. This confirms our initial hypothesis, that NGO employees whose job is to empower the poor and disenfranchised village women do not only resort to rhetoric but also live their own lives significantly differently from that of their clientele. In other words, they 'walk the talk' in their own daily lives. As we observed patterns of significant differences in the E-Index between the "Fieldworkers" and "Supervisors" we attempt to uncover the underlying factors that may account for this difference.

The literature suggests several factors of influence: age, education, income, and family structure. To this mix we add their 'tenure in the NGO'. We do this as we believe being in contact with the mission and values of the NGO, that promotes the empowerment of women, must affect their daily lives. Review of the Independent

Variables in our Model: Age: Mason (1986), pointed out that a woman's behaviour varies across the stages in the life cycle. As a woman grows older, experience can teach her to stand up for her own rights. As her children grow older and are less dependent on her she can assert herself better without the threat to her children's well being. Also within the traditional family structure, as a woman gets older and her sons get married and her own in-laws grow older and die, the Indian woman is promoted from the comparatively obedient daughter-in-law to the role of a mother-in-law, the one 'who must be obeyed'. Family Structure: A women's role in household decision-making: control over money matters and other important household matter is a function of the family structure.

Whether a woman lives in a joint family or where she is a mother in law, or if she lives in nuclear family structure will impact her autonomy. We expect that in a joint family she will have less autonomy than in a nuclear family structure. Of course this may be mitigated by age. Education: It has been argued is one of the indicators of empowerment. Indeed, many of the variables that have traditionally been used as proxies for empowerment, such as education and employment, are better described as "enabling factors" or "sources of empowerment".

Empowerment includes cognitive and psychological elements, such as a women's understanding of her condition of subordination and the causes of such conditions. This requires an understanding the self and the cultural and social expectations, which may be enabled by education. Hence we expect education to be positively linked to the E- Index, as human capital will facilitate empowerment. Tenure at NGO: If the NGO is providing models of empowerment through its leadership and core values, we expect that association and the length of tenure with the NGO will effect the E- Index positively.

Although education may be an enabling factor, experiences allows a woman to see that the lack or autonomy in her life choices not as a given but something that can be changed. We expect that thc interventions made by the NGO for women in general give the employees the wherewithal on how changes can be made and the impetus to make further changes in their own lives. Thus, we expect the E-Index to be a function of age, family structure, income class, education and tenure at the NGO. A bivariate analysis reveals that there are no significant correlations among the independent variables and dependent variable except tenure at the NGO15. In order to understand the combined effects of all the conceptualised variables, we use a regression model using the data for 'Fieldworkers' and 'Supervisors' combined, we do not include the 'Recipient' group, as they all have zero years at the NGO. This will provide an estimate of the combined explanatory power of the independent variable on the E - Index.

We use the equation,

E = F (A, E, I, F, T) where:

EI = E- Index - dependent variable, an aggregate of four separate indexes

E = Education (years of formal education)

A = Age in years,

C = Income class (Dummy variable 0= low income, 1= Middle income),

F = Family structure (Dummy variable 0= nuclear, 1= Joint family),

T = Years of tenure at the NGO

The regression in Table shows that Years in the NGO, and education are two significant explanatory variables. In both the bivariate analysis and the regression model, the years in the NGO are significant. It is interesting to note that education is only significant in the regression model. This suggests, that education, in and of it self, may not be sufficient to give a woman a high E- Index. It is likely that a woman with higher human capital is more receptive to the experiences of a working in an NGO.

Thus we see the explanatory power of education when combined with longer tenure at the NGO. What needs further explanation is why the variables such as age, income class, education, and family structure were not significant in the regression model. One explanation may be, that given the poor rural environment from which these women originate; the social traditions and disenfranchisement of women were similar regardless of their education or age. The income variation was also fairly minor, as our qualitative notes showed. The respondents were asked to say whether they were classified themselves between upper, middle or lower income classes.

Almost all said "lower class". On some prodding, those with any regular source of income put themselves in the middle class. What is surprising to us is how many women lived in nuclear families still scored low on the E- Index. However, they lived in fairly close proximity to their in laws and extended families, and we think that this negated the influence of family structure

QUALITATIVE ANALYSIS

The findings in this part rely on many interviews conducted with the Director, Dr. Shama Metre and attending staff and community meetings over the course of two weeks by both authors. We first report on the challenges encountered by Dr. Metre in hiring employees, the training of local employees and how the NGO functioned.

When Dr. Metre chose to expand her NGO she could not afford to import trained employees from neighbouring cities, for two reasons, the costs were fairly substantial and city folk did not like staying in rural areas for any great length of time. Retention is a major problem given the harsh conditions and lack of amenities. Dr Metre took this challenge and turned it into an opportunity to hire local labour.

Trained local labour was not available, so Dr Metre identified some of women clients of her NGO who showed qualities of leadership and worked with them. Single handedly she counseled this small group of poor and marginalised woman and persuaded them they are entitled to a better life, that acceptance of subjugation is not their karma. She also made them aware of their legal and constitutional rights. She brought about what she and many of the employees referred to as 'jagruti' or awakening. The word 'jagruti' was often repeated in our intensive personal interviews as that moment of epiphany when the women realised that they did not have to accept their low status in society as God given – that they could, and should, fight to better their lot. Over a period of time, she was able to change their lives through personal interventions and guidance. When these women were self supporting and had confidence in their own capacity to make change she recruited them to work for her. Only when she had recruited and trained a handful of them did she start new programmes in the NGO, which hitherto had simply been a pediatric clinic.

It was a slow process, but Dr Metre chose to do this intentionally. Her vision was to use these women to help other women, not only through intervention strategies, but also as role models who would encourage local women to stand up for their rights and take charge of their lives. We noted that in the staff meetings and community meetings these homegrown

'Supervisors' and 'Fieldworkers' were quick to share their own experiences and thus were effective models. They showed village women who came to seek assistance from the NGO that they themselves faced similar circumstances could rise above them.

Stimulating community discussions among women- through organized village women's groups —persuade and encourage women to undertake behaviour changes in a supportive atmosphere where every individual effort is lauded. More importantly the audience can identify with the leaders as they are of the same class, religion and geographical region and are therefore subjected to similar oppression yet they are living examples of empowerment and have managed to rise above the subjugation.

This realistic modeling, in an appreciative and supporting atmosphere as we have suggested, is a powerful from of vicarious learning and more likely to motivate behaviour change especially when combined with persuasion in a supportive and appreciative environment earlier. Though the modeling of homegrown employees is an effective method of empowering women, many of the employees as well as Dr Metre, credited their success to their firm belief in God. This self-efficacy, grounded in a spiritual conviction, is what they conveyed to their clientele. One supervisor put it this way " It is not your karma to be subjugated, rather God expects that you take control of your life and help yourself". This message was reflected in many ways by many of the "Supervisors" and "Fieldworkers".

This spirituality, we were told, acts as social glue among the employees and clientele, connects and engenders trust amongst them and gives support to the overall agenda. This is no means an overtly religious NGO; the spirituality is often an unspoken bond and simply frames the norms and values of the organization. Several authors have written on the relevance of spiritual and religious capital, and this idea of promoting behaviour change with the added benefit of such capital is gaining currency.

Further research with spiritual capital in mind may point to the success of CRTC from another perspective. We suggest that because of the frequency with which it was mentioned, and despite the fact that this is not a religious NGO and the fact that our questionnaire did not elicit any information related to religion or spirituality, this issue may have potential in explaining some of our findings.

We are unable to say more given our research did not systematically address this point. Our in depth interviews allowed us a glimpse into the manner in which the 'Supervisors' had managed to transform their own lives before training to assist other women to bring about similar changes into their lives.

Although it is not possible to document all their stories what is indicative from our findings is that all of the women employees who had come to the NGO for assistance, despite their education level, would have scored very low on the E-Index before being employed. We give one story to show many of the stories, all of which have common denominators of subjugation, poverty and helplessness. Murma used to be a poor helpless woman with four children who was beaten regularly by an alcoholic husband. There was not enough money to buy food or clothing for the children and Murma would eke out a subsistence living by begging and borrowing form neighbours and relative. Lacking education, skills and finance, Murma had resigned herself to a dismal fate until she heard of the CRTC programme. Skeptical that she would be accepted, she ventured to join a women's group run by the NGO and enrolled her children in a children's programme. Thereafter she received informal help with health and welfare services and some training to make her functionally literate. She later joined a micro credit group and received entrepreneurial training.

She was spiritually convinced that she could and should improve her lot and help her other sisters achieve the same enlightenment. Murma was one of the first local women hired to work in the NGO 18 years ago. Today she owns a mushroom farm and is economically self-sufficient. She even managed to support her errant husband until he died recently. She is now senior supervisor and has also trained in political leadership. Though she lost in the elections of the local village council or 'panchayat' she plans to try again. Murma is now a model of empowerment devoted to helping empower other rural women; she also lobbies for change and liaisons with government.

Employment Guarantee for Fural Women in India

The National Rural Employment Guarantee Act is one of the most progressive legislations enacted since independence. Its significance is evident from a variety of perspectives. First, it is a bold and unique experiment in the provision of rural employment – in India and indeed in the world at large. Second, it is the first expression of the right to work as an enforceable legal entitlement.

In a country where labour is the only economic asset for millions of people, gainful employment is a prerequisite for the fulfilment of other basic rights – the right to life, the right to food, and the right to education.There is much that the NREGA promises from the perspective of women's empowerment as well.

Most boldly, in a rural milieu marked by stark inequalities between men and women – in the opportunities for gainful employment afforded as well as wage rates – NREGA represents action on both these counts. The act stipulates that wages will be equal for men and women. It is also committed to ensuring that at least 33 per cent of the workers shall be women. By generating employment for women at fair wages in the village, NREGA can play a substantial role in economically empowering women and laying the basis for greater independence and self-esteem. Government figures indicate an impressive participation of women in the NREGA. It is above 33 per cent in 15 states. Tamil Nadu, with 82 per cent, shows the highest participation with Kerala and Rajasthan also showing impressive figures.

At an all-India level, women's employment as a percentage of total employment in NREGA works was 40 per cent in 2007-08. The first four months of 2008-09 have already seen this figure go up to 50 per cent.

Table. Women's Participation in NREGA
(women workers as a percentage of all NREGA workers)

States	2008 – 09 (%)
Tamil Nadu	82.01
Kerala	71.39
Rajasthan	69.00
Andhra Pradesh	57.75
Karnataka	49.77
Gujarat	46.54
Tripura	44.51
Uttaranchal	42.77
Chattisgarh	42.05
Madhya Pradesh	41.67
Maharashtra	39.99
Sikkim	36.73
Orissa	36.39
Haryana	34.44
Mizoram	33.62
Manipur	32.80
Meghalaya	30.87
Assam	30.85
Himachal Pradesh	30.11
Arunachal Pradesh	29.58
Nagaland	29.36
Jharkhand	27.17
Bihar	26.62
West Bengal	16.99
Punjab	16.29
Uttar Pradesh	14.53
Jammu and Kashmir	1.08
All India	49.33

With this in mind, the National Federation of Indian Women (NFIW) carried out a survey to assess the impact of NREGA on women. The basic objective is to measure the tangible benefits that women have received from the implementation of the NREGA over a period of two years. A second aim of the study is to shed light on possible improvements that can be introduced to make NREGA more effective and responsive to the needs of women, particularly given its extension to all of rural India from April 2008.

The survey was carried out in one district each of four states where the NREGA had been in force since February 2006: Rajnandgaon (Chhattisgarh), Jhabua (Madhya Pradesh), Mayurbhanj (Orissa) and Cuddalore (Tamil Nadu). In each of the districts, two blocks and five Gram Panchayats per block were randomly selected.

A random sampling was also done to select women workers from completed worksites' muster rolls of 2007-2008. Two sets of questionnaires were used for the data collection. One was addressed to members of the Gram Panchayat and the second was addressed to women workers. The target number of sample workers was 800 (200 in each district). A total of 776 women workers and 40 Gram Panchayat members were actually interviewed.

Close to half (49 per cent) of the interviewed women were Scheduled Tribes; the rest were SCs (20 per cent) and OBCs (27 per cent). Out of the total sample of women workers 68 per cent were illiterate. Half of the respondent households had less than 5 acres land, and 35 per cent had no land at all. Most respondents reported agriculture or manual labour as the households' main occupation.

Table. Sample Areas of the NFIW Study

State	District	Blocks
Chhattisgarh	Rajnandgaon	Rajnandgaon
Dungargarh		
Orissa	Mayurbhanj	Shamakhunta
Bangriposi		
Madhya Pradesh	Jhabua	Pethlawad Rama
Tamil Nadu	Cuddalore	Mel Bhuvanagiri
Kurinjipadi		

NUMBER OF DAYS WORKED AND WAGES

Employment at NREGA worksites seems to have raised both enthusiasm and expectations among women workers. Women workers unanimously affirmed that the benefits from NREGA employment were high and that they would like to get more days of work in a year. The challenge of the situation becomes clearer when we look at the small proportion of women surveyed (only 7 per cent) who got more than 75 days of work in the last year. Almost half of the respondents (43 per cent) reported that they had worked for fewer than 25 days in the previous year.

Regarding wage payments, we found, in Cuddalore district, that most women workers were receiving the stipulated minimum wage, *i.e.* ' 80 per day. In the other three districts, however, the average wage was generally around '60 per day (as compared to a minimum wage of ' 69 in Madhya Pradesh, ' 70 in Orissa and ' 66.70 in Chhattisgarh) in the financial year 2007 – 08. Nevertheless, even where the full minimum wage was not being received, it is clear that NREGA wages are far higher than the wages otherwise locally available.

For example, Bhagwati w/o Ram from Gram Panchayat Khaira of Dongargarh block in Rajnandgaon district said:

- "Before NREGA, we were forced to work as agricultural labourers or casual labourers in brick kilns for ` 25/- to 30/- per day. But under NREGA, we are getting `62 to 64 per day, more than double, which is almost an unexpected amount for us."

It is also clear that, by and large, men and women are paid equal wages at NREGA worksites as has been mandated by the Act. Given that wage gaps between the male and female casual workers have been the norm in rural India, this is an extremely significant development.

Table. Women Workers' Access to MinimumWage and Days of Work

Districts	Statutory minimum wage* (Rs/day)	Per cent women aware about min. wage(Rs/day) workers	Average wage paid to women under NREGA getting the full	Proportion (%) of sample womenmini. Wage
Rajnandgaon (Chhattisgarh)	66.70**	33	62	18
Jhabua (Madhya Pradesh)	69	25	60	10
Mayurbhanj (Orissa)	70	51	60	40
Cuddalore (Tamil Nadu)	80	84	80	93

Contribution to Women's Independence

By putting cash incomes into their hands, NREGA is beginning to create a greater degree of economic independence among women. This was one of NREGA's main aims: with the increased participation of women in household income-generation a positive contribution to gender relations can be made.

The survey data (both qualitative and quantitative) suggest that women workers are more confident about their roles as contributors to family expenditure and their work decisions, and that they are also becoming more assertive about their space in the public sphere. More then half of the respondents felt that the NREGA has brought a significant change in their villages as well as in their own lives.

This is because employment is being provided within their village, generating community assets and enhancing their spending capacity. In each of the four survey districts, most of the women felt that the Act is "important" or "very important" for them. In Rajnandgaon and Cuddalore, the proportion who felt that NREGA is "very important" was as high as 70 per cent and 61 per cent, respectively.

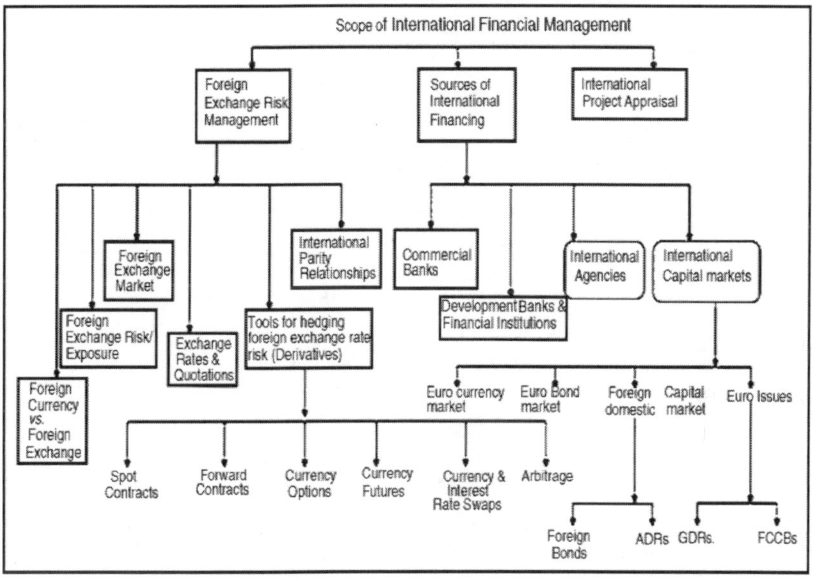

When asked about their decision to work under the NREGA, most respondents said that the decision to work at NREGA worksites was their own. Rajnandgaon was exceptional in this regard: 93 per cent of the women said that they had taken their own work decision. In the other three districts as well, this figure was remarkably high: 81 per cent in Mayurbhanj, 68 per cent in Cuddalore, and 67 per cent in Jhabua. Evidently, NREGA employment has encouraged women to take the decision to enter the sphere of the cash economy.

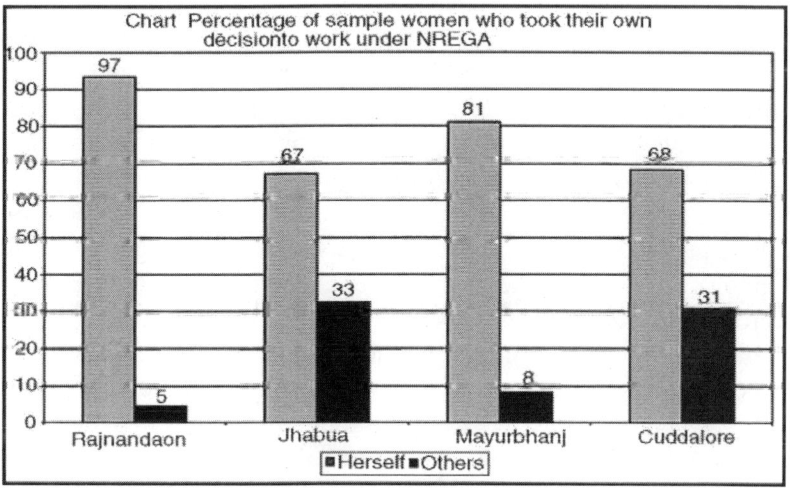

Another important point that emerged from the survey is that women workers were, by and large, receiving their wages in person, rather than through husbands or other proxies. In Rajnandgaon and Cuddalore, over 91 per cent of the women collected their own wages. In Jhabua and Mayurbhanj this figure stood at 60 per cent. Despite the substantial proportion of women not receiving their wages in person in these last two, this is also an encouraging finding.

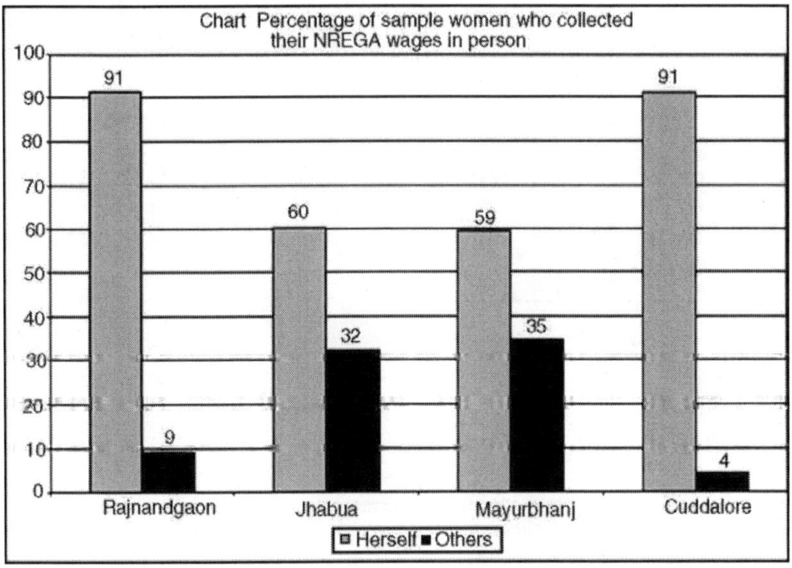

Inevitably, women's NREGA earnings are increasing their contribution to household income. A large majority (72 per cent) of the respondents said that they spent wages earned at NREGA works on regular food and consumer goods. The increased income locally available through NREGA work, they felt, was helping ensure at least two regular meals a day.

For the most part, the amounts earned through NREGA are insufficient to repay debts. Nevertheless, 28 per cent of the respondents said that they had spent their wages on repaying small debts. Further, it helps them to keep themselves away from the clutches of local moneylenders. A significant percentage of workers – almost 34 per cent - also spent their NREGA wages on their children's education.

The other large expenditure regularly met through NREGA wages is health care, with around 40 per cent of the respondents having spent earnings on this. All this taken together seems to sketch out the beginnings of a marked shift from the previous role of women. While women's labour (farm and non- farm) has always been an essential component in the functioning of rural households, it has been made invisible due to the absence of any monetary remuneration. By putting cash earnings in women's hands, NREGA has both increased and diversified the contributions that women are making to household incomes as wage earners.

MIGRATION – CHANGING TRENDS

One of the most positive trends in all the districts studied has been the impact of NREGA on migration patterns. 73 per cent of the respondents said that neither they nor their family members had migrated in 2007. The sole exception to this pattern was Jhabua, where 59 per cent respondents stated that they had migrated last year. That being said, even in Jhabua there is evidence of a shift in the pattern of migration. Respondents stated that where earlier entire families would migrate, now only one or two persons tend to leave for seasonal work in neighbouring states or elsewhere in Madhya Pradesh. NREGA seems to have created reasons and opportunities for people to work and remain in their own villages. The strengthening of this perception in rural areas can have significant impacts on questions of security, health and children's education, all of which are often compromised, in one way or another, during migration.

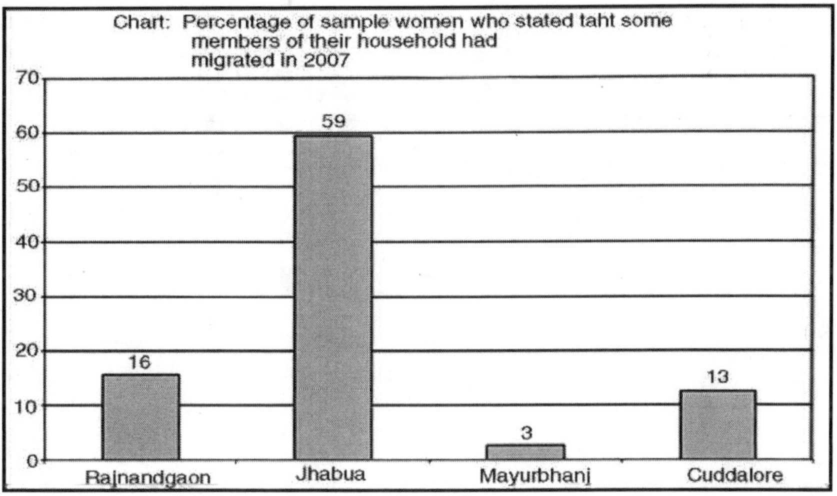

AWARENESS

It is perhaps predictable that awareness about the provision of NREGA will be low among disadvantaged communities. Less than half (48 per cent) of all sample workers were aware of the level of minimum wage in their respective States. Cuddalore is the only survey district in which awareness levels were relatively high (84 per cent were aware of the minimum wage).

Most women were aware that under the Act each household is guaranteed 100 days of work in a year. But awareness regarding operational guidelines, household registration, the job card distribution process, work applications and entitlements such as worksite facilities and unemployment allowance was inadequate. Only 43 per cent of women workers reported having made a formal application for a job card. In all four districts, most people just applied orally or gave their names when asked whether they wanted a job card. The situation was even worse with respect to applications for work. Only 18 per cent of thewomen surveyed were aware of the work application process and had appliedfor work themselves. The low level of awareness, even in districts where NREGA has been implemented for over two years, are indeed worrying. Generating much higher awareness about NREGA work clearly constitutes one of the key challenges for authorities, NGOs and popular movements.

POOR WORKSITE FACILITIES

The NREGA is committed to ensuring a workplace conducive toproductivity and workers' welfare. With this in mind, NREGA funds have been allocated for the provision of safe drinking water, shade for periods of rest, first aid and child care facilities at the worksite.

The last of these, in particular, is significant in order to make NREGA work a viable option for women with young children who cannot be left alone at home. It is disturbing, therefore, to find that most of these facilities are routinely absent from worksites. Only 68 per cent of worksites had drinking water facility. Most striking, however, is the almost complete lack of child care facilities in any of the four districts surveyed.

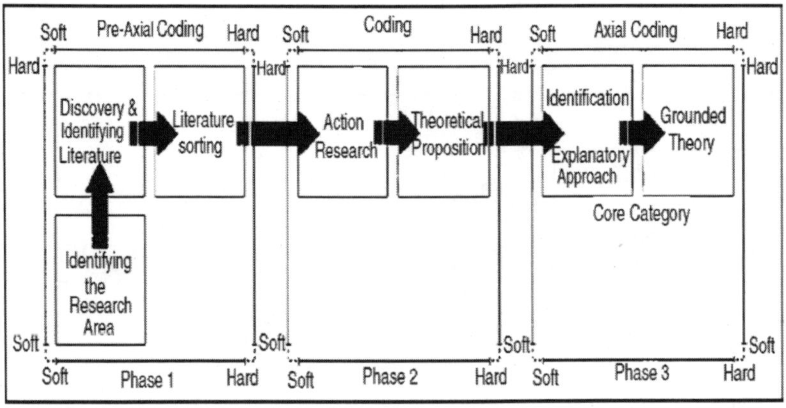

Women's Needs, Women's Action for Rural Communties of India

I must begrudgingly admit that as a product of the west, it is not easy for me to conceive of the toilet as an item of great luxury to be harboured, treasured, and valued. However, this is exactly what the toilet means to hundreds of millions of Indians whose access is limited to one toilet per every 1500 people at best, and at worst, who are denied access to this basic technology because no infrastructure exists in their villages. Consider a story that is prevalent throughout India. The way the story goes is that a young man gets a job in one of the major urban centres in India. He leaves his young bride at home while he commutes during the week to his job. Many times he is forced to spend weeks in the city without being able to return to the village to see his wife.

During this time, they correspond with each other via letters. In her letters, she often writes of the many goods that she wishes he would bring home, items that are not available in the village stores. However, her number one desire is not for silk saris, cashmere pashmina shawls, or for fancy jewelry; her number one wish is for him to bring home enough money so that they may build a toilet in their home. This anecdote was repeated often throughout the many rural villages I visited in India's Uttar Pradesh state. To the women of these rural areas, the toilet is the number one status symbol; and like the Gateway to India, the toilet is the gateway to a life of luxury, wealth, and opulence.

The same is true of India's urban centres where slum communities comprise the vast majority of the urban population without access to a toilet. Once again, being born and raised in the west, it is not my first inclination to see areas of urban slums and think of it as indicative of a majority of urban life. My initial tendency is to think of it as a pocket of society neatly tucked away from mainstream city living. This was sadly my first reaction to slums I visited throughout the city of Mumbai. Although I could see that the slum area was vast in scope, I didn't think it was representative of a majority of urban society in India.

After all, this is the city of glamorous Bollywood, with its beautiful stars and starlets dancing among the opulent mansions of Malabar Hills, picnicking in the lushness of the Victoria Gardens, or frolicking in the exotic waves, where the Indian Ocean meets the Bay of Bengal and the Arabian Sea. However, even though slums are rarely depicted in Bollywood storytelling, they are anything but a pocket of Mumbai's society. Slum dwellings are the mainstream of India's urban centres; juxtaposed between the gardens and mansions of great wealth, these slum societies are not tucked away out of sight of the rest of the population as they so easily are in the west. Instead, slum communities are an integral part of the social fabric of Indian cities.

The picture portrayed throughout this document through the statistics regarding those who do and do not have access to a toilet is a vivid representation of urban and rural life throughout India; they create a portrait of immense urban sprawl and an impoverished universe within which personal health and hygiene is a tremendous challenge. The toilet plays a critical role in this challenge either because of its unavailability to the masses through disparate numbers or because of its total absence in these areas.

But before we can turn to the specific case examples of rural and urban women's relationship to the technology of the toilet, we must first grasp the history, as well as the many different physical and cultural characteristics of the Indian toilet. This is especially important for those of us who rarely give our western-style porcelain, flush-toilets more that a passing thought. Because of the uniqueness of the Indian toilet in physical design and character, it is important to take a moment to look at and distinctly describe the various types of toilets found in India. This concrete description of what is classified as a toilet in India is crucial to our story and the impact the toilet has had on Indian society, especially the women of India. Those that do have access to toilets in India have traditionally relied upon some variation of either the pit or dry latrines. These latrines are usually contained within a small room, several metres away from the main house. The technology consists of no more than a hole in the ground that opens into a container that is situated within a compartment below the hole.

In pit latrines, the waste empties into a jute bag. There is no seat to the toilet. To use the facility, one squats over the hole. This is of importance because a main concern for toilet design among women is the fact that children can easily fall through the hole; the size of this hole is one of the main differences between the toilets designed by Indian women and those designed by western NGOs. The fact that the women designed a toilet with a "child-friendly" hole size has played a huge role in why their toilets have been more readily acceptable than western-designed toilets made for the Indian market. Those that do not have access to pit or dry flush latrines often rely upon the bucket privy rather than defecating in public.

This small amenity is exactly what the name suggests. People that have a bucket privy excrete their waste into the bucket and then, when the bucket is full, take it to dumping grounds to empty.

Western-style flush toilets are a luxury only available to the wealthiest in the country. Options to convert dry flush into flushable toilets containing a septic tank also exist, but only for those whom can afford it and in areas that have adequate sewage and sanitation facilities, which would again be the rich areas of India. Therefore, less than twenty per cent of the houses have septic tank toilets. After using the latrine of any type described above, water, not toilet paper, is used to clean oneself; so there is generally a spigot or bucket with a ladle to rinse soiled areas. Toilet paper is not an amenity that is widely used as traditionally there has been no water to flush it down with and it creates extra waste. To clean these toilets, a person must crawl into the compartment and empty the receptacle, a job traditionally assigned to the Dalits, or the untouchable class.

While the physical description of the Indian toilets is important in showing the technology choices available to Indian society, the cultural history of the toilet technology defines how those choices came about and shows the uniqueness of adapting a technology to the society it serves. To those of us in the west it may be difficult to comprehend how toilets can be intertwined in all aspects of a culture. The history of the toilet in India exemplifies how a seemingly neutral technology like the toilet both helps to define and is defined by the culture it serves. The culture of the toilets in India can be said to have its roots in the Aryan Code of Toilets written in the historic Vedas of 1500BC that describe the ritualistic rules of defecation, toilet constructions, and daily ablutions. This code outlines various chants to be said before, during, and after defecation. It outlines the rituals to be performed before and after going to the bathroom, such as rolling the sacred thread, that Hindu males wear across their chests, and putting it behind the right ear; covering one's head by a cloth; and using the left hand for cleaning of the body after urination or defecation.

It also explicitly describes where defecation should take place and where toilets should be constructed; one should not urinate within 10 cubits from a source of water or defecate within 100 cubits from a water source. The distance is increased if one is in proximity to a river, temple, or other holy site; in these areas, one should not urinate within 40 cubits of a river or temple nor should they defecate within 400 cubits of such a site. It is ironic that a nation that has records of the first known toilets in existence, suffers such a problem as lack of toilets in the modern day.

In 2500 BC the Harappa Civilization is said to have had water borne toilets in each house that was linked with drains covered with burnt clay bricks. This sophisticated sewage system was even equipped with manhole covers and sewage draining chambers. With such a well equipped sanitation system, as seen in the Harappa Civilization, such ritualistic rules were easy to abide. However, with the decline of the Indus valley civilization and the subsequent histories of outside rule and colonialism, the science of sanitary engineering disappeared from India.

In 1556 AD, Muslim rulers transformed ideas about the toilets. King Jehangir built a public toilet at Alwar about 70 miles from Delhi. This became the first community toilet in India and the Mughul rulers were quick to build them throughout the empire. However, the idea was not so well received by the majority of the population. Because the community toilet facilities were not properly cleaned and maintained, most of the Indian people preferred open defecation to the dilapidated and dirty toilet blocks. It was also about this time that open air defecation became the norm in agricultural societies because it was a means to fertilise the soil and increase crop yields.

Luxurious bathing facilities were established for Mughal rulers only and became common primarily in palaces and homes of the very wealthy. As a result, those that had a toilet and those that did not became a way of separating the rich colonizers from the poor colonized population. During this empire, the Mughals established practices that would become cultural standards within Indian society up to the present day. For example, the ruling Mughals established notions of hiding female bodies, such is exemplified by burguas to cover women's faces.

From this cultural practice, it became a cultural norm that women should remain modest and covered in public. This established that women would not be able to defecate in public, as could the men; to do so would cause public humiliation and deep shame. Such was the advent of the bucket latrines, which are designed to allow women to be able to defecate in public. The Mughals also predominantly depended upon captives to clean the latrines and bucket privies. These captives were also forced to transport the human excreta to distant places for waste removal. Once these prisoners were done with their years of service, they were no longer accepted by their Hindu castes because they were seen as unclean according to Hindu standards of cleanliness, as established in the Vedas. As such, they were forced to form a separate class, known as the Dalits, or "untouchable" caste. This is the beginning of the scavenger class whose hereditary duties are to clean and remove waste from the dry latrines and transport it to separate dumping areas. These hereditary duties, initiated by the Mughal rulers, have fixed their role and status in society to that of the lowest on the caste hierarchy.

Under British colonial rule in the 19th and early 20th century, the trend continued to keep the toilet as an amenity accessible only to the rich rulers. When sanitation improvements were made in India by the British rulers, they were done only when they would be beneficial to the economic resources of England. The first priority of the British Empire was to protect its investments by protecting its military and trading companies. Thus, resources for sewage and improved sanitation were reserved exclusively for the homes of English serviceman and merchants who peddled English goods to the native population. Initially, Britain did not want the extra cost of providing amenities to their colonized subjects; only when more and more British civilians were forced to interact with the native population, which increased the British likelihood of coming into contact with such diseases as cholera or smallpox, were improved sanitation initiatives brought to the Indian masses.

However, the British elite proposed innovations that were too capital intensive for the majority of Indians. As a result, the infrastructure that was put in place by Britain could not be afforded by Indian civilians and could not be maintained by the new Indian government once India won independence in 1947. The story of the toilet today in India is a vastly different tale from the one of the Harrappa Civilization of yesteryear. Today only thirty-five per cent of the urban population and fourteen per cent of the rural populace have access to a toilet; this means that nearly two-thirds of all Indians do not have access to a toilet. Without access to a toilet, this population has no choice but to defecate in the open, on the sidewalks, streets, and rural fields of India's cities and villages. It is estimated that more than seven hundred million people defecate in the open throughout India. Like the Harrappa civilization, the contemporary government of India has tried to build toilets and sewage systems, but most of these endeavors have failed because they were forced to rely on assistance from foreign investors.

Because they controlled the capital resources, these foreign investors were able to impose their own western-designed toilets and to contract their own companies to build them; the Indian government had no input into what kind of toilets would be built to serve the Indian population. The resulting toilets that were built by the western companies were not conducive to India's unique cultural needs. Without this outside "aid", the Indian government simply lacked the funds necessary to initiate toilet-building projects on their own. The 2,47,72,500 ` billion is needed to provide all of India's population with a conventional water supply and sewerage system. At this expense, it would take two hundred years for every Indian to have access to a toilet. Given this fact, it is easy to understand why toilet building projects are a standard platform in political election campaigns and have remained a top political priority since India won its independence in 1947.

When scanning the local Indian newspapers and political news magazines, it is not uncommon to see toilets referred to by many politicians seeking election. Sarpanch's, the head of the state governments, and election into the local gramsabhas are won or lost on their ability to recognize toilets as an issue; seats in these governmental institutions are then retained or lost on the elected official's ability to bring the toilet technology to fruition in their village. The country's forefathers, Gandhi and Nehru, recognized the importance of this simple technology on the political, economic, social, and civil progress of their newborn country.

Nehru famous quote, "the day every one of us gets a toilet to use, I shall know our country has reached the pinnacle of progress," is often referred to in campaign speeches today. Throughout his life, Gandhi believed that, "in our approach to private and public sanitation lies our commitment to true freedom and dignity." He recognized completely that "toilets govern a lot of human issues: Personal hygiene, public health, street behaviour, crime rate and above all dignity and self-esteem.

Gandhi was not naïve when he harped on the centrality of sanitation in development." As such, he was an avid advocate of doing away with the traditional caste custom of having Dalits clean the dry latrines. In his communal ashram which embraced all members of society regardless of race, nationality, caste, or religion, Gandhi deliberately did not permit toilets in the private homes of the compound. This ensured that everyone had to use the row of public toilets at the end of the ashram and, as a rule, every person, regardless of caste or social status, would be rotated on toilet-cleaning duties. In this way, he ensured that all members of the community were equal.

"Gandhi's reasoning was that cleaning public toilets was the contentious issue on which the caste oppression was based. So, the best way of getting rid of the prejudices, equalizing society and teaching people a lesson in humility was to make them do the work they so despised," Caste oppression has always been contentious throughout India's history. In 1993, toilets entered the political arena in the form of laws that govern toilet construction, design, and maintenance, specifically in regards to the dry latrine, in the form of the Employment of Manual Scavengers and Construction of Dry Latrines Prohibition Act.

This law stated that anyone who constructed a dry latrine or employed a Dalit to clean or empty it would be subject to imprisonment of up to a year or a fine of Rs2000. Despite this Act, there are still nearly 7.5 million dry latrines in India. This is because the law was enacted, but no alternative was supplied. In some cases, the municipalities made new water toilets, but because there was no water available in these areas, they still needed to be dry-cleaned by a dalit.

This is a prime example of the local government, through the encouragement of World Bank sponsors, choosing a technology that was completely unsuitable to the terrain, geography, and society that the toilet serves. The Manual Scavengers and Construction of Dry Latrines Prohibition Act directly enforced what types of toilets can be built and how those toilets are to be maintained and cleaned. However, even those laws that do not specifically refer to toilets have had tremendous ramifications on the technological development of sanitation facilities throughout the country.

This will discuss the 73rd Amendment to the Indian Constitution in greater detail and its ramifications upon the women of the rural villages and their relationship with the toilet technology in their communities. This law states that thirty-three per cent of all village government local seats must be reserved for women. While this amendment states nothing directly about toilets and their construction, it has had a huge impact on bringing this technology to the rural countryside. This is because women, as the main caretakers of water, have a vested interest in bringing toilets to their community. Whereas before toilets were not an issue in the local village governments, or gramsabhas, because women participation in these local council meetings were minimal at best, now they are able to raise their voice, and thus, raise the funds, to begin designing and constructing toilets in their villages.

These women have brought the political aspect of the toilet to the forefront of their gramsabha meetings because the lack of proper toilet amenities, as well as the design of those toilets that are available, most adversely affects the women of India in both the urban centres and rural villages of the country. For example, because in India water chores, which include toilet duties, are within the domain of the women, the untouchable worker that cleans the ubiquitous dry latrines is inevitably a woman.

To clean these latrines, the woman Dalit physically removes the jute bag containing human waste and takes it to a waste disposal site. Not only is this type of work degrading, but it is extremely detrimental to her health, as well. All of the women Dalits interviewed for this document stated that they suffered from extreme nausea after a day spent cleaning the hundreds of dry latrines in their community. One woman actually stated that, "the men are lucky, [because] they can drown it all in liquor," another escape that is strictly taboo for women. In rural areas, where open-air defecation by men is rampant, cultural norms make it unacceptable for women to defecate in the open.

Women are not permitted to defecate within the confines of the village parametres. If they did so, they would feel extreme shame, be shunned by their society, or face harassment from men. The only answer that many of these women can find to the problem of lacking amenities is to severely limit their consumption of food and drink. This ensures that they will only have to relieve themselves once or twice a day. But this practice also leaves the women susceptible to many health risks. Primary among these risks is malnutrition because the women simply cannot consume enough caloric value to get the daily dose of vitamins and minerals; to do so would mean going to the bathroom more often during the day.

Many women also suffer from gastroenteritis almost all of the time because they refuse to drink water even when thirsty or to eat even when hungry. The women of India's urban cities suffer many of these same health-related issues. Even though access to a toilet is slightly increased in the cities of India, workplaces, schools and recreational areas still remain inadequately equipped with women's toilets. In these urban environments, as in the rural countryside, women must often walk for kilometres before they can find proper amenities; a fact that is hard to believe given the amount of public buildings in any given block of an Indian city. In many ways, the women of the urban cities are not as controlled by traditional, cultural customs and mores that dictate the domains of men and women.

Women of the cities frequently hold jobs in all areas of business and girls are encouraged to be educated to the fullest extent. However, the lack of toilet amenities impedes women and girls' progress so that they are not able to compete with their male counterparts in both workplaces and schools. For example, one woman interviewed described being greatly hindered because of the lack of toilets in her workplace. She said she and the other women in her office "must rely on a friendly neighbourhood hotel or master ancient yogic retentive techniques,". Another woman recalls having to meet with potential clients throughout the day. Each meeting means another cup of chai and other refreshments.

The office did not have a bathroom, so she had to learn to time her trips to when she would be able to leave the office and walk kilometres away to the nearest women's toilet. If she couldn't time the trips properly, she had to refuse the refreshments, which had ramifications on her professional performance because it was not socially acceptable. Beyond the workplace, the lack of toilet facilities in schools greatly hinders a girl's ability to get the same education as a boy. India strives to ensure that it provides an equal education to all regardless of caste and gender; but to do so the government is beginning to realise how important the provision of a toilet is to ensuring an equal opportunity for both boys and girls. Currently, 82 per cent of schools lack toilets.

Of those that do have toilets, 89 per cent do not have a separate toilet for girls. Another headline reads, "Why girls drop out of school". The answer is because they do not have access to a toilet. The object goes on to state that in terms of providing an equal education to all a, "Lavatory is more important than laboratory" the Planning Commission concluded. The lack of availability of a separate toilet for girls is a, "major impediment in the way of girls' entry into schools," concludes the object. This is because parents refuse to send their daughters to a school were amenities are not separate. To do so would risk the girls honour, decency, and purity.

One local woman interviewed for this document was asked why she sent her sons but not her daughters to school. Her response was, "I cannot because the local school does not have a toilet." These examples have not been used to make the western reader gasp with surprise or to make Indian society sound uncivilised, pre-modern, or bizarre, but to make the point that toilets, as a technology, can have tremendous social ramifications. The illustrations above establish that a technology that is seemingly gender neutral can actually play an important role on the status of women in all societies, not just throughout India. In the instances, the lack of a toilet is inhibiting a fair education and equality in the workplace. But it also shows us a society that is in transition between its traditional customs of a male-dominated workplace and institutes of education to one that is on the cusp of accepting women in these arenas.

The same was true for my alma mater, Drexel University. Drexel bears the remnants of what was once a traditional and cultural standard in America at the time—the fact that women simply did not become engineers. As a predominantly technological institute, Drexel focused mainly on its engineering school to build its reputation. The proof that women were not traditionally accepted into these engineering schools is marked by the absence of women's bathrooms in many of its buildings. To this day in Matheson Hall, there are only women's bathrooms on the first and fourth floors, while all five floors provide a men's bathroom.

There is also a broom closet that was converted to a one-toilet-seat women's bathroom in the basement; the conversion is so crude that it is easy to see that this women's bathroom was installed as an afterthought to the building design and it occurred much later than the original construction to meet the growing population of women enrolling and working at the university. This demonstration of a society extending boundaries to admit women where once before they were not traditionally accepted is a key element to the story of these Indian women. In the following stages as suggested, see how the toilet as a social technology is permitting these women to transition into areas that were never possible before and to improve their lives in ways that many in the west never get the opportunity to do.

These opportunities stem from the transition from traditional gender roles that identify women as the "main caretakers of water and sanitation facilities," to their modern roles in revolutionizing the construction, engineering, and availability of toilets in their communities. So, there is another side to the toilet situation in India. It is one that is drastically different from the images of hardship and neglect depicted above. It is the story of female empowerment and control of a technology to better their social positions and to build healthier communities for themselves and their families. As these women transition to their new roles in Indian society, they are teaching us in the west many lessons.

Primarily these women are proving that citizens can be more involved in scientific and technological development. For example, Robert Hiskes, in his book Democracy, Risk, and Community, discusses how western society can effectively alter scientific research and technological development through community action. The community action that Hiskes describes in an ideal democratic society is the banding together of citizens to become more educated, and thus, more involved in the policymaking of the scientific and technological issues facing society. To Hiskes, this is how western society should strive to shape science and technology discourse.

This does represent one method of society effectively influencing scientific and technological development; but Hiskes' method still clearly delineates the scientists from the rest of society. According to this theory, society cannot enter the scientific arena and shape policy from within, but must remain outside the fringes of science and technology and create policy from outside of this boundary. The women of India are not only living up to Hiskes' model of a responsible and active community involved in shaping the policies of what toilet technologies are available to them, these women are going a step further than what would be viable to them in the west. They are entering the scientific and technological fringes and becoming what we in the west cannot become without the years of training that our western society has made necessary to qualify one as a scientist or engineer.

These women have the opportunity to not only address a technological issue that concerns them, but to participate actively in the designing and construction of a new technology that will improve their lives. This does not happen readily in the west where it is not so easy to cross those boundaries from policy making to hands-on implementation.

So, even though our western society may have a women's bathroom in each building, it may also be limiting our scope of technological and scientific alternatives available to us. We must rely on the scientist to give us alternatives to choose from instead of creating them ourselves as the women in India are doing with their toilets.

The next few stages will show how women are transforming their roles in Indian society by taking control of a technology that has been neglected by their government, rendered ineffectual by foreign companies and ventures, and remained elusive throughout most of their lives. So called illiterate women of the cities and villages are starting enterprises, ventures with financial institutions, and serving in their local governments; all because of the toilet. These very same women are taking their control of the toilet technology beyond western notions of policy-making and are proving themselves to be actual practitioners of science, engineering and technology. In this way, they have defied western notions of licensing, accreditation and standardization and have expanded the boundaries of applicable science and technology. They are showing us in the west that we, too, are a society in transition and through their example we may be able to develop a more sustainable global discourse.

❐

6.

Rural Sector

In the rural areas of India, the statistics regarding who has access to a toilet differ drastically from the urban sector. The numbers are not about how many people use one toilet seat, as we saw in Mumbai, because in many cases not even one toilet seat can be found. Instead, ninety per cent of the rural villages have no access to a toilet. Given the population of these rural areas, this means that over seven hundred million people defecate in the open. In a typical rural area where a census was taken of 1,017 women, only five had a toilet at home; the others used fields and open spaces for defecation. Traditional cultural customs and mores have determined women's control over the domain of the technology of the toilet. For this reason, the statistics associated with the rural sector also often focus on tasks that are considered part of a woman's traditional domain and show how women in these areas are defined by these traditional gender roles most often to their disadvantage. The customs dictate that women are primarily the caretakers of water and sanitation.

This means that they are responsible for all tasks associated with water, from the collection to the management of this precious resource. It is their duty to draw, store, utilise, and manage water as per the daily requirements of their family; they are also responsible for the proper disposal of the family's excreta and other domestic wastes. These daily tasks consume most of a rural woman's day. Seventy-eight per cent of women spend an average of four hours a day in fetching water. The women of these rural villages must walk on average a minimum of six kilometres to transport water from the local water sources. Fifty-three per cent of women polled in the census above complained that they were not able to transport enough water for personal hygiene use, especially during menstrual periods.

What is striking about the case of the women of the rural sector is how this absence of toilets has shaped their communities and how the inception of the toilet that our story will chronicle is defined by a combination of traditional gender roles, current legal reforms, and future economic and environmental endeavors. The traditional gender roles and social attitudes that define women and their daily tasks and chores perpetuate a relatively low status for women in these areas. The main status indicators of the villages are education, ownership of property and resources, and control of new technologies. It is very difficult for women of the villages to have access to any of these resources.

Because so much of a woman's life is spent in collection of water, girls are usually engaged in household activities from a very early age rather than being sent to school for an education. Long-standing family properties are rarely ever transferred to a woman's name; she is unable to gain landholdings through marriage or to buy her own piece of property if she remains single. Because they have no land as collateral, women are unable to have credit extended to them for any sort of economic endeavors. Also, new technologies are usually considered to be the domain of the men of the village; as such, technological initiatives are not taught to women or girls within the village communities, which, in turn, deprives these women of technological developments that could enhance their status and daily quality of life.

These customs also dictate the day to day interactions that take place within the village community on several levels, such as between men and women, and also between women of differing castes. Due to the traditional, cultural taboo against menstrual blood, women and men are not allowed to defecate at the same place. Because defecation is done is the open, in fields usually outside of the villages perimetres, and not contained in sanitary containers, there is the possibility that menstruating women could taint others with their menstrual blood. There is also an extreme cultural sensitivity to the possibility that women will be exposed to the eyes of men, thus tainting the women's chastity, while they are in the compromising position of defecating in exposed fields. Both of these examples mean that women are deprived of basic services that are provided during the day in public areas.

In addition, women of the "untouchable" caste are not allowed to use public sources of water and sanitation neither during the day nor at night for fear that they will pollute the rest of the village. They must travel even farther distances than women of higher castes to transport their water and perform their daily ablutions.

Because of the lack of women-only public sanitation facilities, all women, regardless of caste, must wait until after dark to relieve themselves and defecate in the open. This has led to many health-related concerns such as bladder and urinary tract infections directly caused by prolonged periods of not being able to urinate and dispense with other bodily wastes. To reduce their need to excrete during the day, women drink and eat less. Not only do they not receive proper nutrition because of this, but they often suffer from dehydration because of the lack of fluids consumed. Being forced to travel long distances away from their village after dark, unaccompanied by men, also poses a personal threat to their safety. Assault and molestation are not rampant in the villages, but the odds of it occurring are increased when women must travel alone at night to isolated areas where they are exposing themselves in order to wash and go to the bathroom. Often their treks to these remote areas take them across train tracks that are notorious "hangouts for unsavory characters prone to drinking".

These train tracks are also hazardous to travel at night as the train conductors cannot see the women in their paths. While the above cultures, customs, and traditions of the village directly affect the health and safety of the women of rural villages, the simple fact of scarcity of safe and adequate water affect the state of the entire village: men, women, and children. Because there are not wells, pumps, irrigation pits, or any other infrastructure to bring clean water to the villages, women are forced to rely upon unsanitary sources for their water supply. This water is used to do the cooking, cleaning, and laundry, and is a main source for basic consumption. These sources of water are so unclean and infected that jaundice, viral and gastro-enteric diseases, and cholera outbreaks occur frequently in the rural villages of India. Diseases that are less common and easily treated in the United States, such as diarrhea and dehydration, result in the death of over 500,000 children every year.

Basic productivity, which is the only resource that a village can offer for its subsistence, is highly compromised due to sanitation-related diseases. Each year, 180 million work-days per year are lost due to illnesses caused by unclean water. This is equivalent to 12 billion rupees per year. These harsh conditions not only exemplify the challenges that women face as the main caretakers of their village water supply, but they also serve as indicators of the important role that these rural women play in controlling the environmental hygiene of their communities. This ability to control and choose water resources, limited as it may be, is a source of autonomy and authority for these village women. This autonomy did arise because water-related issues are not viewed by the village councils as critical to the villages' needs. Men are not concerned with how the laundry got done, how the dishes are washed, food is cooked, or where the water for their bathing comes from as long as it is always accessible to them when they come home from the fields in the evenings. And the women are sure that it always is accessible because it is their place within the community to ensure that it is.

The choices these women have for gathering water may not seem ideal to western standards, but at least the choice is theirs. Women control what water sources are used in their daily routines, whether it is the murky water hole used for doing laundry that is located 6 kilometres away, or whether is the less murky rain-water hole to be used only for precious consumption located 8 kilometres away. Women use their traditionally defined dharma, or duty, to influence the sanitation practices of the village. Part of their water duties entail teaching proper hygiene habits to the children of their community. As teachers, these women influence their family's sanitation habits and are consulted on the design of facilities to improve the cleanliness of the village.

Even though women do have control of the sanitation facilities within their village, their power remains quite limited in scope when it comes to initiating new technological improvements, such as toilets and sanitation systems. This is because women have never been given a forum in their local village meetings and governments to voice their concerns and their interests in bringing new water technologies to their communities. Traditionally, only men were allowed to participate in these local government meetings and to address the needs of the community.

Toilets were rarely an issue under these male-dominated village meetings because sanitation, including toilets, was not considered vital to the village's needs. This is because it falls within the women's dominion; only those technologies that concerned men directly were considered issues worthy of discussion within the village gram sabhas. These primarily focused on bringing new farming technologies to the area in the form of machines and fertilizers.

So women's drudgery in obtaining water continued and the village's sanitation and environmental health remained stagnant because women did not have a voice to propose new ideas for technological improvements in the water supply that would be beneficial to their villages. To repeat, this may not exemplify an ideal autonomy over a technology. But it is this symbiotic relationship to water that women have been able to use as an impetus for change through a new Indian law giving women a chance to discuss their issues within the local village governments. This law is helping women to prove that not only are toilets a valid technology, but also a technology that can improve the health, efficiency and productivity of the entire village. The women are seizing the opportunity that this new law gives them to completely control the toilet technology and to retain autonomy over all realms of its creation.

The autonomy that before was quite limiting in scope is now giving these rural women the opportunity to show their village how important sanitation is to overall productivity and, as a result, to bolster their status as women in society-all through the technology of the toilet. In fact, what was previously considered a hindrance, the lack of any sort of infrastructure for sewage and sanitation, is ironically proving to give the women even more freedom.

Unlike the urban sector where the women had to work with the infrastructure that was already in place, be it improving dilapidated toilet blocks or using the sidewalls and facades of the buildings where they chose to build their sidewalk communities, the women of the rural sector are given the freedom to choose a technology that will be the most beneficial to their village. This new law being instituted throughout the rural states is a mandate from the national government that women participate in the local village and state governments through a reservation of elected seats. It is these village meetings that prioritize projects for the entire community. Even though, historically, these village gram sabhas were always present to discuss the needs of the village, they functioned mainly as informal, village council meetings among the men of the community. As part of the independence movement, Gandhi envisioned making these meetings part of a recognized local and state government. He often spoke of Gram Swaraj in which adult villagers would annually elect the government and which would have authority and jurisdiction in the fields of legislation, jurisdiction and executive decision- making without interference from the state government.

Thus, by 1948, twenty native states had enacted Panchayati acts. However, even these covered few villages, were extremely limited in their functions, and did not include women participation. In the period between of 1959-1964 the Panchayat Raj Institutions became the institutionalised three-tier model that it is today and were conceived as local bodies meant to ensure peoples' participation in development. This trend continued through the 60's and 70's. The three tier model was accepted by all states but neither sufficient powers nor sufficient finances were given to, thereby leaving the panchayats to languish to their fate. In such a scenario the importance of ensuring the participation of women took a backseat to having the PRIs institutionalised and recognized. The function of the PRIs was nowhere defined in the constitution and its meaning and scope were never authoritatively interpreted by the judicial guardians of the Constitution, the High courts and the Supreme Courts.

Therefore, there was a growing realization that it was the lack of constitutional support that kept the PRIs from reaching their full potential. As a result, the government of India wrote the three-tier panchayati raj institutions into the constitution of India with the enactment of the 73rd Constitutional Amendment passed in 1992. It was at this time that the 73rd Amendment also incorporated the political participation of women into state and national law.

Previous gram sabhas and panchayati initiatives did propose women representation in the forums; however, participation was not mandated and, therefore, never fully accepted by the states. Because participation was voluntary, most women did not participate in the local governments; they feared speaking out in the village forum because they were regarded as illiterate and unimportant simply because of the fact that they are women. The men of the village certainly did not force the women to take part in the councils because they were happy to keep that distinction for themselves.

In those states where the provision for women to be able to optionally participate in the village gram sabhas was proposed, the panchayati raj system of government was accepted, but the provision for including women was rejected. Without this provision in the previous government, less than 7 per cent of parliamentary seats were won by women. Therefore, a mandate reserving seats for the "poor, marginalised, and the oppressed," was needed to ensure their representation in local governments. The state of India realised that if development initiatives and poverty alleviation programmes were to succeed at the rural level, they needed the local involvement and participation of women. To ensure an effective presence of women in these institutions, the amendment stated that 33 per cent of the local government seats are now to be reserved specifically for women of the rural districts. This Amendment that was passed in 1992 was enacted for the first time in the 1993-1994 state elections.

Before looking at the impact that this law has had on the women of the villages, it is important to understand the structure of the local governments and the areas where women are becoming prominent due to the amendment. This description shows the vast web of bureaucracy that is Indian local government.

As will be seen by all of the villages, districts, jurisdictions, blocks and official, ex-officio, non-official levels, elected, non-elected, and appointed posts and positions and the division of labours and controlling of funds for development, working within the system can be very confusing to say the least.

It is very hard for members who have studied politics at universities and institutions to know the proper channels to get a project funded. The task can be overwhelming if you are a woman from a rural village that has never attended school, village meetings, and never before had a voice of your own. These local governments are known as the Panchayati Raj Institutions. Below is a diagram that shows the basic pyramid structure of the PRIs. The PRIs are comprised of a 3-tier organizational structure of elected posts and positions. The elected tiers of the PRI are the gram panchayat, the panchayat samiti, and the zilla parishad.

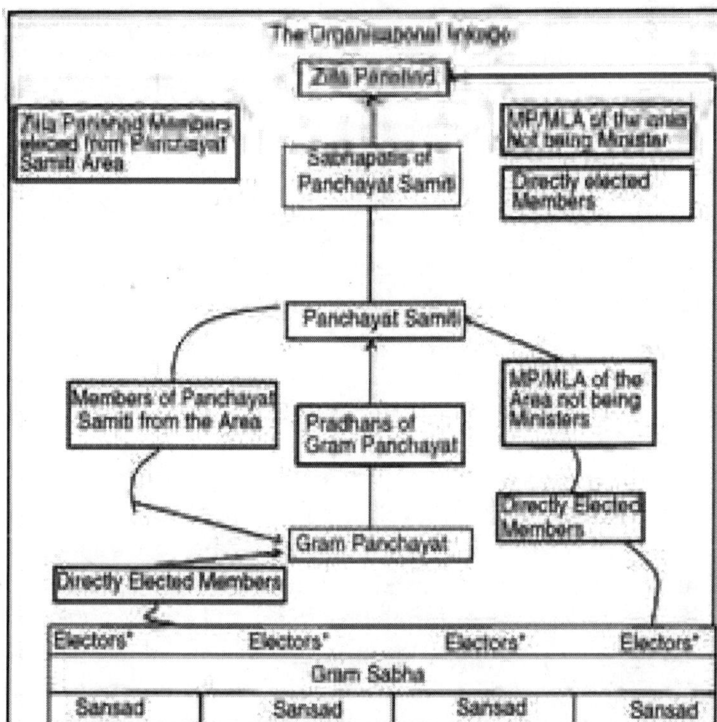

Fig. Panchayati Raj Institutional Structure

These can have slightly different variations of name according to the dialect of the rural district they serve. No matter what the name, the pyramid structure remains the same as does the function of each tier. "The provision of a three-tier structure, except in states with less than a population of Twenty Lakh, is designed to bring uniformity in the structure and pattern throughout the country which in time will strengthen planning processes at the grass roots level.". The main goal of the PRIs, which provides for electing all members of Panchayats at every level directly by the people, will also contribute to accelerating democratic processes at the grass roots levels. Thus, it will "boost local people's initiatives and enhance their involvement in the system, through the electoral process,".

At the base of the PRI structure is the gram sabha. The gram sabha is not an elected branch of the local government. Instead, it is comprised of the entire body of citizens that are eligible to vote in a village. Eligibility is based only upon age; anyone 18 years of age or older is eligible to be a part of the gram sabha. Each village has its own gram sabha that is expected to meet twice a year to discuss improvements that are necessary to the functioning of the village, important issues relative to the community, and to act as a watch dog of the elected Gram Panchayat tier.

It is also designed to be the place where "villagers will discuss development issues, begin the planning process to initiate development programmes and select beneficiaries for these schemes,". Located just above the gram sabha on the pyramid structure is the Gram Panchayat. This is the basic unit of village democracy as it is the first elected body of the panchayati raj institution and has jurisdiction over a village or a group of villages. It consists of five to thirty-one members elected by the Gram Sabha through a secret ballot; each elected member serves for a period of three to five years. The elected officials of this tier are chosen by the voters of the gram sabha usually because they are prominent members from this base structure.

This means that they have already served the gram sabha by being proactive members of their village and have already effectively been able to bring many developmental projects to their communities. The members of the Gram Panchayat are called Panchas and the President of the Gram Panchayat is the Sarpanch. The Sarpanch is directly elected by the gram sabha members. The intermediate tier of the Panchayati Raj Institutions is the Panchayat Samiti. This is a vital link between the village served by the Gram Panchayat and the district level of the Zilla Panchayat; the Panchayat Samiti serves as an intermediary between these two tiers in terms of planning and administration. This level of government is known as the 'Block' level; a Block is consisted of all of the Gram Panchayat districts and the villages it serves; they all come together to form a Block at the Samiti level. Each Panchayat Samiti consists of official and non-official members. "The official members are the Block Development Officer and the Officers of various State Government departments ordinarily stationed at the Block level, such as the Chairman of Primary Co-Operative Agricultural Development Bank, Director of District Co-operative Central Bank, and the President of Primary Co-operative Marketing Society,". The non-official members include the Panchayat Samiti members and the Sarpanchs of the Gram Panchayats.

The Panchayat Samiti members elect a Chairman to head this body of government. The main functions of the Panchayat Samitis are "planning, execution, and supervision of all development programmes in the Block,". It also supervises the works of Gram Panchayats within its jurisdiction. The Zilla Parishad is the apex of the PRI structure. All tiers of government below and the villages encompassed by these tiers comprise the jurisdiction of the Zilla Parishad. This district-level tier is the direct link to the state governments of India. The various Rural Development Works being done at the Villages, Gram Panchayats, Block and District levels are planned, implemented, monitored and maintained by the Zilla Parishad. The Zilla Parishad supervises the works of Panchayat Samities as well as Gram Panchayats within its Jurisdiction. This completes the pyramid structure of the Panchayati Raj Institutions.

The enactment of the 73rd Amendment to the Indian Constitution is now permitting these women an opportunity to beintegrated into the political system. With a mandatory reservation of 33 per cent of the seats being held for women in every tier of the Panchayati Raj Institutions, rural women are now being politically empowered to bring their issues to the forefront of their local governments.

"The political empowerment of women by providing this reservation means that about seven to eight lakh women will be participating in and contributing directly to the development process. About fifteen to twenty lakh women will be office bearers at all levels of Panchayats,". Not only is this reservation mandatory for the elected tiers of the PRIs, but it is also mandatory to have this 33 per cent representation in the gram sabhas, as well. A gram sabha meeting cannot take place unless this requirement for women's participation is met. Because it is the gram sabha that basically sets the agenda for the developmental needs of the village, women's participation is fundamental in addressing their issues and needs for reform. Below is a table that outlines the specific areas that gram sabhas have addressed as key developmental issues. These 29 areas were commonly indicated as important areas for development by India's 638, 365 villages.

The "areas marked in bold are areas where independent observers have indicated that women bear primary responsibility,". This is primarily because these bold areas lie within the traditional domain of a woman's responsibility to her village.

Panchayat responsibilities: The "Eleventh Schedule" of the 73rd amendment specifies 29 areas of responsibility that states may devolve to the panchayats:

- Agriculture, including agricultural extension
- Land improvement,implementation of landre forms, land consolidation and soil conservation
- Minor irrigation, water management and watershed development
- Animal husbandry, dairy and poultry
- Fisheries
- Social forestry and farm forestry
- Minor forest produce
- Small scale industries, including food processing industries
- Khadi (homespun cloth), village and cottageindustries

- Rural housing
- Drinking water
- Fuel and fodder
- Roads, culverts, bridges, ferries, waterways and other means of communication electrification, including distribution of electricity conventional energy sources
- Poverty alleviation programmes
- Education including primary and secondary schools
- Technical training and vocational education
- Adult and non-formal education
- Libraries
- Cultural activities
- Markets and fairs
- Health and sanitation, including hospitals, primary health centres and dispensaries
- Family welfare
- Women and child development
- Social welfare, including welfare of the handicapped and mentally retarded
- Welfare of the weaker sections, and in particular, of the scheduled castes and the scheduled tribes Public distribution system
- Maintenance of community assets

As can be seen from the list, about one-fourth of the areas falling under women's responsibilities have to do with water directly. However, what is not obvious is that all of the areas in bold are indirectly related to water in one way or another. Health and sanitation, means not only providing hospital resources, but also mean that clean sources of water and effective means of dispensing of wastes need to be available within the village. Furthermore, health care is a primary concern because women are traditionally responsible for the overall welfare of the family unit, but also because so many deaths and illnesses are caused by unsafe water.

Agriculture, animal husbandry, fisheries, and minor forest produce are possible only with convenient sources of water nearby. Education, including primary, secondary, and adult and non-formal, is directly intertwined with the need for toilet facilities. The number one reason why girls drop out of school, women do not teach in rural villages, and women cannot go back for an education, is the lack of toilets in village schools. Poverty alleviation programmes, maintenance of community assets, and women and child development are directly related to women's control and autonomy over the technology of the toilet. As a result of their active participation in the local governments, these women are now able to wield quite a bit of power and influence through their increased participation in the PRIs. The women elected into the PRIs are able to set their agendas and have their concerns heard by all in the village; they are taken seriously by their male counterparts and are not seen as merely figureheads as was feared when the law was initiated.

Direct proof of their influence comes in the re-election campaigns that have taken place since 1993. In these elections, women are surpassing the thirty-three per cent reservation of seats held for them. In some states, as many as forty-three per cent are being elected to the PRIs. Currently, there are over a million women elected to local governments; overall women's participation in local governments is three times this number, with increased women voting in these elections and helping to run campaigns.

It is not unusual for many women that have been elected to the PRIs in 1993, have now become the Sarpanch of their gram panchayat. As a result of their increased numbers and positions within the PRI system, women are finally able to bring toilet building projects and sanitation endeavors to fruition. They have established 'pani panchayats,' which literally translates into 'water committees,' within the their respective gram sabhas and gram panchayats to ensure that water issues become part of and remain on the agenda for their villages.

These pani panchayats are usually comprised of all of the participating women of the gram sabha. Through the pani panchayats, women's traditional gender role as custodians of water and sanitation has led to modern-day business ventures in which they are firmly in charge of all stages of the development process. The first step of development is getting toilet blocks and toilet initiatives on the agendas of the gram sabhas and gram Panchayats. Once the women are able to convince their gram panchayat to bring toilets to their village, the next step, the Initial Project Stage, begins. In this stage, the pani panchayats meet with local engineers and organizations to decide what sort of toilet would be right for their village. Once this has been decided, the women are then responsible for selecting the actual source and location of the toilet and beginning the implementation of the construction process.

When construction has been completed, the pani panchayats educate the village on proper use of the toilet facility and ensure satisfactory operation and maintenance of the toilets. By having this sort of control over a technology, women are improving their status within the villages, bringing outside business initiatives, which brings wealth and prestige, to their communities, and maintaining one of the most vital assets that their community has to offer.

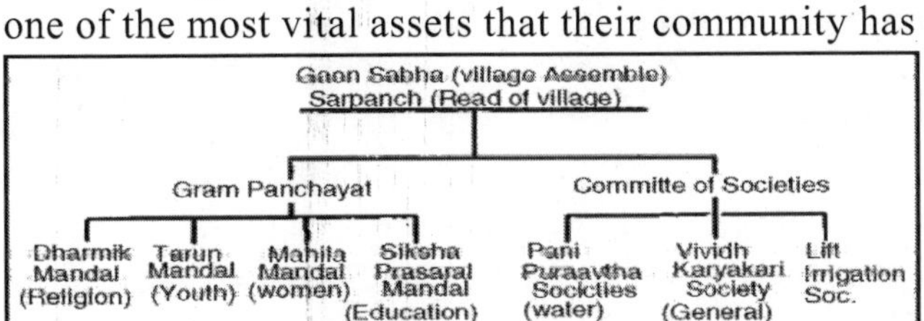

Fig. Typical Gram Sabha Structure Showing Institutionalization of the Pani Panchayats

The results that the pani panchayats have brought to their communities in terms of toilets, water, business, and increased quality of life have made them an institutionalised part of the panchayati raj governmental system. The diagram is one example of many in which water committees have become a fixed structure of the local system. Because of the different dialect of this village, the water committee is called 'pani puraavtha,' in this instance, but the roles that are assigned to them and the mission they take on is the same as pani panchayats across the many villages of India.

Because the pani panchayats have become a formalised part of the panchayati raj institutions, they are now able to provide a wide array of technology choices of toilets for their respective villages. This is extremely important to the rural areas of India as their complete lack of infrastructure makes it necessary to choose the right sanitation system for their needs. Obviously, without any sort of infrastructure, a western-style flush toilet would not be appropriate for these villages.

The materials needed for construction are too cost intensive; the time needed to build sewage systems is too time intensive; and the water needed to flush them are too resource intensive. Therefore, the pani panchayat must take into account their villages' unique set of conditions ranging from temperature, climate, and water supply to village population and fiscal economy.

This has enabled the villages to choose a viable alternative to the "one model fits all" approach to toilets offered by the government through World Bank sponsored programmes. Prior to women's participation in the local governments and the establishment of pani panchayats, this "one model fits all" was the only toilet choice, if any, offered to the village. In many cases, this choice was not offered so much as thrust upon the villages through "good will" ventures sponsored by the World Bank and initiated by a government run programme known as the Central Rural Sanitation Programme.

The design that was promoted by the government was a twin pit, pour- flush latrine with a brick superstructure. The cost of this design is 2500 rupees; a cost that is not so exorbitant by western standards, but is well beyond the means of most villages in India. This meant that the government would have to provide a subsidy to the cost of the toilets in order to move ahead with the World Bank programme.

The subsidy they provided was Rs2000 per toilet. The high subsidy price being paid by the Indian government meant that the government could only then afford to provide one or two latrines per village. As a result, only the most prominent members of the village would likely be the recipient of the toilet subsidy because they could afford the remaining Rs500 and because they had access to 'favours' from the local governments. Instead of sharing the latrines with the rest of the village, the lucky few that owned toilets flaunted their obvious wealth and used the toilets as an emblem of their prominence. Like the toilets in the urban sector, a vast majority of the toilets that were built through the CRSP are not being used for the purposes intended. A recent government study revealed that "only 3 per cent of these latrines were used for the purposes for which they were built,".

In many cases, people have converted the latrines into storerooms or kitchens.

This occurred because the one model promoted by the government was not conducive to the great variety of terrain, environment, and economies found in villages throughout the rural areas. The toilets were designed with the "total absence of people's participation. Local village masons were not even contracted to undertake the construction of the latrines,".

Instead of utilizing local materials, labour, and skills, construction was done by outsiders or volunteers from the west who either took toilets for granted or were not vested in the outcome of the project. As a result, the construction quality was so poor that many latrines remained incomplete or damaged. Repairs could not be made the damaged latrines, because bricks and other out-sourced materials were not available to the villages.

When women began to form the pani panchayats, they evaluated these World Bank sponsored toilets and realised that they obviously would not meet the needs of their village. The immediate need for toilets could not endure the length of time it would take to build the infrastructure for these toilets. At the current rate of government sponsored construction and population growth in the rural areas, it would take "over 200 years for every Indian to have access to a toilet,". Furthermore, it would cost over 24772500 ` billion to provide India's rural population with a conventional water supply and sewerage system, so traditional western-flush toilets were definitely not an option.

Many rural areas do not have enough water available to meet daily needs for drinking, bathing, and cleaning, let alone to flush a toilet. A western-style flush toilet uses at least 100,000 liters of water a year for flushing. This is simply unsustainable for the rural villages of India. As such, a primary role for the pani panchayats became exploring alternatives and affiliations with organizations that would suit the varying needs of their villages. They explored the option of have other western non-governmental organizations give training seminars and discuss options for toilets. However, the women felt that a majority of these foreign NGO training meetings were "useless" and "impractical". Non-Indians simply could not understand the cultural sensitivities of the women and their villages. Based on these inadequacies that they experienced first-hand from outside, foreign organizations, it became very important to the water committees that the toilet technology should remain within the domain and control of the local women.

From the creation of the pani panchayats themselves to local efficacy groups involved in supporting women's new found political careers, the organizations that were most effective were the ones that sprang up internally. In fact, pani panchayats are one of the most successful of these groups. They grew internally from the village women's singing groups which would gather to sing at weddings and festivals. From this connection, a natural committee with the same concern for toilets was formed.

Internal did not necessarily mean from within the village itself but from among other Indian women who shared the same culture, concerns, and hardships and understood the basic need for toilets. Another source of inspiration as well as a proven valuable resource for the women of the rural areas are the women's toilet organizations of the urban sector. These women understood their rural sisters' plight and need for the toilet technology.

They also understood the political process through their own situation in the urban cities, and were able to help organize, educate, and encourage the village women to participate in the government seats that were now reserved for them. These urban women created non-profit organizations specifically to educate the rural women in how to effectively participate in the panchayati raj institutions. They taught the rural women how to overcome the traditional stigmas of interacting with men and women from other castes, how to revive defunct gram sabhas, and how to set up self-help groups. As a result, the internal organizations that the women chose to consult with on the toilet building projects were ones in which local women were given opportunities for employment as masons and block makers, either independently or attached to production centres and that allowed them to retain control over the project.

Working with such organizations provides the women with the forum they need to discuss their needs in designing the toilets for their villages. Through this they are able to specifically meet their villages' cultural specifications as well as to take into account their village's unique geography and environment. Furthermore, by collaborating with such organizations, as opposed to relinquishing control to an outside company, the women are able to control the project after the initial design stage into the building and construction process. These endeavors have resulted in lasting employment opportunities for the village women.

Through the knowledge gained by consulting and collaborating with these organizations, most of the pani panchayats chose a toilet system that was far different from the one the World Bank programme wanted to impose upon them. The most common model chosen was a lower-cost single pit pour-flush latrine. This system uses less water than the other options, about 1.5 – 2 litres per flush; this was a high priority for the women considering they must travel such long distances, many times a day, for water to flush the toilets. The design is conducive to use by up to ten users and it usually take four to five years for the pit to fill before it must be emptied.

This means that the toilet can be shared by multiple households within the village. However, just as the World Bank's one model could not fit all varied situations in India, even this type of toilet could not serve the varied topographies and climates that make up India. Furthermore, with their new- found voice in the village gram sabhas, their training and expertise from their counter-parts in the urban sector, and their desire to create a better environment for themselves, their families, and their village, the women of the rural villages have created an opportunity to be at the fore-front of implementing an environmentally sustainable technology. In some instances, the pani panchayats are determined to find an "environmentally-friendly" alternative to meet the needs of their village.

They have learned through experience that some forms of pit latrines and other waterless toilet models can be detrimental to both the environment and their health. Traditional pit-latrines, where excreta is dropped and stored in a deep pit, can contaminate the ground water, which can threaten the entire water supply of the village. They also attract flies and other insects, which can increase the risk of air-borne infections. Another big deterrent to these models is simply the smell they emit; this can make them unbearable to many villages. Ecologically, both models avert the natural fertilizers found in human waste from making its way back into the depleted soil. Thus, chemical fertilizers are often used in these villages, which cause further environmental damage in the form of desertification and soil erosion, which virtually halts crop production. Beyond these very persuasive reasons for seeking an alternative toilet design to the traditional pit-latrines, the pani panchayats are exploring environmentally-friendly compost toilets for a variety of other reasons. Many villages do not have access to electricity and it would take many years and most of their capital resources to complete the infrastructure required to bring electricity to them. These toilets do not require electricity or a great amount of capital to build, operate, and maintain.

The environmentally-friendly design of the toilets protects the surface and ground water from sewage pollution as they do not produce any sewage at all. This fact alone combats the problem of disease outbreak and infant and child mortality due to diarrhea. Another big benefit of this toilet design is that they do not smell or create foul odours of any kind. And perhaps most importantly, the end result of the toilets is that soils are steadily improved by the regular addition of good compost returned to the earth. This has helped to boost crop production in quantity and quality and diminishes the dependence on fertilizers that can only be obtained from foreign exports and damages the earth.

One such example of the ecologically friendly toilet is the compost toilets that are currently being used in the many villages in the state of Kerala. These toilets have many advantages over the flush and pit pour-flush toilets in that compost toilets are low-cost, can be modified to meet the needs of many different geography types, and can easily be located anywhere in the village because they are not dependent on sewage lines. Compost toilets can be used by a single family or it can be established for community use.

Each compost toilet contains two chambers, built above ground and plastered with cement internally to prevent soil seepage of the excreta. Waste is collected in one chamber at a time. When one chamber becomes full, it is sealed off, and the other chamber is used. The waste in the full chamber is allowed to go through composting, which again takes about nine months. The compost produced is "an almost dry, crumbly, black product having a light, pleasant, earthy odour," The compost produced can then be sold or used by the village for household food production.

Many women have become local entrepreneurs by using this compost in home gardens and using the sale of the produce to increase personal incomes and also by contracting out their knowledge of these toilets to neighbouring villages. The village as a whole also improves as scarce water resources are used to drink or water crops, instead of being wasted on flushing toilets. Also, once endangered biodiversity is protected from the harmful effects of detrimental fertilizers.

This crossover of the technology of the toilet and its effects into the technological realm of farming brings more status and power to the women as they are crossing boundary lines into a traditionally male dominated realm.

In some instances the men may feel threatened, but mostly this is squelched by the fact that through these endeavors the women are bringing more wealth and status to the village as a whole. These "sustainable" forms of the toilet not only give the women more leverage within their society, but serve future generations by improving the environmental and economic health of their villages. The once unheard, unsought-after voices of the women are now speaking out with confidence through their village gram sabhas and gram panchayats.

They now demand copies of the village budget and are proactive in affiliating themselves or creating themselves into organizations that allow them to retain control over the technology of the toilet. They do not hesitate to speak out against foreign organizations that do not fully serve the cultural, environmental and fiscal nuances of their village or to deem as ineffectual a toilet construction project that would never meet their communities' needs. Where, once before women were sequestered to the boundaries of their village, they have now been able to expand into areas that were once completely unattainable to them— socially, culturally, politically, and technologically. These women are now able to transcend these boundaries and form a community network of women interconnected the many villages of India.

Those that have been initiated into the process of participating in grassroots democracy are able to now educate and mentor women of other villages of their legal right to participation in the raj panchayati institutions, how to speak effectively in the governing bodies, and how to have their agendas realised and materialised, thus continuing this circular continuity of the rural women's journey of empowerment.

HISTORY OF FAILED AID, PAST AND PRESENT

Imperialism, both past and present, has had a tremendous impact on the practice, administration, professionalization, and sovereignty of India's scientific and technological development. Imperialism in the past, throughout the eighteenth and into the early twentieth century, is a well known and often studied phenomenon; but, imperialism still exists under the new guise of global market rules and structural adjustment by the major international financial institutions, which will be discussed later in this stage. Both of these stages of imperialism have influenced the way in which traditional science has been perceived and practiced.

As will be seen, British colonizers sought to discredit indigenous science as an unprofessional and unstandardized practice of "witchcraft" when it was economically advantageous to discredit the native healing practices. However, the perception of indigenous science would gain more credence when it was economically more advantageous for the colonizers to exploit the natural resources associated with fabrication of medicines or when it was more profitable for the British to tout indigenous scientific practices. Not only does this economic determinism still occur in the new form of imperialism, but under the new global market, today's imperialists seek to control both the industry and the intellectual property of India's endeavors in the realm of science and technology and to define who can be classified as qualified practitioners in both of these fields.

This stage will take a look at imperialism, both in the past and in the present, to provide a framework for India's skepticism in accepting foreign aid. Part One will focus on the rise of science and technology in Indian culture and show how advanced its scientific fields were in comparison with much of the rest of the world. This stage will further explore how British economic motivations sought to discredit India's accumulated knowledge in order to advance the west's burgeoning industrial trade within its colonial empire.

Part Two will address modern-day economic loans and sanctions and their existence as a façade for the perpetuation of western economic dominance. Rather than helping developing countries utilise indigenous scientific and technological resources, modern-day colonialism, in the form of structural adjustment loans, keep developing nations dependent upon the west by establishing the rules of development. Under the laws of capitalism, the west continues to suppress native industries, steal their resources, and discredit their science and technology so developing countries have limited ability to equally compete in today's global economy. The first occurrence of established Indian science practices can be traced to the 3rd millennium B.C. and then followed through two major phases, the Vedic and post-Vedic, occurring in 1500 B.C. and 600 B.C. respectively. During these periods, the Indian scientific system was completely intertwined with the rise of the Hindu religion in India because medicine was codified and documented in the sacred writings of the Vedas. To see how completely religion and science were intertwined it is necessary to refer to the different books of the Vedas and what they represented.

The Rgveda and Samaveda "formed the backbone of India's religious life for over three thousand years and still represent the most important canonic books of Hinduism;" the Atharvaveda contained the beginnings of the practical knowledge of science as practiced in ancient times. The Vedas show that India had established a medicine system that contained, "anatomical, physiological and pathological views which were neither magical nor religious and of treatments that were rational,". Religion became interwined with these scientific and medical practices because the Brahman priests were the custodians of all knowledge; they were also the custodians of the Vedas.

As such, the Brahmans were in charge of codifying and appropriating the developed practices of Atharvaveda and, in doing so, gave them a religious origin. The Atharvaveda would become the dominant indigenous medicine system in India,

Ayurveda. Ayurveda, through its elaborate texts describing the application and collection of drugs in ancient medieval times, thrived throughout Indian society. With the advent of Buddhism in India in the 6th century B.C., medicine, science, and religion became further enmeshed.

The Buddha codified his rules of medicine in the religious texts of the Vinaya pitaka and the Mahavagga, which described various therapeutic measures. Also at this time, both the Brahmans and Buddhists established medical training for practitioners which were also very deeply rooted in the religious training of priests for both sects. The reinforcing of this religious foundation of science in India had several important effects for the development of science at this time.

First, as followers of Buddhism traveled throughout the sub-continent to spread the religious beliefs, they also took with them their practice of Ayurveda. This helped Ayurveda spread throughout Southeast Asia and even to influence many of the Greek practices of medicine during the 6th century B.C. The strong influence that Ayurveda had on scientific practices throughout Asia and into Europe is important because this is what eventually brought native medicine to the attention of India's future colonizers as a viable science with economic potential.

However, when the economic potential became too great that it interfered with the profits garnered by new practices of western science, Indian science would have to be discredited. This leads to the second important effect of the religious foundation of Indian science and its worldwide development. The intersection of religious and scientific practices is important when discussing the effects of colonialism on Indian science because it provides a fundamental basis for the misunderstandings of the British colonists towards the indigenous population and it also helps to explain the deep rooted convictions of Indians towards their practice of medicine.

This point directly correlates to the example of toilet construction in India, as will be seen in Stages Three and Four. The medieval age ushered in India's first experience of colonialism and imperialism by Muhammedan conquerors. Once again, the intersection of religion and science in Ayurveda caused initial conflict between the new Muslim rulers and Ayurvedic practitioners. But, unlike the British, the Mughal rulers did not try to discredit or suppress native scientific practices. In fact, the Mughal rulers of this time encouraged the practice of both the Unani and Ayurvedic forms of medicine and allowed each to practice within the palace, showing Mughal tolerance for native medicine.

In addition to native practices, the new Mughal Empire also brought its own form of science, the Unani system, which was based on "the significant medical concepts of Egypt and Greece, and developed in Arabia and Persia under the aegis of the Khalifas of Baghdad,". Both the vaids, practitioners of Ayurveda, and the hakeems, practitioners of Unani, were encouraged to compile their systems of practice into large compendiums of knowledge. In the same way that the Mughal rulers overcame their initial reluctance to Ayurveda's religious foundation, India recognized that the Mughals also had a great wealth of science to share, but they could not fully accept that system because it did not fit into India's culture and its certain taboos. However, the Brahmans priests practicing Ayurveda were willing to allow some concessions in the practice of Ayurveda in order to facilitate and incorporate the scientific essentials of a new system of scientific practices.

As a result, Ayurveda was able to incorporate some of the systemizing standards of the Unani systems, particularly in respect to surgery; and the Unani system incorporated the vast medical knowledge of Ayurvedic pharmacopoeia into its medical repertoire, resulting in two systems that eventually became fully integrated. This example of integration is a very important characteristic of Indian society as a whole. Indian culture has always been open to new ideas from the outside and if these ideas seemed conducive to developing knowledge and enlightenment according to Hindu philosophies, they were easily absorbed into the fabric of Indian society. What is important about this integration, though, is that these new philosophies were not seen as coming from outside of India, they are accepted by Indian society and then remolded into something distinctly India in nature and culture.

"Thus, with each new form of government in India, indigenous science came to acquire a new form of medical system," because it would be accepting of other practices of science and take these ideas until it easily fused with Indian society. This was demonstrated in the case of the Mughal Unani system in the case above. This strong native integration characteristic of Indian science is the crucial quality that helped to define India's history with its British colonizers.

While Britain's main motivations were economic, India sought to further the pursuit of pure science by integrating those scientific ideas and practices that worked, even though they came from outside their system of beliefs. These two qualities were able to merge harmoniously during the early years of the British's arrival in India, when what is referred to as a "peaceful assimilation" endured throughout society. During this time, it was economically more advantageous for Britain to employ native knowledge and medicines, because they had yet to develop their own pharmaceutical trade. Also, during this time, Indians were able to learn from British scientific developments, while still practicing their Ayurvedic cures. As such, the peaceful assimilation continued into the early years of Britain's arrival in India.

However, as will be discussed later in this psrt, this assimilation would not be tolerated when Britain needed India as a market for its mass produced pharmaceuticals. From the period of British control in Bengal, 1757, until about 1835 "there was a peaceful co-existence and incorporation of the indigenous forms of medicine," One reason for this is because both the European and Indian scientific systems were very closely related. From the first contacts of European travellers to India, in the late 15th century and becoming more common in the 16th and 17th centuries, scientific technologies were on a par with those practiced in Europe. "European science drew heavily on Islamic knowledge, but this in turn had been influenced by the Hindu achievements,". Because of this influence, European travellers perceived Indian science as being homogenous with their own practices.

Both systems relied on the notion of the four humours as a foundation for their humoural pathology. According to these systems, "disease was a result of an imbalance or impurity of one of the four cardinal humours, which in turn, affected one's temperament,". In those instances where science was not homogenous between the two cultures, the British actually saw advancements in the Indian system, which they could learn from. Among these advancements were the use of urinalysis in testing for disease and the rise of rhinoplasty as a treatment of nasal congestion.

During this period, the British seemed to have had respect for the vast amounts of knowledge that the Ayurvedic practice had accumulated because it was economically advantageous to the British empire. The British had no flourishing scientific and medical fields of their own to force Indians to accept. At this time, Britain was seeking to gain this knowledge to better position themselves economically in the fields of science and technology that they used Indian research to help build this foundation. As a result, Britain used this knowledge as just another resource extracted from their Indian colony. But, beyond the knowledge gained during these years of strategic "peaceful coexistence," economic motivation still remained the determining factor of strategically appeasing the natives.

The Europeans chose to acknowledge that Indian medicines were better suited to treat Indian diseases or other European forms of diseases that occurred in the Indian climate and that Indian doctors were much better equipped to analyse, treat, and cure these diseases. To not acknowledge this would be to antagonize Indian scientists and to lose access to valuable knowledge that had been accumulated. The British saw indigenous science as an area of opportunity suitable for research into the investigation of indigenous drugs and saw production of these drugs as a profitable import/export venture. In the early years of the British East Indian Company, the British were eager to find local alternatives to medicines that were often expensive to import, such as the Peruvian bark, cinchona, used to treat malaria.

"Given the cost and scarcity of imported drugs, there were strong financial as well as therapeutic incentives to find local substitutes,". As a result, several indigenous remedies were cultivated and used by the British living in India as an import substitution to the highly priced pharmaceuticals of Europe. In turn, these locally produced medicines were then exported to Europe as valuable remedies for various ailments. Not only does this example lay the foundation for the economic motivations that would influence British rule over India, but it also gives us glimpses of colonial intentions from the early years of Britain's first arrival to Indian shores. Even though these instances show that the Europeans acknowledged the efficacy of Indian cures and doctors for Indian diseases, it also shows that they thought of the people and the diseases and cures as different from their own. By personifying these sicknesses as "Indian" and qualifying the medicines that treated them as "Indian," the British were able to retain their own identity as English and not be assimilated by Indian society as had happened to other rulers. Through this labeling and ability to retain their identity, the English were able to position themselves to truly rule and conquer India.

Pearson argues that the true distinguishing point that separates European rulers from others colonizers, like the Mughals described earlier, is European dominant authority and perceived superiority; they actually perceive their subjects as being completely different from their British ruling class. Pearson sees these Europeans, in this case the British, who are classifying the people and diseases as different, as "harbingers of a future intolerance and overt assumption of superiority,". These differences are only exacerbated when economic influences, such as the Industrial Revolution, come into effect. Economic incentives increase the motivation for separating the ruling class from the colonized and to perpetuate not only the differences, but the superiority, of western modes of practicing medicine.

This shows that the conquering, colonial mindset was already instilled in the British and that they had every intention of controlling the knowledge and resources that India had to offer because theses resources would generate more wealth for Britain. These European mentalities of superiority were motivating factors of colonization from the inception of trade with India. The "harmonious" and magnanimous acceptance of native medicine was primarily selfserving and economically motivated.

During the eighteenth and early nineteenth centuries, this acceptance came easily for the Europeans because of the similar humoural pathologies of both systems of science and even more, because there was much to be profited from the accumulation of Indian "materia medica, accumulated over centuries of empirical trial and observation".

But with the start of the Industrial Revolution, Britain generated greater wealth through the mass production of items such as books, clothes, tools, and medicines. As a result, Britain was able to accelerate their scientific research fields and, through industrialization, was able to make chemical cures that could be mass produced cheaply and sold at a much higher price than natural therapies. Therefore, it became economically disadvantageous for the British to validate any form of Indian science because in doing so they would be discrediting their own manufactured goods and eliminating a vast market for their finished end products.

Now, for Indians to be deemed qualified scientists by the British Raj, they had to be trained, practiced, and skilled in the British manner. Only this would qualify them for positions in the institutes and universities where only western systems were allowed to be taught. Indian scientific texts were only proven authoritative when they had been published and "scientifically" proven by British physicians. Indigenous research was strictly forbidden in British institutions and its practice outlawed throughout Indian society. It is also at this point, when integration was not allowed, that British and Indian cultures began to clash as India was not able to absorb British practices and mold them to meet their needs.

This clash of cultures is exemplified by the smallpox treatment in India and the native variolation techniques of treating the Indian population versus the European vaccinations. The treatment of smallpox in India was initiated by the

British to protect civilians and army personnel who were employed within the service of the Crown. "From the British perspective smallpox was too dangerous a disease to be ignored, and the lives of European soldiers and civilians would continue to be threatened unless effective measures of control were introduced,". Proof of this economic determinism comes in the fact that it wasn't until Britain had the ability to manufacture, and more importantly to sell, its cure for smallpox in the form of a British made vaccine that vaccination began to rival the native cure of variolation.

In fact, Indian variolation was initially used by the British in 1767 as proof that inoculations were a successful means of disease prevention. Tikadars, who were primarily Brahmin priests, would travel from village to village shortly before the beginning of the smallpox season in January or February. In a festival devoted to Sitala, the Hindu goddess whose presence was manifested in the disease's fevers and eruptions, the tikadars would perform their inoculation on the members of the village. In this manner, it is estimatedthat up to sixty per cent of the population was protected from the disease. In the late eighteenth century, the British themselves took up the practice in order to protect themselves from the deadly Indian disease.

When the smallpox vaccine was created in Britain in 1796, it became economically necessary that British vaccination conquer its native rival, variolation, because of the chemical and pharmaceutical industry that was newly forming in Europe in the mid-nineteenth century which would manufacture and sell the cure to smallpox in the form of a British vaccine. But, to make this possible, the tikadars first had to be discredited by the British as quacks who were involved in "a murderous trade,". However, the general native public was not to be swayed from their religious festivals and in their confidence in their native practitioners.

Furthermore, they were distrustful of the vaccine introduced by their colonizers and were not welcoming of a medicine that used the lymph of their sacred cow. As a result, there was much cultural resistance to colonial medical intervention. To overcome this resistance, the British rulers simply made vaccinations mandatory and outlawed the practices of the tikadars. "Ultimately, by outlawing the tikadars' trade, by making vaccination more widely available and overcoming initial resistance to it, the British were able by the close of the nineteenth century to effectively suppress a once widespread practice," and to reap the economic benefits from the monopoly they created. In their increased efforts to discredit native scientific practices, Britain began to enforce standardization and licensing in scientific and technological fields of study.

As a result more and more Indian practitioners of science and medicine were deemed unprofessional because they did not meet these British standards, eastern medicine was not within the realm of science that could be licensed, and they were not 'educated' according to western texts and manuals. In scientific fields, Indians no longer met British qualifications of being called true scientists, doctors, or engineers. Instead, much of the Indian population was merely trained to be menial and cheap labourers which would be more cost efficient to serving the needs of the

British army than bringing manual labour over from England.

Indian designs are discouraged by these western institutions as not being as acceptable to western standards. While the smallpox case establishes the historical precedence of a dominant group demeaning native forms of science and medicine to promote western made products and services, the next example of the cholera epidemic establishes India's precedence of distrust to foreign "aid" initiatives. The cholera epidemic has its roots in the devastating poverty that was induced in India mainly as a result of British colonialism. Because many resources that were indigenous to India or produced in India were shipped back to England to generate greater income for the colonizer, the majority of the Indian population became poverty-stricken. This poverty and India's status as a colony meant that economic resources were not available to the native population to create proper sanitation facilities and it is at this point that sanitation becomes a major issue within India.

The poor sanitary conditions only added to the perceived superiority of the British colonizers and the further discrediting of all native practices of science and technology. The British began to tout the natives as unclean and, therefore, uncivilised. Because India is an uncivilised nation, the British would argue, native scientific practices must also be primitive and unclean, why else would they live in these conditions? According to the British, this argument was proven by the severe cholera outbreaks that were now rampant in the villages and cities of India.

The British were not motivated to do anything about these outbreaks initially because it was only the Indian population that was at risk for contracting the disease. The British citizens' encampments were afforded all of the luxuries that England's opulence could offer, including functional privies and safe drinking water. They were effectively kept segregated from the unclean masses so British civilians were not in danger of coming into contact with cholera. These conditions of economic oppression by the colonizers that led to the poverty and conditions described above sparked the Indian National Movement of 1857 which was India's first attempt to "Quit India" of British rule.

Ironically, this movement was officially initiated after yet another incidence of cultural technological insensitivity by the British towards two major populations in India, the Hindus and the Muslims. While training natives for the British army serving in India, the British introduced a new gun whose shell was encased in the grease of both the pig and the cow; the first is taboo to the Muslim, the latter is sacred to the Hindu.

The casing of the bullet shell had to be ripped open with teeth, thus causing contact with the taboo and defilement of the sacred. To do this meant that both the Hindus and Muslims would become outcastes of their respective societies. When they learned of this new technology, a "Quit India" movement led by Mangel Pandey ensued that quickly incited the entire country. After this incidence, the British raised their army presence in India by sixty per cent. Because the British population was so drastically increased, the odds were now in favour that some of its citizens may have to come into contact with the natives and, thus, the risks were increased of coming into contact with cholera.

It is only at this point that the Royal Commissions were assigned to look into the sanitary conditions of the army barracks in India. The number one priority of the Royal Commissions in improving sanitary conditions and controlling the cholera outbreak at this time remained the health of the British Army. The army would not be able to serve and protect the economic interests of the British Empire without first controlling sanitation and cholera. This economic motivating force is exemplified through a comparison of how public health initiatives grew in Britain compared to that of India. Two popular works spurred the advent of public health measures in Britain in the mid-nineteenth century.

These were the investigations of Edwin Chadwick, who established the relationship between poverty and the rise of cholera, and Robert Koch, who identified the cholera organism as the cause of the epidemics. Before this time, the British widely believed that "cholera was sent by the Lord in punishment of sins, individual and collective," -a theory that is ironic given that these ideas are what led the British to discount indigenous Indian medicine mystical and religious.

With the introduction of a concrete cause of cholera and the push made by Chadwick to create measures to alleviate those conditions of poverty that increased the spread of cholera, Britain quickly established public health acts that reduced the occurrence of the disease within England, but these measures did not come so quickly to the British colonies. For example, the first governmental public welfare act, the Poor Law Commission, was established in Britain in 1834 to study the causes of destitution in London. Similar acts were not passed in India until 1859, even though the first cholera outbreak occurred in 1817. The British did not enforce measures to eradicate cholera during this first outbreak in India because the Europeans seemed to have "had a greater immunity from the disease than the bulk of the Indian population," which the British understood had a direct correlation to their better state of sanitary conditions.

Because cholera rarely affected the English population in India at this time, the British government was not economically motivated in solving the cholera problem. It was only when increased numbers of English army personnel were sent to India to maintain order and to ensure that another nationalist uprising would not destabilise the colony that the British government establish measures to research and eliminate the cause of cholera in India. But, even then, these measures were targeted to improving only those areas where British personnel were stationed. The prime concern of the British government in establishing these acts was "to assist in all matters relating to the health of the army and to supervise the gradual introduction of sanitary improvements in barracks, hospitals, and stations on a continuing basis,".

Maintaining a healthy army community was economically in Britain's best interests as it was the army's responsibility to maintain authority over the native civilians. It would have been too much of a financial drain of Britain's economic resources to initiate such public welfare endeavors in the native population. Instead of improving sanitary living conditions by increasing social welfare among the Indian population, the British treatment of the cholera epidemic in the native population was restricted to hospitals and dispensaries.

European practitioners often demanded higher salaries for living and practicing medicine in the Indian sub-tropical environment and medical duties were often combined with a wide range of colonial bureaucratic administrative responsibilities. Sickness and mortality rates were high which led to a paucity of European doctors to attend to the needs of the ever-growing British population in India. Furthermore, because the British considered it unsafe to "entrust the lives of Company servants to indigenous practitioners who had no training in Western medicine", it was necessary for the Company to train Indian subordinates to perform menial duties and for these native subordinates to have some appropriate form of western medical education. Thus, the British established the Calcutta Native Medical Institution to provide a regular supply of native doctors, trained in Western medicine, to the British East Indian Company. These institutions made it acceptable for natives to be educated only if they provided training in western knowledge; native institutions that taught native sciences were not worthy of the term "education," and were demeaned by the British.

This educational 'reform' was becoming the predominant philosophy of the British colonizers throughout India at this time. A major proponent of introducing this type of educational "reform" that stressed western-only lessons and philosophies was Thomas Babington Macaulay. Macaulay served as Supreme Council to India between 1834 and 1838. He was an outspoken essayist on the need for educational reform among the Indian population until his death in 1859. Macaulay was a "convinced colonialist and a believer in European, especially British, superiority over all things Oriental.". His now infamous "Minute on Education" stressed this need for educational reform among the Indian masses and expressly stated that this "assistance" to that native population was needed in order to ensure a bountiful market of British produced goods and manufactures.

To prove that educational reform needed to occur, he first had to denigrate the Indian population as being crude, unrefined, and uncivilised. He did this by stating that, "The dialects commonly spoken among the natives of this part of India, contain neither literary nor scientific information, and are, moreover, so poor and rude that, until they are enriched from some other quarter, it will not be easy to translate any valuable work into them." He went on to tout the superiority of the British educational system by completely dismissing all native literature by saying, "It is, I believe, no exaggeration to say, that all the historical information which has been collected from all the books written in the Sanskrit language is less valuable than what may be found in the most paltry abridgements used at preparatory schools in England,".

Macaulay's goal in initiating this educational "assistance" to the masses was to produce a population that was, "Indian in blood and colour, but English in taste, in opinions, in morals, and in intellect." It was necessary to make the Indian population have the same "civilities" as the English, so they would have the same wants and desires for material comforts. As Macaulay states, "It would be far better for us that the people of India were ruled by their own kings, but wearing our broadcloth, and working with our cutlery, than that they were performing their salams [sic] to English collectors and English magistrates, but were too ignorant to value, or too poor to buy, English manufactures." And he ends by simply saying, "To trade with civilised men is infinitely more profitable than to govern savages,". As a member of Parliament and primary orator of the ruling Whig party, Macaulay's words reverberated the thoughts of most Englishmen of the time. He was seen by the English to be an authority on Indian affairs because of his position as member of the supreme council on the East India Company. As such, his "Minute on Education" was representative of British colonial thought on how to tame the savage native. This speech is often referred to as a primary instigator of the 'Quit India' movement through which India eventually gained independence in 1947.

During this period, an Indian who chose to adopt a Western culture as a lifestyle was spitefully referred to as "Macaulay's Child." This was meant as a derogatory term for someone who was disloyal to India and the Indian heritage and was a direct reference to Macaulay's statement being "Indian in colour, but English in taste." This speech was often used to incite and rally Indian nationalists so that one of the key factors in winning Indian independence was the rejection of the mass manufactured goods of England. Instead, Indian nationalists urged fellow Indians to locally produce the goods that India would consume. Cutting England off from the huge Indian market was crucial to the non-violent strategy of defeating Britain. Gandhi urged Indians to make salt themselves with his famous 1930 March to Dandi on the Indian coast to make natural seasalt; thus, defying the British law that stated only the British could produce salt and garner the income generated from salt taxes. Images of Gandhi creating his own broadcloth at a spinning wheel in order not to wear English fashions are indelible in the minds of all Indians as he encouraged his fellow compatriots to embargo English textiles and instead buy or make homespun themselves.

When Jawaharlal Nehru became the first Prime Minister of India, he quickly undid the "reforms" of Macaulay's times and peers. Instead of focusing on British literature and poetry, he mandated that science and technology would become a priority. No longer would India be subject to the importations of other countries when it came to high-tech goods, but they would position themselves to be a prime competitor of such items in the global market. Everyday, when they look at their national flag that has at its centre the spinning wheel, Indians are reminded of this ideal of creating for themselves what they consume in the markets, of not being beholden to others, which causes dependency, but instead, to be self-sustaining and self-sufficient.

This, Nehru urged, is the ultimate path to freedom. Indian politicians believed that functioning as a sovereign nation, they would be able to ordain their own course of development. Even though they knew they required aid, they believed they controlled where this aid came from and that they had autonomy over how it should be used within their country. They quickly realised this was not the case as certain sectors, like the example of the toilet as discussed in stages three and four, remained under a new form of colonialism in the form of the old guise of "aid" and "assistance" programmes. One such example is the SITE satellite that India strove to develop in the early years after its independence. As India entered the global political arena as an independent sovereign nation in the 1950s and 1960s, it began to explore areas where it could compete technologically with other nations. As a newly independent country, it was necessary for India to request aid from other countries for technological initiatives they sought to develop.

And, as a politician applying for this aid, Nehru basically applied the Hindu principle of Advaita, that "all are one" in his strategy of political non- alignment. As such, aid was sought from all sides of the political spectrum, from the United States and Russia. The prevailing thought was that these countries would freely give "alms" to India and that their mendicancy was justified because it would be good for these countries' karma. But the SITE satellite development quickly showed India that with the "politics of foreign aid…nothing comes free,". They soon began to realise that with western "aid" of developing the tools to support the technological infrastructure of the SITE satellite, the United States was merely supporting its own political agenda in the Cold War against Russia by setting up military posts and spy surveillances through the satellite in India.

As a result, the "archaic Hindu notions of philanthropy, coupled with political Vedanta cast partially as non-alignment prevented India from establishing a comfortable working relationship with the United States," and the West. This was yet another realization for India that colonialism still existed in the new global system, even though in theory they were an autonomous nation. Examples like this were happening all over the globe as many countries throughout Latin American and Asia vied for their independence during the midtwentieth century. India, like other newly independent countries of the time, found itself struggling to compete with markets that had had centuries to establish and gain a firm foothold in global economics.

Furthermore, these developed markets had extracted or ravaged all the viable resources from their former colonies; this left these newly independent countries with little to offer the global market place which, in turn, led them to realise that the age of imperialism had not yet fully ended for them. To be able to survive in the new global market, they would be forced to accept loans from the western countries.

With the loans, came developing contingencies, called Structural Adjustment Policies that ensured that these new countries developed according to the West's standards. To understand how these structural adjustment policies represent a modern form of economic imperialism on the part of the west towards the lesser-developed countries of the Third World, it is necessary to first understand exactly what they are and what they mandate. As the major contributors to the IMF and World Bank, the G-8, especially the United States, control the conditions for these loans. Countries that accept loans from the IMF and World Bank must go through a variety of these structural adjustment programmes which usually involve forcing the loan-accepting country to rapidly remove its trade barriers, increase its exports to earn hard currency for debt service, and promote foreign investment through privatization and deregulation of its labour and environmental laws.

Export promotion policies such as tax breaks and subsidies, bargain basement privatization sales, and lowering of wages are encouraged to help attract investments from multinational corporations. The IMF's cure in a nutshell is: cut government spending, reduce economic growth with high interest rates, and liberalise the rules for foreign investment and trade through free trade. "Privatizing state enterprises is a key element of structural adjustment; World Bank policy is essentially a device to shift the larger burden of curative services to the private sector, where it is thereby accessible to foreign investment,". Under these SAPs, the third world countries were forced to privatize certain sectors of their economy, such as initiatives in medicine, science, and technology.

As a result of this "liberalizing" of the global market, it is often the indigenous technologies that are jeopardized because they simply cannot compete with the large, corporate manufacturers. Such is the case in Tibet where it is often the Tibetan monks who practice and administer indigenous remedies to the local population. Because they are not-for-profit, they often rely on government subsidies and protection to maintain their trade.

Structural adjustment policies will force the Tibetan governments to remove the subsidies given to the monks and force the monks' health-aiding charities to compete with foreign, private corporations seeking to sell their manufactured pharmaceuticals abroad. Furthermore, the Tibetan monks do not retain global patent rights for their local medicinals. Because they are not protected by these western laws and systems, the very same foreign corporations can steal the monks' ancestral knowledge of indigenous medicines and make a substantial profit off of the expanding alternative medicine craze. There is no way that the local, native practitioners of indigenous medicine who "will find themselves transformed in the competitive atmosphere of the private sector, where they must compete for patient fees, sell medicines and support clinical facilities," will be able to withstand the multinational forces unless they are subsidized by government agencies.

However, the government agencies cannot subsidize such local ventures because they would be going against the loan conditions of their structural adjustment policies and, hence, would have to forfeit their much needed loans. The structural adjustment policies that are placed as loan conditions by the West are meant to be facilitators of free trade and an opening of global markets. However, the logic of this sort of forced free trade seems to increase the economic advantage of those that already have it, namely the West. The rule of the free market is that countries should specialise and trade according to their comparative advantage, what they can produce most efficiently. Much of the Third World, therefore, has a comparative advantage in mainly agricultural products, while the First World would specialise in technological goods.

"An average of about 30 per cent of the economic output of low-income developing countries comes from agriculture; in the industrialised world, this value is about 3 per cent,". And, according to the economic principle of a product's life cycle, agricultural goods yield a low market price because they have already reached the mature stage of the product life cycle, when demand has leveled off and prices have stabilised; meanwhile, technological goods are continuously being updated and reintroduced into the market. Therefore, these technical goods are subject to the entire product life cycle of a new product. This means that during the early stages of the life cycle, a country that specialises in technological goods can take advantage of the increased demand for this good, which generates revenue for these countries. From this revenue, these countries now have the capital to create new products, once the old products have matured, continuing the cycle of another product's new life on the market. Instead of helping these developing nations move away from a reliance on an agriculture-dependent economy and fostering new technological developments, the west's structural adjust policies focus primarily on keeping the Third World mired in the agricultural realm.

Many of the structural adjustment programmes focus only on those technologies that will bolster crop yields or "modernize" traditional methods of farming. Some of the most devastating effects of SAPs have been incurred by the women of Third world countries. Structural adjustment initiatives that have encouraged the adoption of western technologies and the privatization of native industries have led to the steady, systematic disempowerment of women in the globalization process. Prior to western 'assistance' programmes in many areas of the Third World, women had established dominions were they were able to control decisions made within that realm, as well as the technologies that feel within their domain. This document discusses how the technology of the toilet was controlled by the women because it was a part of their traditional gender role of controlling all water resources.

As a result, they are able to achieve a sort of independence by controlling the means of the toilet technology and bringing it to their villages. In other areas of the Third World, women cultivated the fields, distributed the harvests among their village, and disposed of any surplus through trade with other villages and nearby urban centres. Out of these activities, trading networks controlled exclusively by women emerged, as surplus grain would be traded for livestock and the latest in farming technology. This direct involvement in trade and owning the technological means of production gave women a considerable degree of autonomy. However, when international development agencies enter Third World countries and impose structural adjustment programmes, they systematically channel new technologies of efficiency mainly towards men. In those rural areas where women were able to establish dominion over a technology and then their governments accepted western loan programmes, women's productivity was reduced and any progress they had generated for themselves was stunted. For example, the Land Resettlement Programme in Zimbabwe, which was initiated by the Zimbabwe government to show compliance to the structural adjustment contingencies of its loans from the World Bank, redistributed land only to individual males and new technologies of farming were taught exclusively to males.

Through the World Bank's push to open these markets up to foreign investment and private competition, the women are no longer able to control the seeds of their craft because they do not have the capital resources that western corporations have. As a result, control of the seeds are given to the corporations who are then able to patent the "knowledge" of how to cultivate and use these seeds. To bring our examples full circle, this mirrors what is happening in Tibet as monks are losing their sovereignty over their medicinal remedies and cures. For these women seed keepers, Intellectual Property Rights of herbal remedies would be taken away from these longtime Ayurvedics and given to the multinational corporations, thus taking away these women's livelihood. Not only is the concept of Intellectual Property Rights unfamiliar to many in the Third World, it represents another tool used by the free market to take control over native technologies and to implement another form of economic imperialism.

Toilets, while not obviously a technology which promises great profits to those who implement it, nonetheless follow the same course of development under western initiatives as though described above. When the World Bank decided to "help" India build toilets for the multitudes of the Indian population without access to a toilet, the World Bank once again imposed contingencies for lending their capital and aid. World Bank initiatives forced the government of India to privatize the toilet-building sector and to open up contracting to the competitive market. When this occurred, western contractors vied with local Indian endeavors and won the opportunity to construct toilets in India.

However, the World Bank models were not conducive to nor were they sensitive to the cultural norms of an acceptable toilet system in India. For example, the World Bank's model toilet had women and men's stalls facing each other, meaning that men and women would have to interact while waiting in line and there would be no privacy between the sexes when performing their ablutions inside of the stalls. This is an idea that is anathema to Indian culture. The World Bank did not choose to consult with the people the toilets would be serving and, as a result, the World Bank had no concept of what would actually be used by the people, what locations were the most desirable, and what would be sustainable for the environment they were building for. The toilets built by these western initiatives were often constructed in isolated dirty spaces, with septic tanks that cannot be sustained by India's population of urban pavement dwellers and could never be used in India's rural areas, and they were made out of flimsy materials that deteriorated rapidly. Because local materials and contractors are not used, and because upkeep and maintenance are not a priority on the World's Banks agenda, the toilet blocks cannot be maintained by the poor population they serve. As a result, eighty per cent of all World Bank sponsored toilets in the urban areas of India lay in disuse and disrepair.

This is why the women of India have decided to take the technology of the toilet into their own hands, literally. They have learned what foreign 'aid' will bring them and they do not want the kind of help the west is offering. Their experience of denigration at the hands of colonizers, both historically and presently have made them very skeptical of any form of outside aid, especially those with strings attached.

Furthermore, their cultural/religious standards have engrained in them that it is better for them to do for themselves rather than increase another's karma by allowing outsiders to help them. Historically, they were taught that to be a strong nation, individuals have to make and sustain their own goods. By doing so, they can overcome any kind of colonialism. As a result, these women strive to develop the technologies of the toilet according to their cultural standards. The following examples drawn from urban and rural sectors reveal what happened when they did.

Promotion ofrurallivelihood Through Women Self Help Groups

Most of the women Self Help Groups promoted under different development and microcredit programmes are involved in savings through periodic collection from the members, recycling of this money among the members as micro-credit for consumptive and productive purposes and training of women members for initiating various micro-enterprises.

Many Self Help Groups have progressed further to deal with various social issues such as education for girls, prevention of child marriages, struggle against liquor sale, promotion of community health, sanitation, establishment of community grain banks and protest against violence. Promotion of micro- enterprises and various income generation activities is an important aspect of women empowerment. Although it is extremely difficult to find remunerative selfemployment, there are enormous untapped opportunities in the rural sector. These include both on-farm and off-farm opportunities.

Advantages of Agro-Based Activities: While promoting various income generation activities, agro-based activities have advantages because of the following reasons:

- Target groups are acquainted with most of the basic skills.
- Easy access to inputs.
- No problems of marketing, as most of the outputs are locally consumed as food. Market outlets for even cash crops have been well established.
- As over 75-85 per cent of the rural families own land and livestock, income generation activities can be initiated immediately without heavy capital investment.
- Risk of failure due to improper technology, poor quality, low demand and poor price recovery are very low. Hence, the chances of success are high.
- Infrastructure required for promotion of on-farm activities has been very

well established. Hence, the entrepreneurs can progress even in backward regions, which are deprived of regular power supply and electronic information connectivity.

It is therefore advantageous to tap all the opportunities to promote various on-farm activities. The experience of BAIF has confirmed that the best strategy to promote income generation activities through SHGs is to analyse the on- going agro-based activities undertaken by the members and introduce suitable interventions to enhance the production. There are also excellent opportunities to improve post production management of the produce through grading, storage, processing and marketing. Establishment of direct linkage with the consumers through establishment of consumer stores and farmers. open markets in small and large towns will not only reduce the cost of marketing but also help in receiving feedback from the customers.

Such direct interaction with the customers will help the farmers to improve the quality and variety of produce and enhance the profitability. Most of the agricultural products have stable prices and steady demand. Hence, the risk of price fluctuation and market glut is limited. As these products have good local demand, marketing cost is low. Most of the surplus can be stored to ensure food security in the future. In case of non-farm activities, most of the skills and inputs will have to be brought from outside. There is very limited scope for marketing these products locally. As some of the activities are new to the local women, the cost of starting the enterprise is very high. As a result, chances of success and sustainable growth of these enterprises are also very high.

The non-farm enterprises are often affected due to glut in the market, fall in prices due to competition and poor market distribution and outlet network. The enterpreneurs are not able to sustain such shocks and end up in deep financial crisis, which threaten their food security as well. It is therefore suggested that agro-based activities be promoted, followed by different non- farm activities, which will have greater chances of success and risk bearing ability. While the on-farm activities address food security, supplementary non- farm activities can contribute to rural prosperity.

❐

Index

□□□